ebXML Simplified

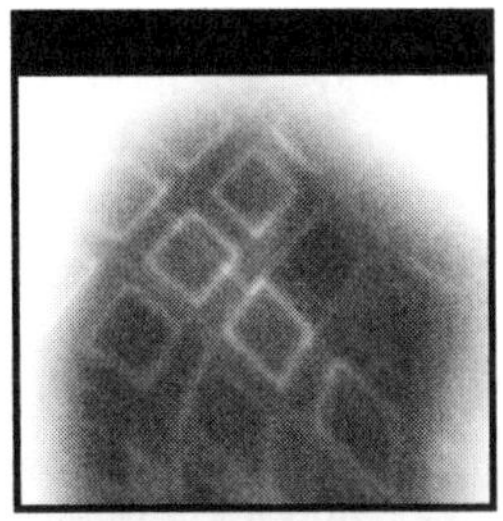

ebXML Simplified

A Guide to the New Standard for Global E-Commerce

Eric Chiu

John Wiley & Sons, Inc.

Publisher: Robert Ipsen
Editor: Robert Elliott
Assistant Editor: Emilie Herman
Managing Editor: John Atkins
New Media Editor: Brian Snapp
Text Design & Composition: John Wiley Production Services

This book is printed on acid-free paper. ♾

Published by John Wiley & Sons, Inc.

Published simultaneously in Canada.

Wiley also publishes its books in a variety of electronic formats. Some content that appears in print may not be available in electronic books.

Library of Congress Cataloging-in-Publication Data:

Chiu, Eric, 1970-

EbXML simplified : a guide to the new standard for global e-commerce / Eric Chiu.
p. cm.
Includes index.
ISBN 0-471-20475-7 (PAPER/WEBSITE : alk. paper)
1. Electronic commerce. 2. XML (Document markup language) 3. Web sites—Design.
4. Internet programming. I. Title.
HF5548.32 .C475 2002
658.8′4—dc21

2002006570

Printed in the United States of America.

10 9 8 7 6 5 4 3 2 1

It's a joy to dedicate this book to Maurice and Joan Chiu, who made it possible.

Contents

Acknowledgments xiii

Introduction xv

Part 1 Overview of ebXML 1

Chapter 1 An Overview of E-Commerce and ebXML 3

What Is E-Commerce? 4
- The Economic Value of E-Commerce 4
- B2B versus B2C 5
  - B2C E-Commerce 6
  - B2B E-Commerce 6

Building B2B Systems 8
- Developing Applications and Application Programming Interfaces 11
- Web Services 12

Electronic Trading and Interchange 13
- EDI versus XML 14

Electronic Trading Standards 15
- What Is a Standard? 15
- Standard versus Specification 16
- Open Standards versus Proprietary Standards 17

Why ebXML? 17
- ebXML Players and Politics 20
- Arguments for and against ebXML 22

Summary 23

Chapter 2 Building Blocks of ebXML: EDI and XML **25**

Electronic Data Interchange 26

EDI Technologies 27

ANSI X1 28

EDIFACT 29

Business and Technical Issues with EDI 29

Extensible Markup Language 31

Structure of the XML Document 33

Elements and Attributes 35

Document Type Definition 37

DTDs, Schemas, and Namespaces 42

XML Standards 43

ebXML: Convergence of EDI and XML 44

Summary 44

Chapter 3 Web Services and ebXML **47**

What Are Web Services? 48

How Web Services Works 51

The Parts of Web Services 53

Simple Object Access Protocol 54

RPC or Messaging? 54

The SOAP Envelope 55

Encoding 56

Request/Response and Invocation 56

ebXML and SOAP 56

Universal Description, Discovery, and Integration 57

UDDI and ebXML 59

Web Services Definition Language 60

Who Is Using Web Services? 61

Why Use Web Services? 63

How Does Web Services Relate to ebXML? 64

Summary 64

Part 2 ebXML Technologies **67**

Chapter 4 ebXML Technical Architecture **69**

Architecture, Frameworks, and Platforms 70

Architecture 70

Frameworks 71

Platforms 72

ebXML Architecture Overview 72

XML as the Common Language 73

ebXML as the Unifying Architecture 74

Methodology 75

ebXML Technical Architecture in Detail 79

Business Process 81

Core Components 83

Messaging Service 84

Registry 85

Collaboration Protocol 87
Security 89
How Does ebXML Work? 91
Major B2B Frameworks 93
BizTalk 94
Comparing ebXML and BizTalk 94
RosettaNet 95
Comparing ebXML and RosettaNet 96
Summary 97

Chapter 5 The ebXML Business Process Model 99
Business Process 100
The Business Process DTD and Schema 102
Using the BPSS 103
Collaboration: Interchange in ebXML 104
Interchange between Two Parties (Binary Collaboration) 105
Interchange Between Multiple Parties (Multiparty Collaboration) 107
Transactions 108
Business Document Flow 109
Choreography: A Sequence of Activities in the Interchange 113
Business States 114
Summary 116

Chapter 6 Using Core Components 119
What Is a Core Component? 120
Basic Object Concepts 120
Definition of Terms 121
Identifying Core Components 124
Using Core Components 126
Step 1: Find a Business Process That Meets the Requirements 127
Step 2: Identify Contexts 128
Step 3: View and Select the Core Components and Associated Business Information Entities in the Registry 128
Step 3b (Optional): Create New Business Information Entities 128
Step 4: Create an XML DTD or Schema 128
Context 129
Overview of Context 130
Context Categories 130
Business Process 131
Geopolitical 131
Product 132
Partner and Supporting Role 132
Official Constraints 133
Industry 133
System Capabilities 133

Context Rules 134
Example of Using Context Rules 135
Assembly 138
Example of Document Assembly 138
Summary 140

Chapter 7 ebXML Message Services 143
Messaging Basics 144
RPC versus Messaging 144
XML in Messaging 146
SOAP Basics 147
SOAP Message Structure 148
Encoding Rules 150
SOAP Transport Architecture and Mechanism 151
SOAP Messages with Attachments 152
SOAP as a Standard 153
ebXML Message Service 153
Overview 154
Design Criteria 154
Architecture 155
Architectural Levels 155
Formatting Messages 157
Message Package 158
Header Container 160
Header Processing 160
ebXML SOAP Extensions 161
SOAP Header Extensions 161
SOAP Body Extensions 162
Payload Container 162
Handling Messages 163
Reliable Messaging 164
Message Status Request 165
Ping/Pong Services 165
Lost Messages 166
Duplicate Message Handling 166
Failed Message Delivery 167
Error Reporting and Handling 167
Security 167
Persistent Digital Signature 168
Summary 169

Chapter 8 Using the ebXML Registry Services 171
Who Uses the ebXML Registry? 172
Business Semantics and the Registry 173
Meta Data and Shared Context 174
Shared Semantic Discovery 176
Directory Model 178
Registry Model 179

What Is the ebXML Registry? 181
Compliance 184
How the Registry Works 184
Registry/Client Communication 185
Classification System 187
Universally Unique ID (UUID) 188
Managing Objects in a Registry 188
Searching for Objects in a Registry 194
Using SQL Queries 195
Registry Security 196
Summary 197

Chapter 9 Trading Partner Profiles and Agreements 199
Interbusiness electronic interactions 201
The Electronic Trading Partner Agreement 202
tpaML Overview 203
Overall Structure 203
Business Protocol Layer 204
Document Exchange Layer 205
Transport Layer 206
Delivery Channels 206
Role 207
Collaboration Protocol Profiles and Agreement 207
Inside the Collaboration Protocol Agreement 208
Using the Collaboration Protocol Agreement 213
Inside the Collaboration Protocol Profile 215
Summary 219

Chapter 10 Implementing ebXML in the Organization 221
Why ebXML? 222
Shared Context and Semantics Management for XML 224
Standard Technical Infrastructure 225
Moving from Theory to Practice 226
Managing Workflow 226
Service Provider Model 229
ebXML Project Life Cycle 230
Planning 231
Pilot 234
Implementation 235
Summary 237

Appendix Additional Resources 239

Glossary 243

References 255

Index 261

Acknowledgments

An author never has enough space to acknowledge all the people who make a book possible. I will try my best to acknowledge all those who helped create this book.

My first acknowledgment is to the ebXML organization, which did an incredible job of putting together this important milestone in IT development. I worked with a great team of technical reviewers, including Scott Nieman (Norstan Consulting), Mike Rawlins (Rawlins EC Consulting), Martin W. Sachs (IBM), Rik Drummond (Drummond Group, Inc.), Betty Harvey (Electronic Commerce Connection), Kurt Kanaskie (Lucent Technologies), Farrukh S. Najmi, Christopher Ferris, and Anne Thomas Manes (Sun Microsystems). Thanks to Ed Roman at the Middleware Company—the visionary for Web services—who introduced me to the publisher. I thank the great editorial team at John Wiley & Sons, Robert Elliott and Emilie Herman, for their dedication and persistence. Shannon Casey at University of Nevada-Reno reviewed drafts and provided critical feedback to make this book more readable.

Introduction

"There's wind, and then there's a typhoon. In this business, you always have winds. But a 10X force is a change in an element of one's business—a typhoon. Is the Internet a typhoon, or a bit of wind? Is it a force that fundamentally alters our business?"

—Andrew Grove, Chairman and founder, Intel

ebXML is an emerging e-commerce standard that leverages the flexibility of the Extensible Markup Language (XML) to build e-commerce infrastructure. XML is a markup language used to create data and documents for application communications and storage. The "eb" in ebXML stands for "electronic business," and the phrase is pronounced as simply "ee-bee-ex-em-el." In this book we will discuss how ebXML fundamentally changes the way information technology (IT) handles online business transactions.

The ebXML standard is the result of a joint international initiative of the United Nations Centre for Trade Facilitation and Electronic Business (UN/CEFACT) and the Organization for the Advancement of Structured Information Standards (OASIS). ebXML is a concerted effort to combine the best of two existing standards: electronic data interchange (EDI) and extensible markup language (XML). Prior to ebXML, members of both EDI and XML groups disagreed over details but wanted something from the other side. XML users wanted access to the EDI community's vast inventory of business semantics and standards development, and the EDI community wanted to use XML technology. Joining forces in the ebXML initiative was a win-win situation. Together they set the following goal, according to the published ebXML vision on the organization's Web site:

"The vision of ebXML is to enable a global electronic marketplace where enterprises of any size and in any geographical location can meet and conduct business with each other through the exchange of XML-based messages."

Why Is ebXML Important?

Why are standards important in e-commerce? The following analogy should help demonstrate. When the home video industry started, movies were available in two popular formats, VHS and Beta. The VHS video format was less expensive, but the Beta offered a higher-quality format. Eventually, however, VHS won out over Beta. Why? Because VCR manufacturers adopted VHS, which—unlike Beta—was not controlled by Sony, one of their competitors. This led to a lower cost for VHS players and cassettes. People that bet on Beta lost out.

Industry standards like VHS and Beta help coordinate the behavior of market players to make wise investments, whether it is a 16-year-old buying the latest Hollywood release or a videocassette player manufacturer building a multimillion-dollar production factory.

The story did not end there, because today there are still more formats for movies. Today we can also purchase movies on DVD or download them as an MPEG on the Internet. New standards come into play in the marketplace, and the market players such as consumers, manufacturers, distributors, and retailers decide whether the standards thrive or die.

How does ebXML fit into this? Technically, ebXML is not a standard yet, but it stands a good chance of becoming an important electronic commerce standard. (See the detailed discussion on a standard versus specifications in Chapter 1). Each year billions of dollars are at stake in business-to-business (B2B) transactions. Companies large and small have to invest in infrastructure to enable trading of goods and services between them. As a whole, industry players decide on the common architecture and applications for exchanging trading information.

ebXML is a uniform solution for building the e-commerce infrastructure. Instead of diverging proprietary standards, ebXML unites the competing factions under a common banner of international trade. The battleground for ebXML is the backdrop of existing standards such as electronic data interchange (EDI), as well as newer trends, such as the Internet and B2B.

Who Should Read This Book

This book is intended to help technology, business, and sales professionals understand ebXML and how it can be applied to meet business requirements. The goal is to help readers quickly get a grasp on what is involved, whether your role is selling, buying, planning, or implementing a project involving ebXML. The book assumes no previous knowledge of ebXML, XML, or other programming languages, but it is helpful if you have a technical background in IT.

You may or may not already be familiar with ebXML. For those just starting out, this book will give you a sound understanding of the basic concepts and principles, a look at what others are doing, and an understanding of the business and technical solutions that ebXML can address. In short, you will have the background information you need to ask serious questions about ebXML and to plan a project involving ebXML.

For those who are more advanced in their knowledge of ebXML, the companion Web site for the book will help with mastering advanced technical topics and provide additional programming code and reference information for your project.

How the Book Is Organized

There is no way one book (even one filling several volumes) could poke into every nook and cranny of an evolving area as complicated as ebXML. Even if we could lay out all the little pieces in one place, it would be obsolete within a few months. Thus, this book is designed to provide a broad overview, which while fluid, does not change nearly as quickly, so we will have a bare tree on which to hang the leaves of our own experience. It is easier to pick up the details from Web sites, trade publications, and industry conferences than it is to learn the structural overview, because few people have the time and patience to sit down and discuss it. For some of the ebXML resources, you can check out the Resources appendix.

This book is divided into two major sections: Part 1 provides an overview of ebXML, including the basic foundations built on EDI and XML; Part 2 provides a detailed discussion of components of the ebXML architecture, such as business process, core components, messaging, registry, and collaboration protocol agreement and profile.

Part 1: E-Commerce Basics

Chapter 1 provides the business context for ebXML within e-commerce and B2B. We look at how companies can benefit from B2B. We also look at standards, why we need them, and ebXML as an emerging standard versus a set of specifications.

Chapter 2 provides the technical context for ebXML within EDI and XML. What is EDI and XML? We explore basic concepts of XML such as format, namespaces, document type definitions (DTDs), as well as work through some XML examples to learn how to use XML.

Chapter 3 provides a technical context for ebXML within Web services, which are interactive services built using XML- and HTTP-based technologies. We define Web services and explore how to use it. Web services technology includes languages such as XML and Web services Definition Language (WSDL); protocols such as Simple Object Access Protocol (SOAP) and Universal Description, Discovery, and Integration (UDDI); and enterprise XML frameworks such as the Microsoft-driven BizTalk initiative and RossettaNet.

Part 2: ebXML Technologies

Chapter 4 provides an overview of the ebXML architecture. First, we discuss the business and technical rationale for the overall architecture, framework, and applications. We look at the specific technical pieces such as the business process model, core components, messaging, registry, and collaboration protocol.

Chapter 5 discusses the ebXML business process model. We discuss the business process model in ebXML and how to use it with some examples of documents, transactions, and collaborations.

Chapter 6 looks at the core components of ebXML. We discuss the component architecture and how to use it with some examples of context and assembly rules to put together core components.

Chapter 7 covers ebXML messaging. We discuss what messaging is in an ebXML context and how to use it to send messages between trading partners.

Chapter 8 reviews the ebXML registry. We discuss the registry architecture and its usage with some examples of browsing and querying a registry.

Chapter 9 provides an overview of the ebXML collaboration protocol. We discuss using the protocol as a handshake between partners and show this process using examples of the collaboration protocol agreement and profile.

Chapter 10 shows you how to apply ebXML in your projects. We discuss how to apply the concepts in real-world situations to gather user requirements and manage stakeholder expectations.

Appendixes

The appendixes include listings of ebXML-related resources, references, and a glossary of ebXML terms. The glossary includes a brief explanation of ebXML technical jargon, and it could be useful for navigating through technical discussions. The lists of resources and references serve as a starting point for further research on your own.

About the Web Site

The companion Web site for this book (www.wiley.com/compbooks/chiu) serves as an information resource for further investigation into ebXML. The companion Web site includes references to the ebXML specifications, sample code, demos, and discussion groups.

Detailed technical topics and code examples are posted on the Web site. What language and middleware will we use? ebXML is the business rules for how two different systems talk to each other. Those systems need to be written using a specific application programming language (XML, Java, C, C++, Visual Basic, and so on), executed in a specific middleware (J2EE and COM+), and designed using a specific modeling language (UML, UMM, and UBL).

For a focused presentation without technical clutter, we will use XML as the sole technical language of choice. This philosophy of XML minimalism means you do not have to bother reading other books on XML or programming languages before reading this book. You will discover all you need between the two covers, and the Web site provides a more detailed reference for examples and pointers to other online resources.

PART

One

Overview of ebXML

CHAPTER

1

An Overview of E-Commerce and ebXML

"Historically, standards within the information technology industry have been pushed by vendors. Uniquely ebXML has been pulled by its user community."

—Simon Nicholson, OASIS director and marketing strategist, Sun Microsystems

AREAS COVERED IN THIS CHAPTER

- **What is e-commerce?**
  - **What is its economic value?**
  - **Business-to-business (B2B) versus business-to-consumer (B2C)**
  - **What is B2C e-commerce?**
  - **What is B2B e-commerce?**
- **How do we build B2B systems?**
  - **Developing applications and application programming interfaces**
  - **How would applications talk to each other?**
  - **Electronic trading and interchange**
  - **EDI versus XML**
- **Why are there standards for electronic trading?**
  - **What is a standard?**
  - **Standard versus specification**
  - **Open standard versus proprietary**

(continues)

AREAS COVERED IN THIS CHAPTER *(Continued)*

- **Why ebXML?**
  - **Before ebXML: Brief history of e-commerce standards**
  - **Who is involved in ebXML**
  - **Should you be involved in ebXML**

In the introduction to this book, we learned that the Extensible Markup Language (XML) and electronic business XML (ebXML) standards are intended to define an e-commerce infrastructure for worldwide trading partners. In this chapter, we discuss the business context for ebXML, including different models of e-commerce, electronic trading, and related standards. We begin by defining e-commerce, and then we examine the different types of e-commerce business models.

What Is E-Commerce?

Electronic commerce (e-commerce) covers a broad spectrum of online businesses, including:

- Individual consumer buying collectibles on an auction site such as eBay
- Real estate agents advertising representation services and listing properties
- Large corporations with a multitude of products and services

In the following sections, we examine why companies engage in e-commerce. We discuss the potential benefits of e-commerce and the economic value of ebXML as an e-commerce standard.

The Economic Value of E-Commerce

Every business is part of a *value-added supply chain* (value chain), with suppliers on the buy side and customers on the sell side. Cost-saving methods usually focus on the buy side of the value chain and on improving the productivity of systems and processes that interact with suppliers. Revenue-enhancing benefits usually focus on the sell side of the value chain and on improving the productivity of systems and processes that interact with customers.

The benefits of e-commerce from both the buy side and sell side include:

Improved productivity. This benefit is usually measured in terms of the cost savings that result by lowering the cost of transactions. For example, a company can automate a paper-based manual process such as requisitioning by using a purchasing application on a computer.

Improved policy compliance. Policy compliance measures improve the quality and efficiency of business operations. For example, a company can set rules on specific general ledger codes that eliminate manual corrections or restrict purchasing to a list of approved vendors.

Better data for more informed decisions. Better data results in useful information for predicting future business events, such as next month's orders. More accurate data means that the company can adjust inventory levels accordingly. If the demand forecast is accurate, the company can move to a just-in-time inventory solution.

New sales channels. Establishing new channels such as a trading exchange, a new distribution network, or direct selling can provide new revenue opportunities.

New customers. Establishing a new channel may result in reaching customers that the company is not currently serving effectively.

New information products. Technologies may capture data previously not available, and the packaging of this data may provide another product to sell.

New services. Extending a business process may facilitate providing value-added services, such as dispute resolution, financial settlement, logistics, and authentication.

Higher customer satisfaction. By having a better and deeper relationship with customers, we can ensure happier and more loyal customers who spend more money and return more often. If the company is the easiest and simplest channel to buy from and offers rich customer value (most variety, best information on availability, highest quality, and so on), then the company has a competitive advantage.

Next, we look at different categories of e-commerce, including business-to-consumer (B2C) and business-to-business (B2B).

B2B versus B2C

Business-to-business (B2B), business-to-consumer (B2C), and consumer-to-consumer (C2C) e-commerce business models describe who is the target buyer market and who is the target seller market. We will focus only on B2B and B2C, since C2C is a relatively small segment by comparison.

B2B describes online transactions between one business, institution, or government agency and another. B2C describes online transactions between a business and a consumer. Examples of B2C sites include Amazon and Yahoo.

Note that although for the most part major e-commerce sites fall into either B2B or B2C, they need not be mutually exclusive. Dell Computer, for example, is both a B2C and B2B site.

B2C E-Commerce

B2C e-commerce, also known as online retailing, offers the convenience of home shopping over the Internet or by phone, along with lower prices. The business model is based on the lower overhead costs of online sales in comparison to sales at traditional brick-and-mortar stores.

A simpler form of B2C e-commerce, called brochureware, uses an online product catalog and a one-to-one selling technique. The buyers receive product information from the merchant's Web site and can then place an order with an email or phone call. From the Web site, the order is manually entered by a customer service person into back-end systems such as accounting and inventory management, rather than automatically processed by a computer system on the back end.

Most retail Web sites include a product catalog, a shopping basket, and an automated payment system. Products are usually grouped into categories and displayed on the Web site. The shopping basket allows consumers to select and purchase multiple items at once. Automated payment systems accept and approve credit cards online. Many sites have customized advertising, cross-selling and up-selling promotions, and product searches.

Web sites such as brochureware sites that require orders to be manually entered into back-end systems are clearly inefficient. Their lack of integration can also prevent the organization from exploiting potential business opportunities. For example, a computer system that can interchange and aggregate data on a standard platform can also be used to aggregate products across multiple catalogs, create a database of customer preferences, and create effective cross-sell and up-sell promotions.

A business driver for a new standard such as ebXML is to make system integration easier and automate manual processes using a standard platform. A business can handle a higher volume of transactions and reduce overhead costs by processing Web site orders in an automated way.

B2B E-Commerce

Dell Computer is a B2B site that has uses the Web to implement a build-to-order direct sales model to effectively reach different target audiences. While the majority of Dell's sales are to large companies, its Internet sales are much more weighted toward small businesses. The business model allows the company to reduce inventory-carrying costs and avoid the markups of resellers and distributors. Using the Web, Dell has also reduced service and support costs.

Vertical B2B sites serve a specific vertical industry, such as chemicals, foods, and telecommunications. These sites focus on understanding industry practices and resolving industry constraints. This means eliminating inefficiencies that lower margins. By automating the vertical supply chains, the B2B sites succeed in making the market more efficient.

Horizontal B2B sites focus on providing e-commerce capabilities that are common to all industries, such as maintenance, repair, operations procurement, sales and marketing, and human resource services. Horizontal B2B sites seek to make these processes more efficient across different industries.

An *intermediary* aggregates data and facilitates transactions by bringing buyers and sellers together. Many B2B sites serve as intermediaries for other businesses. The intermediaries become virtual marketplaces, with multiple vendors and products, and fall into different pricing models, such as exchanges and auctions.

An *exchange* model is a two-sided marketplace where buyers and suppliers negotiate prices, usually with a bid-and-ask system, and where prices move both up and down. These work best with easily definable products without complicated attributes, such as commodities, perishable items such as food, or intangibles such as electric power. An exchange has fluctuating market prices, and this is useful if a true market price is hard to find. The exchange model works where brokers make high margins by buying low and selling high to purchasers who don't know the original sellers. Exchanges are also known as digital exchanges, online exchanges, dynamic exchanges, and dynamic trading exchanges.

An *auction* model lets multiple buyers bid competitively for products from individual suppliers. The auction is suitable for hard-to-move goods such as used capital equipment (forklifts) and surplus or excess inventory. Prices only move up, but buyers can buy below list prices while sellers sell for more than a liquidator pays. Auctions are becoming a feature of many markets, but some use auctions as their primary market mechanism. One example is OnSale, which has created a marketplace for the market of business surplus (that is, excess inventory and idle assets). OnSale gathers qualified buyers and sellers, facilitating transactions and increasing efficiency. Sellers save such expenses as warehousing, and surplus goods are more accurately priced. Buyers access a global supply of business surplus, benefiting from shorter sales cycles and comparable product information.

A *hub* is an intermediary that aggregates demand from small buyers to negotiate better terms with large sellers. This process can involve horizontal (operating supplies) or vertical manufacturing. The hub model is used for spot

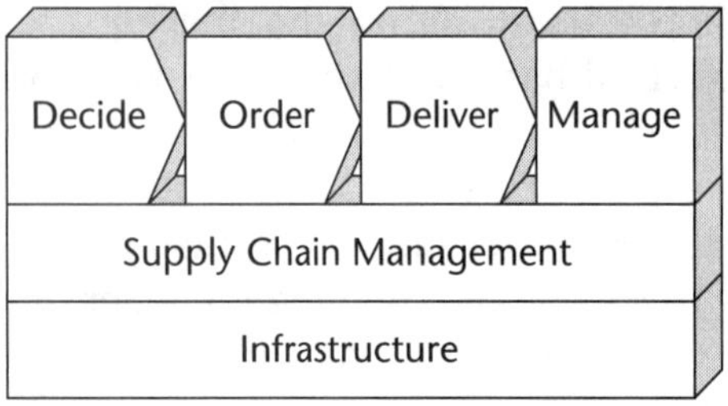

Figure 1.1 B2B interaction between buyer and seller.

purchasing (using exchange or auction) or systematic purchasing (catalog mechanism). The horizontal purchasing hubs use horizontal logistics (UPS, for example), while the vertical purchasing hubs generally need vertical logistics (for hazardous chemicals, for example) for working with existing distributors.

A new concept in B2B is *business webs*, as defined in the book *Digital Capital* (Tapscott 2000). Business webs are places where buyers and sellers come together to communicate, exchange ideas, advertise, bid in auctions, conduct transactions, and coordinate inventory. They are also known as e-hubs or electronic marketplaces. A business web can either be organized horizontally or vertically. The many-to-many connectivity made possible by the Internet enables buyers to link up with customers, suppliers, and other members of their value chain in business webs so that they can exchange information and trade products and services electronically.

In B2B, whether an exchange, auction, or a vertical or horizontal hub, the opportunities to improve communications between customer and suppliers provide cost savings and sometimes revenue possibilities. *Supply chain management* is an effort to coordinate processes involved in producing, shipping, and distributing products, generally with large suppliers. Supply chain management (as shown in Figure 1.1) provides a foundation for the B2B interaction between the buyer and seller. The B2B business driver for a new standard such as ebXML is to make system integration easier and automate manual processes using a standard platform or shared infrastructure.

Building B2B Systems

Integration is a buzzword in IT systems. How do we make different applications or components of the same application work together? Most companies, large and small, have a hodgepodge of different systems built at different times from different vendors. The Internet and World Wide Web have only made it harder to keep up, as now the common expectation is that the companies can and will interface their systems to customers and suppliers. Using their Web storefronts, companies can communicate with back-end operational systems for fulfillment and customer interaction.

In certain B2B models, such as the public online exchange, new technologies may also mean opening up the business model to rivals and competitors. Exchanges enable buyers and sellers to meet new actors and compare prices. In the past, buyers and sellers within the energy industry have negotiated prices and conditions informally, such as at impromptu meetings at industry conferences. It has gathered suppliers and service providers from all over the world to take part in its online exchange, where the participating actors buy and sell energy on a spot market.

Another e-commerce model that has emerged is software enablers, who provide vertical and horizontal B2B with an effective technical infrastructure. An *application service provider* (ASP) provides outsourced hosting services for applications, which allows companies to rent rather than buy applications and services, such as auctions, exchanges, and catalog aggregation. ASPs are often not tied to any one application, plugging a feature of one application into a marketplace when appropriate and using another feature from another vendor elsewhere. Many application software vendors are moving to an ASP hosting model to add revenue opportunities. ASPs provide information publishing tools, catalog software, transactional capabilities, payment services, and customer relationship management functionality, among other services.

B2B exchanges may be an extension of enterprise software or service companies (such as procurement software or IT outsourcing services). In this case the company frequently offers software solutions, such as procurement software, enabling users to conduct purchases more efficiently. Along with providing software products, the companies operate their own Web sites, which provide transaction capabilities and content services, such as industry news and reports, and Internet portals that bring together vendors using a standard format for reading and posting transactions.

In large companies, *enterprise application integration* (EAI) is used to integrate applications among multiple enterprises. In certain industries, such as retail, transportation, and distribution, companies typically need to integrate supply chains tied to fulfillment, shipping, and other internal systems.

A *back-end system* is an enterprise system that handles order processing, inventory, and receivables management for both buyers and suppliers. A B2C or B2C Web site may link to a back-end financial system to process purchases, and an inventory management system may be used to maintain products in stock.

An *enterprise resource planning* (ERP) application is a complex application used by large enterprises to manage inventory and integrate business processes across multiple divisions and organizational boundaries. The ERP system is often the application backbone in many large enterprises. To deploy an online trading platform, companies must often integrate new technologies with the back-end systems, which can include mainframe or ERP applications.

Many B2B initiatives focus on extending legacy ERP systems, such as purchasing and order entry, to wider audiences inside the enterprise (such as e-procurement) or outside the enterprise (such as digital storefronts). These technologies are a natural evolution of ERP solutions (purchasing and order entry), and much of the value in these B2B systems lies in unlocking and extending the value in existing ERP implementations.

Middleware is the integration software that ties together different software platforms and exchanges content and transaction information between companies. Popular middleware platforms include the Java 2 Enterprise Edition (J2EE) from Sun Microsystems, Common Object Request Broker Architecture (CORBA) from Object Management Group, and .NET framework from Microsoft. Vendors have been fighting for ownership of middleware platforms and communication between distributed applications: UNIX vendors pushed the CORBA, while Microsoft backers rallied behind another interoperable technology, the Distributed Component Object Model (DCOM).

Middleware applications can translates messages and transactions into specific formats and integrate data flow from departments such as purchasing, ERP, accounts payable/receivable, and financial reporting. Middleware enables linkage between multiple value chains and the formation of new e-commerce infrastructure. The right middleware can enable companies to rapidly deploy transactional or process interactions. As shown in Figure 1.2, middleware systems provide users with a simplified view of highly complex and technical e-commerce support infrastructure.

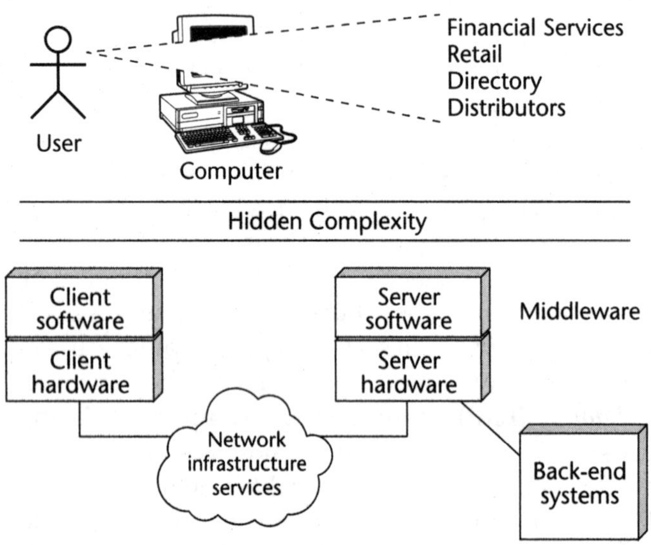

Figure 1.2 How services are provided to users by middleware systems.

An aspect of e-commerce deals with how to exchange data between businesses. A variety of techniques, employing both proprietary and public standards, have been used to manage B2B e-commerce. These methods include developing e-commerce applications and application programming interfaces.

Developing Applications and Application Programming Interfaces

Interoperability is a major theme in a distributed environment. How do we get proprietary applications from different vendors to talk to one another for B2B interchange? (These include both proprietary applications that are developed in-house as well as shrink-wrapped, off-the-shelf commercial applications.) One solution is to define a document interchange format, which is a set of rules for representing documents for the purpose of interchange.

Companies can choose to use the proprietary applications of their trading partner to solve such interchange problems. Rather than building application connectors and other programming plumbing to communicate with the trading partner, they roll out a single proprietary application platform to all partners.

However, this creates other problems—increased cost, complexity, and missed business opportunities. It is difficult to design integrated internal systems that will work with multiple businesses. Adding new trading partners is costly, since the proprietary application has to be rolled out to all partners. Additional manual data entry work is required because of duplicate data inside each trading partner's operational systems. A solution to this problem is using an open system approach to provide a standard interface, using techniques such as an application programming interface to integrate data from different sources within the enterprise.

An *application programming interface* (API) allows usage of specific data or functions in a computer system or application. The data or functions can then be used for writing custom programs that tie into the original program or for modifying the original program. The API per se is just a programming interface; it requires developers to write code to support the desired API functionality. A proprietary API is owned and developed by a company, such as Microsoft's DirectX on Windows, as opposed to a public standard API such as Common Gateway Interface (CGI) on the Web.

Trading partners who want to exchange data can use this API to develop connector code. However, there is a learning curve associated with any API. A new set of APIs is needed for each trading system. The connection mechanism between the companies may create security problems and consume a large amount of system resources.

Another requirement is that data sent through the API has to be converted into a new format. Proprietary solutions for data and document interchange formats have to be decoded in certain ways. They involve communication with other companies a priori, extensive documentation, coding efforts, and reinvention of tools for transmission. This makes a standard language like XML attractive. Using XML for messaging formats is often easier than designing proprietary formats, and it saves time and resources that would otherwise have been invested in developing and promoting nonstandard formats.

Web Services

Current trends in e-commerce are creating enormous opportunities and pressures for automation of business processes across business boundaries. These include the need to truly realize the potential and promise of e-commerce by creating virtual enterprises—that is, networks of applications that automate business processes across enterprise boundaries. One area of convergence between application-to-application communication, Internet, and XML is Web services.

A *Web service* is an application service based on the XML carried over the World Wide Web's Hypertext Transport Protocol (HTTP). Web services are used to communicate between applications. In this context, *application service* refers to an application built as a component that fits into other application services. The idea is to leverage the advantages of the Web as a platform applied to the set of *dynamic* services, not just to *static* information. Modern computer technology and new practices, such as advances in object-oriented technology, have changed the rules of the game. In designing systems, we are not tied to static implementations such as software builds, compilers, or mapping tools, and we can move easily to a dynamic and real-time environment.

For example, a large retail chain might use Web services to integrate its supply chain. Using Web services for such a project is a good idea, since these services eliminate custom APIs. Web services give smaller companies incentive to participate in supply chains because interfaces built according to Web services standards can be used to interact with a multitude of partners. If an 800-pound gorilla wants its partners to build the supply chain services, the partner company can leverage its development effort by using the same interface with other customers.

Many major vendors have focused on the need for application communication in B2B. In 2000, Microsoft introduced their .NET initiative to enable the delivery of software over the Web. Microsoft is staking its future, and billion dollar investments on the .NET business model. Based on the Web service platform, the .NET model will allow applications to talk to each other using the XML format.

Within IT departments, software developers are using tools such as Microsoft Visual Studio to create Web services applications that communicate across a wide area network (WAN). A version of the Microsoft developer product

WEB SERVICES HELPS COMPANY REACH CUSTOMERS

"Right now, the Web is mostly person-to-person, but both our clients and third parties want to gain access to each other, system-to-system," says Tim Hiltenberg, chief technology strategist at Hewitt Associates LLC, a Lincolnshire, Illinois, human resources company. Using a strategy based on B2B technology, Hewitt is working to make life easier for its customers. Hewitt provides employee benefits information, such as 401(k) balances and transactions, to its 250 business customers and their 15 million employees. Hewitt is building its own portal to aggregate all employee benefits information for each client company. Web services will provide the standard application interface to support whatever type of technology is in use at customer sites. The middleware consists of Java servlets, which are server-side programs written in the Java programming language. The middleware resides on the server at Hewitt and contains the business logic for application tasks such as selecting a mutual fund in a retirement portfolio. The company also will be able to give customers easier access to applications provided by third parties such as investment advisers.

***Source:* McDougall, 2001.**

called Visual Studio.NET allows the developer to create Web services using Visual Basic tools. Other Microsoft products, including SQL Server and Exchange Server, allow system administrators to use Web services to communicate with other applications. (See Chapter 3 for more information on Web services technologies.)

Electronic Trading and Interchange

The modern economy depends on moving products and services between businesses that add incremental value to the product or service, or *electronic trading*. The broader concept of computer communications between businesses is referred to as *electronic interchange* or *electronic exchange*, as in electronic data interchange. In this context, a *trading partner* refers to a business involved in electronic trading; typically in a transaction there are two or more trading partners.

Trillions of dollars of transactions take place between businesses each year, most involving paper purchase orders, invoices, and receipts. Electronic trading accounts for a small percentage of all transactions, but it will continue to grow over time as the cost of computer systems decreases while processing power increases. Trading systems allow people to track large amounts of data needed for optimum process efficiencies, which keeps costs down and productivity up. Computers also make it easier for companies to link up with other companies, since an automated system requires fewer people to maintain it over time and eliminates tedious jobs such as manual data processing. An industry standard for electronic trading is Electronic Data Interchange, which is challenged by new technical standards such as Extensible Markup Language. In the next section, we will compare and contrast these two standards and how they can work together.

EDI versus XML

B2B application integration isn't new. For some time now, it has bridged the gap between legacy IT infrastructures and emerging B2B collaboration frameworks and allows the IT infrastructure to provide greater adaptability to the business of the enterprise and easier management of constantly evolving business processes. There are two important enabling technologies: Electronic Data Interchange (EDI) and Extensible Markup Language (XML).

EDI was launched in the 1970s as a standard for high-volume online transactions between large companies and their most significant trading partners. One EDI-based trading system and proprietary network used for transmitting EDI transactions is called the *value-added network* (VAN). EDI was the first of many attempts to create a standard way for businesses to communicate over a network. While successful in certain industries, EDI has proved too complex and costly for most.

XML is a more recent invention for exchanging information between computer systems. XML is a markup language used to create *smart* data and documents for applications. XML coexists with the popular Web formatting language HTML. HTML tells us how the data should look, but XML tells us what it means. XML enables complex linking (using XPointer and XLink) and allows users to define their own elements (using a document type definition or schema). It also provides a style sheet for formatting documents (using XSL).

XML and EDI are not exclusive choices. Some systems provide an EDI-to-XML bridge for supporting both EDI-capable and Web-based systems. A newer standard such as ebXML incorporates as part of its design solution some borrowed ideas from both EDI and XML. (We will discuss XML and EDI further in Chapter 2.)

Internet standards such as XML and ebXML offer businesses the opportunity to build an interoperable e-commerce infrastructure. In a computer system, ebXML specifies the business rules for how two different systems talk to each other. Those systems need to be written using a specific application programming language (such as XML, Java, C, C++, or Visual Basic), executed in a specific middleware (like J2EE or COM+), and designed using a specific modeling language (UML).

To model B2B business processes, an abstract computer modeling language such as UML or the XML language–specific Business Process Modeling Language (BPML) is used. BPML is an XML-based meta language for modeling, deploying, and managing business processes such as order management, customer care, demand planning, product development, and strategic outsourcing.

Electronic Trading Standards

The Internet has created opportunities in strengthening the value chain between businesses and between the customers and suppliers. However, because of a lack of standards for application communications at the strategic framework level, coordinating activities between players can be problematic. In early e-commerce initiatives, the heavy lifting in defining e-commerce communication between companies has been left to the individual companies and their internal development teams. An elegant solution to the difficult problem of coordinating large and small industry players is to use public standards. To be effective, the standard must be adopted by a critical mass of players, be able to meet the requirements of many applications, and be simple enough to implement in a reasonable time period.

What Is a Standard?

A *standard* is an effort to create widespread use of specific protocols and formats to allow software from different vendors to interoperate, often within a vertical industry. Standards bodies or initiatives often work more slowly than entrepreneurial companies in setting up interoperable terms of trade.

A standard is important in an industry where important and complex investment decisions are made independently, but need to be coordinated. For example, compare the lemonade stand business with the computer chip business. As a child, I had a lemonade stand in front of my house. I bought lemons from a farmer (buy side) and sold lemonade to people that passed by (sell side). I would go to a local farm, buy a bushel of lemons. I would clean the lemons and make lemonade by pressing the lemons and adding sugar and water. The business was very simple, but I still had business conventions on buying, selling, and production.

There was no need for standards in the lemonade stand business. This is a cottage industry, and each individual operator had his or her way of doing things. This worked fine because the scope and scale of operations were limited to a small geographical area and a few people. I did not need an automated system to keep track of sales, logistics, or inventory. That would have been overkill and would have added dramatically to my overhead.

On the opposite end of the scale, a large corporation is often interested in business and technical standards in its industry. A standard provides the center of gravity for industry players to orient themselves and coordinate investment decisions. Planning an integrated computer chip production factory that costs billions of dollars involves deciding whether it will produce chips to design specifications from Intel, such as the popular Pentium processor, or its rival AMD. This decision will also impact the factory's suppliers and customers. Hence, because of the greater scope and scale of operations in certain industries, such as technology, automotive production, and commercial transportation, we need public standards for the coordinated planning of independent operators for investment decisions regarding shared infrastructure. In e-commerce this infrastructure may account for billions and ultimately trillions of dollars in trading volume.

How can a standard such as ebXML add value? Assume we adopt a new standard, either a business process standard such as ISO 9000 or a technical standard such as ebXML. If we have new customers or suppliers that use the standard, then we do not need to invest in additional nonstandard infrastructure to support that organization (in theory, at least). This may help create new opportunities to cut costs from the bottom line by coordinating investment decisions between supplier and customers. ebXML focuses on coordinating systems between companies so they can communicate more effectively. With ebXML as a standard, a company can leverage its one-time investment in both IT and business infrastructure over a larger volume of e-commerce transactions over a longer period of time.

Standard versus Specification

There is a distinction between a standard and a specification. A technical *specification* defines how a technology *should* work (methods) and *should not* work (constraints). By contrast, a *standard* is a collective agreement by industry players on a set of technical principles often captured in a specification. A standard organization helps promote wide use of specific standards so software and systems from different vendors can interoperate. To be a de jure standard, a standard body such as the International Standard Organization (ISO) has to endorse the technology and its specification. This can be a long and tedious process.

In practice, technologies may become a de facto standard by the fact that they are in use by most of the important players in the industry. This can occur with or without an official endorsement from a standard organization. For example, the Windows architecture is owned by Microsoft, who can design to its own specifications based on marketing requirements. Since Windows is the desktop operating system on over 90 percent of PCs, we can safely say it is a de facto standard, regardless of the opinions that certain standard bodies may have to the contrary.

Open Standards versus Proprietary Standards

The *open standard* (also known as a vendor-neutral standard) in the computer system context is based on a set of technical specifications for protocols and systems that is jointly created by many companies or industries. An example of an open standard in recording media is the VHS format for videocassettes. The basic idea of *open-ness* is that software specifications are publicly available and a single vendor does not own the architectural design for the software solution. By contrast, a *proprietary system* is based on a set of technical specifications owned by a single vendor and relies on the system and protocol design of the vendor. Windows is an example of a proprietary system, since it is the computer architecture owned by Microsoft.

There are some standard initiatives backed by specific companies, such as BizTalk (Microsoft). These quasi-proprietary standards are attempts to provide some type of standard interface from proprietary applications and platforms (such as Windows) to other systems. BizTalk is a set of guidelines for how to publish schemes in XML and how to use XML messages to easily integrate software programs together in order to allow extended business transactions. BizTalk consists of a message framework and repository for schema written for that framework, as well as a server product from Microsoft. This initiative leverages existing industry data models, solutions, and application infrastructure and adapts them for electronic commerce through the use of XML.

Building systems based on open standards, as opposed to single-vendor solutions, ensures both stability and a larger base of potential trading partners supporting the infrastructure. ebXML is an open standard for electronic trading, and it uses an open process for soliciting input into the specifications, which has pluses and minuses. On one hand, the open process draws in the best ideas from different places into a broad, overarching vision that applies across industries for how to communicate between businesses. On the other hand, the democratic process of decision making in the ebXML committee organization may take a lot longer, compared to defining a proprietary standard where ultimate authority resides in a designated few within the organization.

Why ebXML?

Standards are necessary to promote transparent communications across the many systems operating in the enterprise. Most information technology environments are heterogeneous, rather than homogeneous. This means that the environment is made up of hardware, software, and other components that may not be standard and represent a variety of standards, products, and vendors, rather than an enterprise view with accepted standards. Standards are important in providing the rules via which information technology products interact. They are needed to ensure that systems can communicate, which is essential in an evolving network-centric strategy. Standards such as network protocols and interfaces between applications allow systems on a variety of hardware, and even operating system platforms, to share information and data.

ebXML addresses some of the technical problems in implementing B2B systems with traditional EDI standards. In an interview between the author and Scott Nieman, a technical expert involved with both the ebXML and X12 initiatives, we concluded that some key reasons based on research by UN/CEFACT and X12 for low rates of EDI deployment include:

- The EDI standards, such as EDIFACT and X12, are ambiguous. They were designed to be as generic as possible so that they can be applied to all vertical industry needs and individual company needs. Each company must create an implementation guide to provide context for their usage of the standard. While the intent was that EDI would be *the* standard format for B2B, the end result is a myriad of differing formats.
- The business case expressed in terms of the EDI business process usage and improvement was not published with the standards. Therefore, EDI users, managers, and developers are often confused about how the EDI standards apply to their business process.
- The ambiguity of these formats and lack of process information have led to excess trading partner negotiation that consumed over 70 percent of the implementation time.
- The EDI standards were based on technical capabilities of mainframe systems from over 30 years ago, and data processing was batch-oriented and scheduled, compared to the interactive processing ability and vast processing power common today.

Many e-commerce standards today are based on XML, which provides a flexible way to describe product specifications or business terms. Many businesses are implementing XML solutions based on the technical specifications issued by the W3C and the XML-based business standards of various XML groups. These businesses require a mechanism and migration path for accommodating legacy EDI solutions based on accredited standards and XML solutions already in progress or implemented. Companies like IBM, Sun, Microsoft, and CommerceOne that have major stakes in online transactions are driving to push standardized B2B transaction formats.

Some relevant electronic trading standards efforts to help different industries communicate online with each other include Microsoft's BizTalk, Open Buying on the Internet (OBI) by the industry association CommerceNet, and RosettaNet by the computer manufacturing industry. ebXML may converge with some other standards; for example, Microsoft may introduce ebXML features and compatibility into the BizTalk framework and the associated

BizTalk products based on user demand. One drawback to the competing commercial solutions available compared to a public standard such as ebXML is that the proprietary solutions usually lack widespread support from the business verticals.

As standards are widely adopted, companies will better manage portfolios of B2B capabilities and interface with third parties with limited resources and short technology life cycles. Many industry players will use the industry standard communication languages and protocols, such as XML and Simple Object Access Protocol (SOAP), as well as transaction definition frameworks, such as ebXML, RosettaNet, and BizTalk.

See Chapter 4 for further discussion of ebXML architecture compared with BizTalk and RossettaNet.

BEFORE EBXML: A BRIEF HISTORY OF B2B E-COMMERCE STANDARDS

In this sidebar, we discuss a bit of history on relevant standard initiatives in the last decade (1990 to 2000). ebXML was the end result of pioneering efforts at merging the Internet, XML, and EDI that converged with major industry efforts to create public standards in e-commerce.

Early efforts in combining the EDI standard with modern technology introduced creative innovations but did not reach critical mass in most industries. An early initiative combining the Internet and EDI was Open-EDI. The standard EDI model is based on a closed model of interaction, in which the trading partners are linked through a secure and trusted connection. Each party in the relationship must have detailed knowledge about the other. Open-EDI reduced the tight coupling required between business partners, since the closed model is too restrictive for Internet-based applications. Another early model in combining XML and EDI is called XML/EDI, an idea pioneered by David R. Webber, which drew industry attention to the need to combine the aging EDI infrastructure with the technical benefits of XML. Many of the good ideas and solutions in XML/EDI and other forerunners would be later incorporated into ebXML, and these early models provided significant contributions to the ebXML specifications.

Compared to EDI, XML is more adaptable and easier to use, but the flexibility and lack of constraints in XML has its drawbacks. A major problem was the splintering of XML into different communities of interest, each with its own dialect of the XML language. These efforts by independents lack widespread cohesive support and critical mass. One industry observer commented: "I'm a big supporter of XML, but XML is fragmenting into multiple standards as we speak. The fragmentation of the standards is going to seriously retard the adoption of those standards into B2B environments. We have associations like RosettaNet promoting one version of XML. We have the World Wide Web Consortium promoting its own version. Commerce One is promoting its own version. Ariba is promoting its own version."

(continues)

BEFORE EBXML: A BRIEF HISTORY OF B2B E-COMMERCE STANDARDS *(Continued)*

Industry-specific initiatives such as RossettaNet introduced important technical innovations but failed to attract participants outside the semiconductor industry. A proprietary standard such as Microsoft BizTalk has its advocates among companies using a Windows-based platform with its early-to-market implementation and cohesive architecture, but it lacks uniform support among companies with heterogeneous systems or systems primarily based on non-Windows platform, such as UNIX or mainframes. From the flowering of ideas during the last decade, ebXML emerged as the dominate solution by major standards organizations to address the need for combining modern techniques in XML with EDI and to provide public standards in growth areas in e-commerce, such as Internet-based B2B exchanges.

Early in 1999, members of the United Nations Centre for Trade Facilitation and Electronic Business (UN/CEFACT), as a committee called Techniques and Methodologies Working Group (TMWG), made recommendations for a new standard work based on XML. They convinced the group to approach an international technology business consortium called Organization for the Advancement of Structured Information Standards (OASIS) for the formation of ebXML. The primary authors of the recommendation were Scott Nieman, who is also the vice chair of Strategic Implementation Task Group in X12, and Bob Glushko of CommerceOne, with Mike Adcock as a contributor.

In September 1999, UN/CEFACT and OASIS announced they were joining forces to produce a global XML framework for electronic business. More than 120 companies and standards bodies participated in the ebXML initiative. After 18 months, at the May 2001 meeting in Vienna, more than 1,000 participants ratified the first generation of ebXML and began delivering the infrastructure.

At this ratification meeting a proof-of-concept demonstration was shown where more than two dozen companies and organizations implemented ebXML. Based on ebXML standards, a sample supply chain information environment was built using ebXML architecture. It proved ebXML standards are relatively easy to work with.

On May 11, 2001, UN/CEFACT and OASIS signed a new memorandum of agreement for continuing the ebXML work. The agreement assigned the infrastructure component to OASIS (transport, registry/repository, and collaborative profile protocol). UN/CEFACT kept the business components (business process and core components).

ebXML Players and Politics

As mentioned in the sidebar, the direct sponsors of ebXML are UN/CEFACT and OASIS. In addition, standards bodies involved in ebXML include National Institute of Standards and Technology (NIST) and World Wide Web Consortium

(W3C). OASIS is a nonprofit, international consortium that creates interoperable industry specifications based on public standards such as XML and SGML, as well as others that are related to structured information processing. OASIS, founded in 1993 under the name SGML Open, was originally a consortium of software vendors and customers devoted to developing guidelines for interoperability among SGML products. It has more than 170 organizational members, including the world's leading technology firms.

UN/CEFACT is a United Nations group set up in 1996 to respond to new technological developments and to officially recognize the contributions made by experts. The United Nations also produces the EDI standard called UN/EDIFACT. UN/CEFACT has a memorandum of understanding with the International Organization for Standardization (ISO) and the International Electrotechnical Commission (IEC) that the work efforts each organization produces may be fast-tracked through each other's processes.

ISO is an organization of national standards bodies from various countries established to promote the development of standards to facilitate international exchange of goods and services and to develop cooperation in intellectual, scientific, technological, and economic activity.

The W3C develops interoperable technologies (specifications, guidelines, software, and tools) to lead the Web to its full potential as a forum for information, commerce, communication, and collective understanding.

ebXML supporters include a large number of industrial, shipping, banking, and other general-interest companies, as well as key technology companies. Members of the Global Commerce Initiative (GCI) plan to use ebXML as the backbone of their new data exchange standard for B2B trade in the consumer goods industry. ebXML will provide the technical infrastructure for the Global Commerce Internet Protocol, a set of recommendations governing the management of data for Internet communication and other B2B interactions. The GCI members include 40 major manufacturers and retailers as well as 8 trade associations, which in total represent 850,000 companies around the world. Also included are exchanges such as Transora, the WorldWide Retail Exchange, and GlobalNetXchange.

The UCC has made major contributions to the GCI effort in ebXML to quickly standardize Internet trading in the consumer products industry with the first in a series of electronic commerce standards. The UCC is an organization founded to administer the Universal Product Code (UPC), the standard barcode that can be read and interpreted by a computer, commonly used to mark the price of items in stores. The UCC has extended its role to establishing and promoting global multi-industry standards for product identification, business processes, and electronic communications. Its electronic communication standards are geared to enhancing supply chain management.

ebXML is designed through a collaborative and open process with no barriers to entry. With the open development process, anyone can become involved in the definition of ebXML specifications—in theory, at least. Actual participation in the specification development process is fairly time-consuming and tedious. Certain e-commerce initiatives in specific industries involved with ebXML, such as automotive and transportation, are also open to individuals or companies involved in that particular industry.

Arguments for and against ebXML

To make a rational decision on whether or not ebXML is right for your organization, we need to examine some of the arguments for and against ebXML. The standards promote migration to enterprise solutions with reduced complexity and support. The establishment and governance of enterprise standards require a constant balancing between too much control and not enough. Standards are both beneficial and detrimental, depending on the perspective of the user. The standards must provide the right amount of flexibility so that the business is not constrained.

Klaus-Dieter Naujok, chairman of the ebXML Initiative, and Ralph Berwanger, vice chairman at the American National Standards Institute's Accredited Standards Committee X12, two of the men who helped manage the ebXML effort, offer the following arguments in favor of ebXML (Naujok 2001):

- "The strongest argument for using the specifications is that they are built upon established technology." ebXML uses proven technology as the baseline for all specifications. This did not require inventing new protocols. The ebXML design leveraged from as much existing technology as possible, including the W3C's XML Schema, XML Linking Language, and the XML Signature Syntax and Processing specification.
- Another argument for ebXML is that "the user and vendor communities are being provided with a set of specifications that have been proven to work." During multiple public demonstrations from many companies, the proof of concept trials proved that the ebXML architecture could work and interoperate with other systems. The trials included the entire ebXML infrastructure working end-to-end, ebXML system components that can talk with other components in a network, and components from multiple vendors integrated as a single user-driven solution.
- The last argument for ebXML is that "the infrastructure is the only open, out-of-the-box, standards-based solution available and ready for use." ebXML uses open technology based on XML and is independent of the underlying transport protocol, such as HTTP. The ebXML solution allows traditional Electronic Data Interchange, XML-based or proprietary payloads to be sent between businesses and partners using common or different vocabularies.

The arguments against ebXML are:

- It's expensive and time-consuming to implement. Many businesses have extensive EDI architectures and character sets based on accredited EDI standards. They need to be able to interoperate between these existing solutions and new systems based on ebXML. They also need to account for the costs of building and maintaining the new ebXML systems. Companies are in business to make money, and the return on investment is uncertain at this point.
- ebXML is a risky investment. Naujok states, "implementing version 1 of anything can be risky. Prudent consumers wait while the foolhardy dive in to find undocumented features. Why should either the vendor or user communities implement the first generation of the ebXML specifications?"

Unless there is a good business reason, such as a major customer downstream or a major supplier upstream in the supply chain using ebXML, a standalone business may not have sufficient cause to move to the ebXML standard.

ebXML is not a cure-all for business problems, but it addresses many of the issues in building electronic trading systems, especially with communicating between proprietary applications and systems in a heterogeneous environment.

Summary

E-commerce covers a broad spectrum of online businesses, from the individual consumer buying collectibles on an auction site such as eBay to real estate agents listing properties and advertising representation services to large corporations with a multitude of products and services. The general categories of e-commerce business models are business-to-business (B2B), business-to-consumer (B2C), and consumer-to-consumer (C2C).

A standard is an effort to create widespread use of specific protocols and formats to allow software from different vendors to interoperate, often within a vertical industry. Many e-commerce standards today are based on XML, which provides a flexible way to describe product specifications or business terms.

Electronic business XML (ebXML) is an emerging e-commerce standard for electronic trading between companies. It consists of a set of specifications developed by standards bodies to set guidelines on building e-commerce software that complies with the standard.

The typical large e-commerce system integration project will require a common language such as Extensible Markup Language (XML) and a public standard such as Electronic Data Interchange (EDI), RossettaNet, ebXML, or a popular proprietary equivalent such as Microsoft's BizTalk.

In the next chapter, we dive into the technical details regarding two technologies important for understanding ebXML—XML and EDI. XML is a markup language used to create *smart* data and documents for applications. EDI is a standard, often used for high-volume online transactions between large companies and their trading partners.

CHAPTER

2

Building Blocks of ebXML: EDI and XML

"Without cooperation from industry leaders and XML standards initiatives, it will be difficult to adopt XML broadly across the industry. When the promise for standards is put forth, customers change their expectations. They expect commonality."

—John Rymer, president of Upstream Consulting, a business strategy consulting firm

AREAS COVERED IN THIS CHAPTER

- **What are the EDI standards, such as X12 and EDIFACT?**
  - **What are some business and technical issues with EDI?**
- **What is XML?**
  - **Structure of the XML document**
  - **Elements and attributes**
  - **DTDs, schemas, and namespaces**
  - **What are XML standards?**
  - **ebXML as the convergence of EDI and XML**

In this chapter, we will describe the technical foundation of ebXML by presenting the e-commerce transaction standards for EDI, XML, and ebXML. The grandfather of all e-commerce transaction standards is EDI, from which ebXML borrows its ideas for business requirements. XML provides a foundation as a standard language for e-commerce, and ebXML is the latest proposed B2B standard for business transactions between trading partners.

Electronic Data Interchange

Information exchange between companies often involves trading transactions between customers and suppliers. A common standard is important to building electronic data interchange (EDI) systems in the supply chain.

For example, a retailer stocks products from many suppliers, direct or through wholesalers. The retailer sends orders every day on printed output from a computer. The orders are sorted and distributed to its suppliers. The retailer can benefit from better service and lower costs in electronic data interchange. The quicker delivery and overall greater accuracy in ordering mean better service from suppliers. Improved logistics results in lower storage and warehousing costs. The retailer approaches a major supplier, and together they set up a computer-to-computer data interchange application using a standard of their own design for the system. This can also be extended to other information requirements, such as inventory management and logistics planning. Since it would benefit both of them to increase the number of trading partners using the system, they will want to make similar arrangements with other retailers and other suppliers. If there were no common standard involved, a shared agreement on standards has to be made for every data exchange link. For instance, with 10 trading partners, there could be 10 different in-house standards. Of course, the situation would become even more complex with more trading partners. Many factors would come into play, such as the technical experience or the business clout of a particular company, as well as differences in business processes and conventions across industries. This would result in disagreements, delays, and higher costs. The power of a common standard for electronic data interchange is important for keeping cost and complexity under control. (See Figure 2.1.)

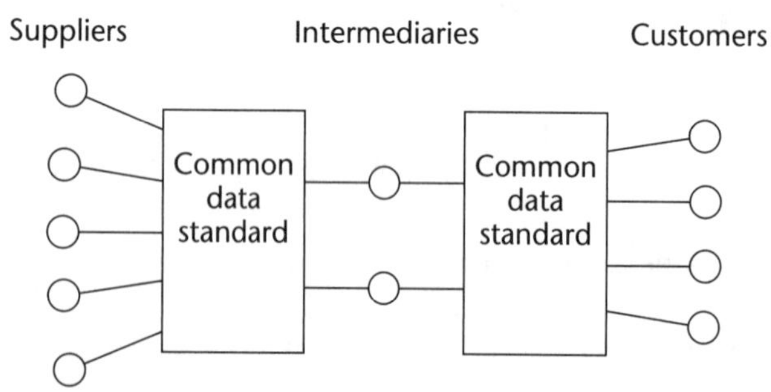

Figure 2.1 Common data standards for exchange in the supply chain.

Before the World Wide Web, e-commerce and EDI—the standard electronic format for transaction processing—were thought to be one and the same. EDI originated from the business and technical requirements of government agencies and large companies to automate trading transactions with each supplier. In many cases, electronic transactions resulted in reduced manual effort while improving quality of services. The industry adopted EDI as a solution to automate handling of high-volume, low monetary value freight transactions. These transactions required significant manual effort to process, and computer automation provided time and cost savings.

In the 1970s, the Transportation Data Coordinating Committee (TDCC) developed the initial standard transaction sets for the air, motor, rail, or ocean transportation business. The transportation industry led in usage of standard EDI transaction sets to conduct business electronically. By switching millions of transactions from paper to EDI processing, carriers and shippers were more efficient in their operations. Defining and handling multiple proprietary formats for each business became a cost barrier for electronic transactions. Industry agreements in the EDI standard reduced this cost of electronic infrastructure. The standard EDI transaction sets were developed with specific documents, such as invoices, purchase orders, and acknowledgments.

These industry dynamics in the transportation industry led to growth in EDI throughout the 1980s and 1990s, and the growth was facilitated by the EDI standards from the TDCC. In the early 1980s, deregulation of the transportation industry in the United States broadened the appeal of EDI for major shippers. This created pricing pressure, as shippers would negotiate their own pricing and payment terms with carriers. Carriers had to compete on *price* and quality of service, which led to a strong economic incentive to create databases of actual transportation costs and shipping patterns. Such databases enabled shippers to negotiate favorable rates and arrange cost-effective carrier selections. EDI usage by major carriers was a cheap and easy solution to the logistics problem. Hence, the industry dynamics created incentives for using EDI by both the carriers and shippers, setting the trend for other industries to follow, such as manufacturing, distribution, and retail.

EDI Technologies

Modern EDI technology is largely associated with the software for formatting electronic messages, data, and forms among computers, as well as with proprietary EDI network services. Trading partners often conduct business using a private network maintained by an EDI service provider. The proprietary EDI network that sends and stores EDI messages is called a *value-added network* (VAN), which typically charges monthly usage fees based on the volume of the transmissions sent through the network. The trading partners in an EDI transaction must agree on the exact content of each document exchanged. Custom translation software is needed to convert a native format used by a company to the EDI format.

EDI messages are composed of segments, and each segment is made up of data elements. A data element reflects the semantics of an equivalent unit of data in a user application. Each data element can be either single or it can be a composite of several elements.

The actual terminology varies according to the different EDI standards. With a specific EDI standard such as EDIFACT, the basic parts are (1) data elements, (2) segments, (3) messages, and (4) syntax. This is analogous to the basic parts of English language as (1) words, (2) sentences, (3) paragraphs/chapters, and (4) grammar. In sum, EDI data elements (words) are put together into segments (sentences), which are grouped into messages (paragraphs/chapters) following rules set by syntax (grammar). The syntax ensures that the order and structure of the data elements make sense by the use of particular rules and special characters, analogous to rules of grammar, where we use commas, periods, spacing, and so on.

The core EDI standards at this time are the ANSI X12 standard and the EDIFACT standard from UN/CEFACT. Both the X12 and EDIFACT standards are similar in concept, but differ in their implementation.

ANSI X1

The American National Standards Institute (ANSI), a standards association in the United States, developed the X12 EDI standard. In the early 1990s, the TDCC standards were incorporated into X12 and endorsed by the ANSI X12

THE MAJOR INDUSTRY STANDARDS GROUPS FOR EDI

- **The Automobile Industry Action Group (AIAG)**
- **National Retail Merchants Association (NRMA)**
- **Voluntary Interindustry Communication Standard (VICS)**
- **Chemical Industry Data Exchange (CIDX)**
- **Electronics Industry Data Exchange (EIDX)**
- **Petroleum Industry Data Exchange (PIDX)**
- **Metals Aluminum Association (MAA)**
- **The American Iron and Steel Institute (AISI)**
- **The American Paper Institute (API)**
- **The National Office Products Association (NOPA)**
- **The Wholesalers Stationers Association (WSA)**

Standards Committee. As the primary format used by many American companies, X12 is a commonly used data format for cross-industry business transactions. However, the standard is only a standard to the extent that it is adopted. Many industries support specific parts of the X12 standard and have created industry-specific guidelines for simplified syntax. Without industry-specific guidelines, companies using X12 have to use the complex X12 format and syntax rules.

X12 standard is a structured, positional format. A *positional format* depends on data elements located in certain positions within a document relative to other data elements. X12 focuses on documents rather than business processes.

EDIFACT

EDIFACT was developed as a combination of X12 and European standards known as "Guidelines for Trade Data Interchange." EDIFACT is an international standard endorsed by ISO and developed by the United Nations Economic Commission for Europe (UNECE). The major differences between X12 and EDIFACT are due to the different data requirements for international trade versus domestic trade.

The EDIFACT format is relatively less structured than X12, and it is not a positional format. EDIFACT transaction sets are more flexible and usable than X12. An EDIFACT message covers a specific business process, which is associated with a specific paper document. Each trading partner in a transaction can process the message segments. Using the business process from the message, the company can engage in e-commerce transactions.

Business and Technical Issues with EDI

The business issues with EDI include the following:

EDI has not penetrated far into the small and medium enterprises (SMEs) markets. This is mainly due to the high cost of doing EDI and the technical complexity involved. Small and medium-size companies can often communicate electronically and send documents. However, thinking that actual costs will outweigh the potential benefits, many have avoided the investment in EDI. Some efforts in large companies have fallen short because they cannot convert the last quarter fraction of their trading partners to EDI.

The application and business process reengineering are expensive if the technology and business processes on either side of the EDI transaction did not keep pace with the technical changes. Many EDI efforts are not fully automated and require dedicated support staff. On the receiving end, too many companies simply send their incoming EDI transactions to the printer while traditional manual processes remain unchanged.

THE MYTH OF EDI STANDARDS

There is no *single* EDI standard. The EDIFACT and X12 standards are only guidelines, and the standards reflect a superset of all vertical industry needs and individual company needs. Each company must create an implementation guide for its usage context of the standard.

Although EDI was intended to be a standard format for B2B, the end result is a collection of different formats.

The ambiguity of these formats and lack of process information lead to excessive trading partner negotiation.

Most trading partners have developed and documented their own interpretations of the standard and expected other trading partners to comply. Disputes are decided in favor of the partner with the most business clout in the relationship (usually a large customer). The end result is that suppliers typically have to maintain some unique code for every trading partner.

Competitors in a particular industry may not completely endorse EDI standards. To survive in a competitive environment, companies have an incentive to differentiate and create proprietary advantages, rather than provide commodity products and services based on a standard. Competitors tend to seek opportunities to differentiate themselves from their peers, which naturally causes deviation from any industry standard.

The technical issues with EDI include:

EDI standards are technically obsolete, since they are based on previous generations of technology. When EDI was first established, product life cycles were measured in years or decades rather than weeks or months, and the pace of change in technology was relatively slow. In a competitive environment, companies must launch new products and services at a tremendous rate in certain industries, with products that often only last for a few weeks or months in the market.

Manual and inefficient processing activities exist in many EDI implementations. EDI focused on automating the flow of information between trading partners, but remaining manual transactions have been the most complex and require the most effort to process. Dedicated EDI staff may have to translate information from its native format to standard EDI.

EDI is typically implemented using a proprietary closed network, such as a value-added network, rather than the open public Internet. EDI using the Internet is becoming more prevalent and far more economical than traditional methods of transmitting EDI transactions either directly or through a VAN. Sending EDI information is usually more involved and more expensive than comparable Internet communication, such as sending email. Businesses that want to exchange data through an open channel such as the Internet need open standards and open technologies on which to build Internet applications.

Since the business requirements for ebXML are partly derived from EDI, it helps to understand the business background for EDI. The next topic, XML, is much more significant as a technical foundation for ebXML. XML presents some technical advantages over EDI. For example, the XML data structure is extensible and the transmission cost is less over a public Internet-based network. In addition, the XML model is open to changes and is flexible for supporting dynamic business processes.

Extensible Markup Language

How do we convert information from the intuitive format for people to use to a logical format for computers to process? We can use a particular computer format such as XML to convert the information in the real world to an understandable stream of information stored on computer systems. It provides a solid set of logical structures with labels. Labels and structures provide recognized information that computers can use to convert input into internal structures for additional processing.

The Extensible Markup Language (XML) is a powerful publishing, data storage, and application and document interchange format—similar to HTML. A critical difference between the two languages is that the XML allows the content provider to define new markup tags for describing data and applications, whereas HTML has a fixed set of markup tags for presentation. XML can be extracted, manipulated, and formatted to the requirements of a target audience or publishing media. XML has spread through many fields of science and into many industries, from manufacturing to transportation to retail.

The strength of XML is its ability to store labeled information, and these labels (also known as markup tags or elements) can be created to represent different kinds of information. In XML, a set of labels for information in a particular domain is called a *vocabulary*. By using a standard vocabulary, various applications on different networks and computers can share a common understanding of the XML document contents. Information stored in a vendor proprietary format can be opened using the XML structured format that labels its contents in plain text. XML provides a set of tools for users to move closer to personalized vocabularies.

The granddaddy of XML is the Standard Generalized Markup Language (SGML), which became an ISO standard in 1986. SGML originated at IBM, which wanted a means of describing document content to publish the same content in different formats. A document markup language, such as SGML, allows content providers to separate the logical content from the presentation. Both XML and HTML are subsets of SGML. XML allows the content provider to define meta data using markup tags for application messages or document content. For example, XML labels the attributes of a book as price, quantity, title, author, and ISBN. By contrast, HTML labels everything by format, such as paragraph, table, and font. XML is a complementary technology to HTML, not a replacement. (See Figure 2.2 for the relationship between these three languages.)

There are two requirements for application and document exchange on the Internet:

Meta data is data about data. Meta data describes what a piece of information is. For example, "book" is meta data about *ebXML Simplified*. Meta data makes it possible to find data and tag data with an explicit description. In addition, the parties exchanging information have to explicitly agree on the overall structure and usage context of the meta data. In B2B e-commerce, meta data should be used with a shared context to fully express its meaning. For example, the meta data "price" attached to "100" may mean euros for one company, U.S. dollars for another company, and Canadian dollars for yet another.

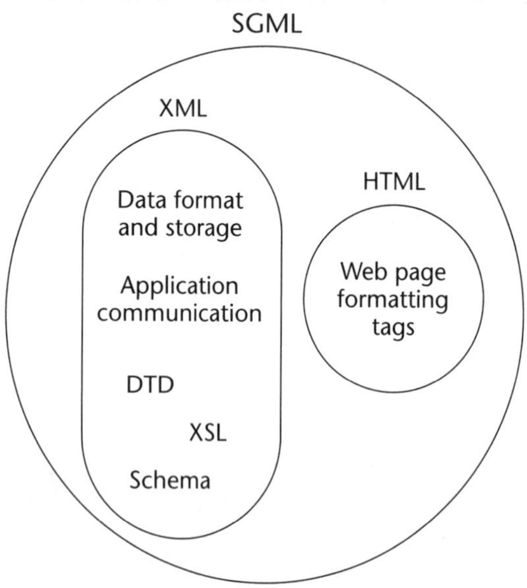

Figure 2.2 Relationship between SGML, XML, and HTML.

Shared context is a formal description of the rules meta data must follow. A shared context applies to a particular type of document and serves as an agreement between the sender and the recipient of the document. The sender agrees that the document conforms to the shared context. The recipient agrees to interpret the document according to the shared context. In B2B e-commerce, two companies would agree to a shared context for documents being exchanged so both parties have a common understanding of semantics. For example, an order can have one or more line items; each line item has a SKU, a unit price, and a quantity; and unit price is a number with two decimal places and represents U.S. dollars.

Both SGML and HTML have drawbacks for defining meta data on the Internet. SGML is complex and is not suitable for automated processing of large volumes of Internet documents. HTML lacks flexibility and is confined to a set of markup tags specific to Web page layout.

Beginning in July 1996, a W3C working group worked on a simplified subset of SGML for use on the Web. Their goal was to find a subset of SGML that was simple to understand but expressive enough to meet the requirement for shared context on the Internet. The W3C released the XML 1.0 specification on February 1998.

The XML language is defined by the W3C specification for XML with two parts, one for XML documents and one for XML document type definitions. The first part defines how to use tagged markup in an XML document to indicate the meaning of data. The second part defines how to define the structure for a class of XML documents using document type definitions.

XML is part of a larger paradigm of Internet documents where XML serves as the foundation. This document paradigm includes related domain-specific standards, such as ebXML for B2B e-commerce and supply chain management, Simple Object Access Protocol (SOAP) for Web services, and so on. This paradigm also includes generic technical standards such as hypertext links (XLink) and page layout (XSL). Figure 2.3 shows the architecture of XML with these related standards. This is a modular design that allows us a choice of what to use for a particular application.

Structure of the XML Document

The XML approach to meta data and shared context is based on using markup tags to indicate meta data and document type definitions for shared context. A *tag* in a document markup language is the meta data attached to an element that defines what the element content is. For example, to indicate that *ebXML Simplified* is a book, we can write `<book>ebXML Simplified</book>`.

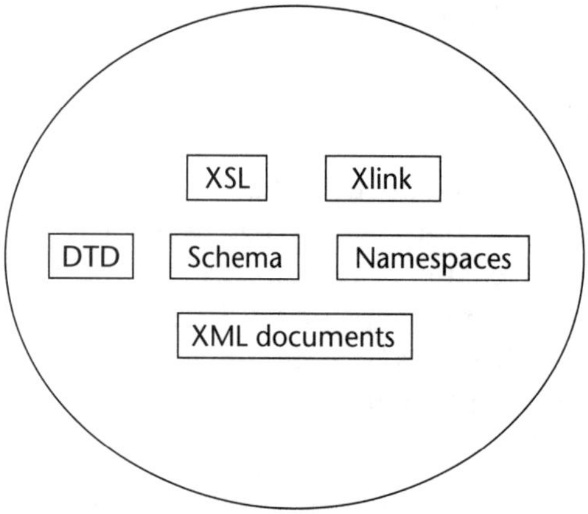

Figure 2.3 The XML paradigm includes a number of related standards.

At the application level, XML documents are containers for information. The primary container holds information and more containers, each of which may in turn contain more information and more containers. These named containers form hierarchical structures, representing an XML document tree, as shown in Figure 2.4. This creates a flexible and powerful framework for storing and exchanging information. XML document type definitions are sets of rules describing the XML document. The parties using or exchanging an XML document can validate using a document type definition that their copies of XML documents follow the same common rules.

The true power of XML to improve business processes comes when multiple documents all use the same public data format. A single software application can process the set of documents, and a single screen layout can display them. If the format is publicly available, then anyone can generate a document that can be processed by the software or displayed in the screen layout.

At the document level, XML uses labels to represent what the information is, not what it looks like. XML uses descriptive tag names (also known as elements in XML) to refer to information, which includes memos, database tables, poetry, program structures, invoices, and so forth. For example, we can use tags to describe the relevant parts of a business document or a purchase order:

```
<BusinessDocument> document content here . .</BusinessDocument>
<PurchaseOrder> order contents here . .</PurchaseOrder>
```

Comments in XML file are declared the same way as comments in HTML, using <!-- for a opening tag and --> for a closing tag. Following is an example:

```
<!-- This is a comment -->
```

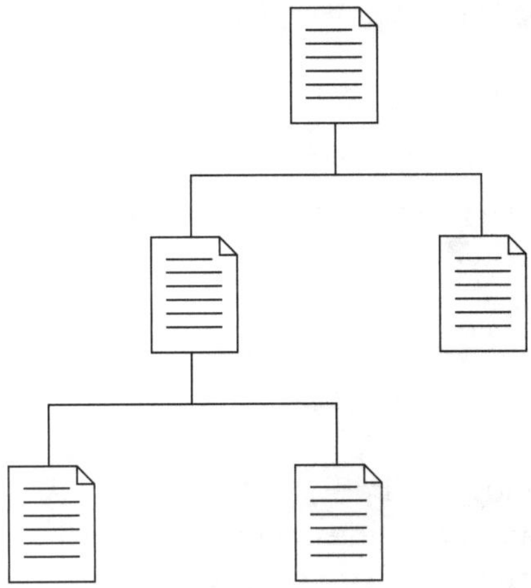

Figure 2.4 XML document tree.

Elements and Attributes

An *element* is a label to define tags in an XML document. An element usually begins with an opening tag such as `<book>`. The element includes an element name, may contain elements and contents with which you vary the results of the element, and may end with a closing tag `</book>`. An XML element may include certain data types or may be empty.

An *attribute* is an option setting that affects the behavior of an element. Attributes can change or specify a piece of information associated with an element. Attributes appear in the open tag and consist of an attribute name and an attribute value, such as:

```
<ElementName attribute="AttributeValue">
```

For example, in XML we can refer to the book, *ebXML Simplified*, with attributes such as price, quantity, title, author, and ISBN (the unique identifying number for published books):

```
<book title="ebXML Simplified" author="Eric Chiu" and
isbn="00000000000">
. . . </book>
```

Most XML tags have elements and associated attributes. An element consists of open and close tags containing the element names surrounding the element content. In an XML document type definition, the value of an attribute is either `REQUIRED` (it must be entered) or `#IMPLIED` (it does not have to be entered).

RULES FOR XML ELEMENT NAMES

- **Names can contain letters, numbers, and other characters.**
- **Names must not start with a number or "_" (underscore).**
- **Names must not start with the letters xml (or mixed-case version such as XML or Xml).**
- **Names cannot contain spaces.**

XML documents have three parts: the prolog, the body, and the epilog. The *prolog*, which includes the data type definition, provides information that an XML reader can use to process the document. The prolog usually contains information describing the root element that follows it, which holds the primary content of the XML documents. The *body* consists of a single root element, which has content including attributes, text, and other elements. The root element is the core of the XML document, sometimes referred to as the payload. The rest of the XML document is just information about how to process the document body. The *epilog* is the part of the document following the root element. The epilog is used for comments, processing instructions, or white space. The root element is the only one of the three parts that must appear in an XML document.

In the prolog, the XML file can contain processing instructions that give commands to an application that is processing the XML data. Processing instructions have the following format, where *target* is the name of the application that is expected to do the processing and *instructions* is a string of characters that embodies the information or commands for the application to process:

```
<?target instructions?>
```

Code Listing 2.1 is an XML document for a book, with an inline document type definition. We will discuss the document type definition in more detail later in this chapter.

```
<!-- Prolog begins -->
<?xml version="1.0" encoding="UTF-8"?>
<!DOCTYPE item [
<!ELEMENT item (book*,description*)>
<!ELEMENT book (#PCDATA)>
<!ELEMENT description (#PCDATA)>
<!ATTLIST book
```

Code Listing 2.1 The structure of a sample XML document for a book.

```
 title      CDATA          #REQUIRED
 author     CDATA          #REQUIRED
 isbn       CDATA          #REQUIRED>
]>
<!-- Prolog ends -->
<!-- Body begins -->
<item>
<book title="ebXML Simplified" author="Eric Chiu" and
isbn="00000000000">ebXML Simplified</book>
<description>This is a book about ebXML</description>
<item>
<!-- Body ends -->
<!-- Epilog begins -->
<!-- This is XML document describing a book -->
```

Code Listing 2.1 The structure of a sample XML document for a book. *(continued)*

In the Code Listing 2.1, the prolog contains a processing instruction that defines the version of XML used and the character encoding:

```
<?xml version="1.0" encoding="UTF-8"?>
```

The prolog also includes a document type declaration that defines the rules for the elements and attributes of the XML document.

In Code Listing 2.1, the root element (item) and its contents describe a book in an item:

```
<item>
<book title="ebXML Simplified" author="Eric Chiu" and
isbn="00000000000">ebXML Simplified</book>
<description>This is a book about ebXML</description>
<item>
```

In Code Listing 2.1, the epilog, which follows the root element, is used for documentation and miscellaneous contents:

```
<!-- This is an XML document describing a book -->
```

Document Type Definition

A document type definition (DTD) specifies the elements, attributes, entities (special or legal characters), and rules for creating one document or a set of documents using XML, HTML, or another SGML-related markup language.

Analogous to the Rosetta stone for archaeologists, the DTD is written with a special syntax for element and attribute declarations that sets the rules for the structure of an XML document. Anyone can access the DTD, interpret the rules, and process the document. An XML document can use a DTD either inline or externally with an uniform resource locator (URL), such as this fictitious example, http://www.ebxml.org/samples/test.dtd. DTDs provide a range of flexibility, with such features as optional and repeatable content models.

Software called a *parser* checks the XML document to make sure that it conforms to the rules set by the DTD for that document. The process of checking the document by the parser is called *validation*. A particular XML is valid if it obeys all the rules of its DTD, as well as the criteria for well-formed documents.

In the software life cycle, a DTD serves as a blueprint during two important phases. During the design phase, using a DTD, the application will produce documents that conform to the DTD. Other applications using the DTD can process those documents. During the execution phase, the XML parser verifies that a document conforms to the DTD, so the processing application knows the document has a valid structure for its content. In sum, the DTD is a contract between the supplier and the consumer of the document.

DTDs give document designers control over both the structure of document elements and the rules that elements and attributes must follow. This allows designers to create DTDs for different applications, including supply management systems and database integration tools.

As DTDs grow larger and more complex, it makes sense to break them into smaller chunks. Developers fragment DTDs to allow reuse of smaller portions, to make the DTD easier to manage and work with, or to divide responsibility among a number of users. XML parsers combine all the modules when it is time to process the document, knitting together parts that may come from disparate sources all over the Internet.

The *document type declaration* (also known as the DOCTYPE declaration) connects the document to meta data describing the document structure and its content, called a *grammar*. This information may be included directly within the document type declaration or included by reference to an external resource containing declarations or both. All the declarations contained within or referenced by the document type declaration form the DTD.

Code Listing 2.2 is the DTD from Code Listing 2.1. The DTD declares the list of elements, which are item, book, and description. The DTD also declares the attributes for the book element, which are title, author, and ISBN. To define the DTD, a document designer starts with the root element. After the root element, the designer moves to the subelements of the root elements. Next, the designer moves to the subelements of those elements, continuing until there are only leaf elements that have data content or are empty.

```
<!DOCTYPE item [
<!ELEMENT item (book*,description*)>
<!ELEMENT book (#PCDATA)>
<!ELEMENT description (#PCDATA)>
<!ATTLIST book
 title     CDATA          #REQUIRED
 author    CDATA          #REQUIRED
 isbn      CDATA          #REQUIRED>
]>
```

Code Listing 2.2 A sample book DTD.

Element Structure

Each *element declaration* begins with `<!ELEMENT` and ends with >. It contains the element name and a content model surrounded by parentheses. A *content model* is the description of the content of an element, including subelements, connectors, and character data.

A DTD specifies the allowable subelements, such as the following declaration to indicate that there are two subelements in the item root element, which are `book` and `description`. The asterisk (*) at the `book` element is an occurrence indicator. The symbol means that the book attribute is both optional and repeatable. If an XML document was created based on the DTD, the book attribute may appear once, several times, or not all.

```
<!ELEMENT item (book*,description*)>
```

An *occurrence indicator*, such as *, ?, or +, is used to define how often an element occurs. The default is exactly 1 if the element appears without an occurrence indicator. * is 0 or more times, ? is 0 or 1, and + is 1 or more times.

For elements with data content, a DTD specifies the type of data it may contain, such as the following declaration to indicate that the book element contains parsed character data:

```
<!ELEMENT book (#PCDATA)>
```

For elements with no content, a DTD specifies an empty content model, such as the following declaration to indicate that the description element is empty:

```
<!ELEMENT description EMPTY>
```

In sum, there are four types of allowable content in XML:

Data content. These elements contain only data. To define this structure, the element declaration specifies a content model of PCDATA, such as <!ELEMENT book (#PCDATA)>.

Element content. These elements contain only other elements. To define this structure, the element declaration specifies a content model that lists the element names, separated by commas. This list is in sequential order, such as <!ELEMENT item (book*,description*)>.

Empty. These elements contain neither elements nor data. To define this structure, the element declaration uses the keyword EMPTY as the content model, such as <!ELEMENT description EMPTY>.

Mixed content. These elements contain both data and other elements. To indicate this structure, the element declaration specifies a content model that includes #PCDATA to indicate that data content is allowed. The element names indicate that elements of these types are allowed.

In addition to these basic content models, DTD designers may use special characters, such as ?, *, +, to encode rules about the number of subelements that an element may contain. These cardinality rules use the following syntax:

0 or 1. The ? character indicates an optional subelement. For example, this declaration defines that a book must have one title, may or may not have one description, then must have one ISBN: <!ELEMENT book (title, description?, isbn)>.

0 or more. The * character indicates a subelement that may appear one or more times. For example, this declaration defines that a chapter may have none or one or more paragraphs: <!ELEMENT chapter (paragraph*)>.

1 or more. The + character indicates a subelement that must appear at least once. For example, this declaration defines that a paragraph may have one or more line numbers: <!ELEMENT paragraph (linenum+)>.

Enumerated alternatives. A list of subelements separated by vertical bars (|), called pipe symbols, indicates that the element must contain one or the subelements in the list. For example, this declaration defines that category must be either fiction, nonfiction, or other: <!ELEMENT category (fiction | nonfiction | other)>.

Content providers can combine different rules in the same element declaration, using parentheses to group subelements together. For example, the following element declaration defines a chapter element that has (1) an optional name, (2) one or more blocks that includes one paragraph sub-element, one or more linenum subelements, and none or more column sub- elements, and (3) either version or updated subelement:

```
<!ELEMENT chapter (name?, (paragraph, linenum+, column*)+, (version |
updated))>
```

Attribute Rules

For elements with attributes, a DTD specifies the list of allowable attributes, such as this set of three attributes for a payment element:

```
<!ATTLIST payment
method CDATA "credit card"
name CDATA #REQUIRED
type (Visa | Mastercard | AMEX) "Visa">
```

Attributes enhance the meaning of element content by providing meta data to elements. DTDs include syntax for defining the rules that attributes must follow. The *attribution declaration* begins with <!ATTLIST and ends with >. There are four parts in an attribute declaration:

Element type. After the ATTLIST keyword, the declaration specifies the element to which the list applies.

Attribute name. The rule for each attribute in the list appears on a new line. The first part of the rule is the attribute name.

Attribute type. After the attribute name, the type specification appears. For example, for character values, the type specification is CDATA.

Default value. After the attribute type, the document designer must specify the default value for the attribute. There are several options, including #REQUIRED, #IMPLIED, and #FIXED. A value in quotation marks indicates an attribute with a default value. If the document does assign it a value, the XML processor will automatically assign it the default value. The #REQUIRED keyword indicates that every document must explicitly assign a value to the attribute. #IMPLIED indicates that a document does not have to assign a value to the attribute; the XML parser will process it even if no value was assigned. #FIXED indicates a fixed or constant value. After the #FIXED keyword, there is an attribute value in quotation marks, which is the value assigned to the attribute in the document.

XML inherited DTDs from SGML. Some shortcomings were also inherited: (1) The syntax of a DTD is different from XML, requiring the document writer to learn yet another notation and (2) there is no way to specify data types and data formats to automatically map to programming languages. XML schemas with the corresponding XML syntax are an alternative to DTDs.

DTDs, Schemas, and Namespaces

DTDs and schema are two different ways of defining meta data for an XML document. XML schemas are more expressive than DTDs. For some content providers, schemas are the preferred way of specifying XML content models. The XML schema standard was developed to improve on DTD limitations and create a method to specify XML documents in XML, including standard predefined and user-specific data types.

The name, content model, attributes, and subelements define the XML element. In XML schemas, the content model of elements is limited to a set of simple and complex content types. An XML document adhering to a schema can have elements that match the defined types. A number of simple types are predefined in the specification, such as string, integer, and decimal. A simple type cannot contain elements or attributes in its value, whereas complex types can specify element nesting and associations of attributes with an element.

In addition to DTDs and schemas, a way to manage the vocabulary for different business groups in XML is namespaces. A *namespace* creates the unique identifier for an XML vocabulary. A set of elements and attributes is associated with a namespace to make the attributes unique. We can avoid naming collisions by associating the vocabulary with a Uniform Resource Identifier (URI), which includes the familiar Uniform Resource Locator (URL) and Uniform Resource Number (URN). An application could include sets of objects that apply to particular namespaces. The applications can use those objects any time the namespace is encountered in a document. XML applications can parse documents and pass off the results to the appropriate application based on the namespace URI.

A way to present an XML document in different forms with the business vocabulary unchanged is to use transformations. Building more flexible systems means planning workflow from input to internal structures to output that adapts to different requirements and business scenarios. The XML applications may be able to create new and different workflow. The key is to express syntax in context in ways that are easy and intuitive for people. This requires breaking down business processes into workflow modeled as XML. Using transformation tools, companies can create the critical information paths to model business processes. By treating the schema as tools for describing structures rather than tools for making structures conform, developers can create systems that adapt to changing circumstances rather than ones that address a particular set of requirements at the beginning of the design process.

While XML has created an unprecedented success for universal data transfer, its flexibility is both a blessing and a curse. The universal appeal of XML has to be harnessed with DTDs, allowing interchange partners to agree on a common vocabulary. Since a single DTD is not enough for most tasks, interchange partners have to agree on a whole set of XML vocabularies. The excitement during the first wave of electronic commerce dissipated once incompatible profiles with different XML standards and dialects became commonplace.

In an effort to catalyze B2B e-commerce, certain industry forums position themselves as clearinghouses. They provide the frameworks for certain industries and business processes to find and exchange schemas. XML is useful for exchanging data between heterogeneous systems. However, the power of industry-wide schemas is in B2B, with communicating systems belonging to different organizations.

The foundations of standards such as ebXML rest on the open content model and usage of DTDs, schemas, and namespaces in XML. For example, if a retailer wants to buy widgets from a distributor over the Internet, the trading partners have to describe their products and business processes in a similar way. The companies will have to share a single dictionary of business vocabulary about every part of the widget business. Using the repository of XML semantics, including tags, DTDs schemas, and namespaces, the end result is a standardization of B2B exchanges based on shared dictionaries of business terms.

XML Standards

Instead of arguing over the technical jargon, with a standard business language (such as an XML standard) we can focus on introducing products to our business partners. This has been a critical aspect of getting information into and out of computers. The key is balancing the formal vocabulary in order to extend the vocabulary as needed in a less constrained approach.

Standards also limit how XML can be applied and used. XML provides a foundation grammar for the structure and labels for information. The basic structure in XML is a system for helping applications comprehend the meaning of a document as a standard across organizations and processes.

An XML standard involves an extensive amount of work on providing practical implementations and technical specifications to enable the development of open, interoperable e-business interactions. This work focuses on utilizing the W3C XML syntax and the Internet as the underpinning technologies. Many critical elements are not set in stone, such as message and document descriptions and XML-based business vocabularies for the majority of industries.

The rising stars of XML standardization are the converging XML initiatives for Web services, such as SOAP WSDL and UDDI. Web services deal with the subject of XML service APIs. (See Chapter 3.)

ebXML: Convergence of EDI and XML

EDI integrated with B2B communities can provide end-to-end services that cover the supply chain and purchasing cycle. The merger of EDI with XML will allow Web-based data sources to be handled by EDI dictionaries. Order entry, purchasing, procurement, and other applications that are built on top of EDI will use the Web as a delivery mechanism.

The Internet platform is widely popular with both large and small players. Internet-based e-commerce can provide rich media support, aggregated information, and speedy installation. Though the Internet has been successful with standardization of low-level communication protocols and data exchange languages, such as HTTP, HTML, and XML, it has yet to produce a consensus across industries on high-level frameworks. The great hope and hype for the IT community is that ebXML bridges the gaps between these existing areas.

The merger of the business requirements of EDI and the technical functionality of XML resulted in ebXML. ebXML was created to make it fundamentally easier to enable integration across industries and between business systems, regardless of platform, operating system, or underlying technology. One of the goals of the ebXML initiative is to build common industry standards for exchanging information and promote adoption of XML as an open standard data format. According to the ebXML initiative, "ebXML is an evolutionary change from EDI to XML technologies. It opens a migration path from EDI and developing XML standards, while providing support for multi-lingual, national, and international trade requirements. As a pragmatic compromise between XML-centric and EDI-centric worldviews, it combines ideas from both into an open integration framework. Within this cross-industry framework, EDI investments in business processes can be preserved in an architecture that leverages the technical capabilities of XML" (from ebxml.org Web site).

Summary

B2B e-commerce systems have to integrate supply chain management and serve as the bridge in communication between businesses. The Internet has been successful as a medium for conducting business, and computer systems among different businesses often have to communicate over the Internet.

ebXML addresses some of the technical problems in implementing B2B systems with traditional EDI standards. Because of the high costs of the infrastructure, EDI usage is limited primarily to large companies and their suppliers. The inability to bring up smaller trading partners on EDI has sidetracked the EDI efforts of large organizations. The available computer technology at the time EDI was developed was more expensive and less advanced than today. A focus of EDI was the development of standard transaction sets. The core EDI standards are the ANSI X12 standard and the EDIFACT standard.

XML may revolutionize network-oriented applications, especially in the area of data interchange, as it is both:

Flexible. XML not only contains data pertaining to transactions; it also contains tags describing data structure, identifying what the data is and what it is for.

Portable. XML documents can be used on different platforms without major changes.

XML has the potential to be the universal language for Internet-based commerce. It can be applied to both informal, ad hoc trading as well as to highly formal, structured B2B exchanges.

The market opportunity for ebXML is the possibility of closer system and process integration and lower cost of shared infrastructure between trading partners. Higher efficiency in the supply chain and new markets open to e-commerce would be major wins for ebXML as a leading XML-centric solution and standard. In the next chapter, we discuss ebXML in the context of Web services, which involves using XML standards on the World Wide Web.

CHAPTER

3

Web Services and ebXML

"Web services . . . are self-contained, self-describing, modular applications that can be published, located, and invoked across the Web. Web services perform functions, which can be anything from simple requests to complicated business processes. . . . Once a Web service is deployed, other applications and other Web services can discover and invoke the deployed service."

—IBM developerWorks.com

AREAS COVERED IN THIS CHAPTER

- What are Web services?
- How do Web services work?
- What are the parts of Web services, such as:
  - Simple Object Access Protocol (SOAP), a format for Internet messaging
  - Universal Description, Discovery, and Integration (UDDI), a specification for building online directories
  - Web Services Description Language (WSDL), which provides the uniform way to describe the interface to a Web service
  - XAML, SAML, and XKMS, which provide XML-based security and transactions support
- Who uses Web services?
- Why use Web services?
- How do Web services relate to ebXML?

The Web—along with a few other platform services—can create fully functional application services over the World Wide Web protocol (HTTP). The Web is the best candidate for the role of universal information distributor, given its simplicity of access and widespread use.

These so-called Web services do not comprise a monolithic all-or-nothing system, but an alphabet soup of smaller technologies that are easy to integrate into other technologies. For instance, Paul Roth, chief technology officer of CommerceQuest, a system integrator, thinks "most businesses will adopt Web services technology in small bites, since applications can be built piece by piece; you don't have to eat the whole watermelon to achieve some benefit."

In B2B e-commerce, a major problem is the complexity of dealing with multiple partners with multiple applications and formats. A potential solution is the integration of XML and Web services into e-commerce transactions. Many vendors already support XML. In addition, the major vendors are ready with their support for the Web services model. HP, IBM, Microsoft, Oracle, and Sun Microsystems have publicly announced support for Web services technologies. The necessary standards are coming together, and major vendors are rallying behind them.

Web services have the potential to help companies save money and generate revenue. Some companies have found ways to market their Web services software externally, while others use the technology to boost sales and customer relationships by building more effective Web sites.

In this chapter, we will discuss the technical underpinnings of ebXML, and, in particular, examine SOAP, UDDI, and WSDL.

What Are Web Services?

The idea of Web services is to leverage the advantages of the Web as a platform to apply it to the services themselves, not just to static information. The services refer to component services that can be used to build larger application services.

At the core, the basic Web service platform is XML and HTTP. HTTP is the ubiquitous protocol behind Web sites on the Internet. Using HTTP in an application makes it possible to work around security issues like firewalls, and technical issues such as different sockets listening on different ports. XML provides the common foundation language for application messaging. By combining XML with other specialized languages, we can express complex interactions between clients and services or between components of a composite service. The XML message is converted to a middleware request, and the results are converted back to XML. The complex programming and processing are hidden behind the simple facade of a manageable Web server.

WHERE WEB SERVICES IS FINDING APPLICATIONS

According to a recent Jupiter survey, 53 percent of companies that plan to deploy Web services will do so to interact with existing suppliers and partners. Only 16 percent of U.S. companies will use Web services technology in the next year to discover and interact with new partners.

"Despite the enormous potential of Web services, the technology will find its early uses in the humdrum role of tying together an enterprise's internal applications."

—David Schatsky, research director at Jupiter Media Metrix

An example of a Web service is the authentication functions offered on the Web by Microsoft Passport. The Hotmail.com email service can leverage the user authentication service in the Passport site instead of developing its own.

Other examples of component services are currency conversion, language translation, shipping, and claims processing. Many large scale Web-based application services like the Yahoo portal services or Amazon bookstore services can be broken down into separate individual Web services as granular, reusable building blocks that can be used for building more Web sites.

The applications built to Web services standards should talk to each other automatically. These applications can be written as software components that can be housed in an application on a local network or on the Internet, and they are accessible by other network applications. As Web sites come to depend on other Web services, they will require support for server-to-server and application-to-application communication.

The following sections provide a brief overview of each of these platform elements. While vendors try to present the emerging Web services platform as a consistent whole, it is closer to a jigsaw collection of technologies in development. The technical functionality in Web services includes open messaging, search, and registry protocols. They enable programmers to build software components that can automatically seek out and interact with other components built to the same standards. These protocols based on XML provide the skeleton for the Web services platform, such as access, identification, and invocation, as shown in Figure 3.1.

The basic Web services platform is based on XML plus HTTP, with higher-level service protocols such as SOAP, WSDL, and UDDI. For additional features like security and transactions, we also need XAML, SAML, and XKMS technologies. These standards and others for security, authentication, and connection management are still evolving.

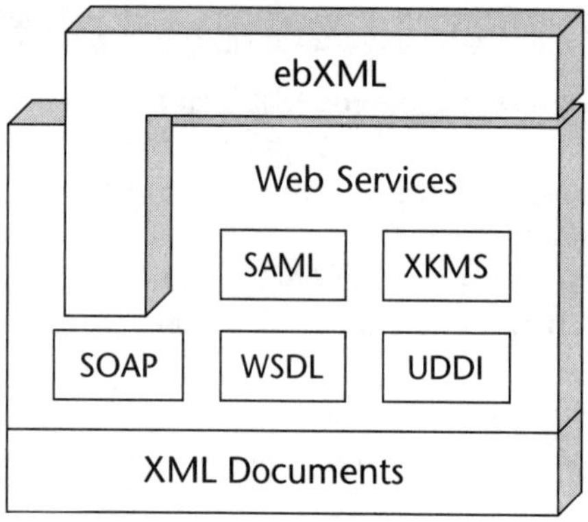

Figure 3.1 Web services model.

Simple Object Access Protocol (SOAP). This protocol is a format for Internet messaging (remote invocation).

Universal Description, Discovery, and Integration (UDDI). This specification is used for building online directories UDDI (directory service). UDDI is a set of protocols and APIs used to discover where Web services are located and to create a directory of services.

Web Services Description Language (WSDL). This language is used for expression of service characteristics.

Both proprietary and standard methods exist for authentication and connection management. However, because the common denominator is XML, all technologies can integrate into Web services in a platform-neutral manner. The additional services include platform support services such as discovery, transactions, security, and authentication:

Transaction Authority Markup Language (XAML). This language is for Web-based business transactions, which support complex Web transactions involving multiple Web services. XAML is a standard that enables the coordination and processing of online transactions in XML Web services.

Security Assertion Markup Language (SAML). This language is for security, access control, and authentication in an XML-based model, developed as an open standard initiative sponsored by OASIS.

XML Key Management Specification (XKMS). This specification defines XML support for authentication and registration involving Microsoft and VeriSign.

WEB SERVICES AND TRANSACTIONS

"Companies are beginning the process of exposing and combining their services on the Internet. As these Web services interactions mature, the need to ensure that the integrity of their customers' transactions becomes more important. With broad industry support, efforts such as XAML could make all the difference between a robust and orderly Net marketplace and one where buyers and sellers spend most of their time resolving fouled transactions offline."

—David Smith, vice president and research area director at Gartner Group

How Web Services Works

An example of how Web services works is a fitness company that provides membership services through a portal built on Web services technology. Registered users will be able to log on and create schedules, plan workouts, and chart their fitness progress. The company offers a Web service–based application to manage membership that it developed for internal use with others in the fitness and related industries. The company will spin off the unit that developed the application into a subsidiary. The company would not have to develop all the applications in-house; instead, it will partner with vendors that specialize in various pieces. The company will use a scheduling tool created by a third-party application service provider, which develops time management and interactive scheduling software. When a registered member initiates the scheduling application on the portal, the action triggers a hyperlink via Secure Sockets Layer (SSL) encryption to the secure page of the scheduling application. The Web sites exchange certificates to verify each other's identity, and the member's information is passed from the application service provider back to the fitness portal via a SOAP interface.

The reuse of Web services functionality cuts development time. By building standard interfaces to existing and new systems, each department can access data in other departmental databases without custom programming on an application-by-application basis. SOAP defines the standard application interfaces, and WSDL describes how to access the data.

Based on the Web services architecture, a company can integrate the supply chain by leveraging legacy ERP systems. For example, a trucking company uses an application to route the job orders from a legacy order management system. The subcontractors use a Web browser to view and bid for the jobs. The subcontractors are needed to haul loads for which the trucking company lacks capacity or local presence. The Java application runs on a Java application server, which supports SOAP, UDDI, and WSDL. The company uses Web services to give customers visibility into the inventory management system so the customers can make better decisions about inventory replenishment.

In the fragmented middleware world, interoperable technologies such as Web services provide a façade for programmatic access to the application service on different platforms and systems. The simple interface hides the complex, vendor-specific implementation in the middleware. In the client/server application architecture, the application access consists of (1) service request handling, such as a listener, and (2) a façade that exposes the operations supported by the business logic, such as an API. The business logic itself is implemented by a middleware platform.

The primary components in a service-oriented architecture are application services. A service is a collection of business or application logic that can be accessed via a messaging protocol such as SOAP, which provides a standard way to couple together software components. This is useful when system changes or upgrades are needed.

Using Web services for database access rather than hard-coded logic adds flexibility into the database application design. The database client application needs to know less information, such as how to send and receive SOAP messages and parse the XML encoded data within each message. The database client needs to decode only the XML data stream and deal with SOAP messages. All other aspects of the database deployment are hidden when both sides have deployed Web services front ends using SOAP and WSDL. The same database client can be modified to connect to other databases by modifying the XML data stream and SOAP message handlers. The modifications become relatively easy, compared with alternative methods of developing application-specific interfaces.

The Web service architecture is resilient in the face of system changes, partly due to the loose coupling of application design. Using Web services, the switch between different databases on different platforms would only involve a few changes in a database client. From the perspective of database client, access to the database service—for example, from a Microsoft SQL Server database running on Windows 2000 Advanced Server to an Oracle database on Solaris from Sun Microsystems—would be a straightforward exchange of SOAP messages.

It's been possible to build similar service-oriented architectures for some time, but because no universally common standards have existed. Several previous approaches have been tried to create distributed applications, such as (1) Microsoft's Distributed Component Object Model (DCOM), (2) Java's Remote Method Invocation (RMI), and (3) custom message-passing interfaces running over HTTP. Unlike Web services, none of these approaches offer a platform-independent, standardized method of accessing services.

SOAP, UDDI, WSDL, and XML are interoperable, platform-neutral standards. Hence, Web services are not dependent on specific aspects of middleware platforms such as Sun's Java 2 Enterprise Edition (J2EE) or Microsoft's .NET framework. Companies can use multiple middleware platforms and applications from different vendors, such as Java 2 Enterprise Edition and .NET. Web services enable applications to communicate together without regard to the development platform or tools. This means that Web service applications built using J2EE and .NET will be able to interoperate using standard protocols.

In addition, a supply chain management system can support transactions using a Web service protocol such as XAML. Should one of these services fail to commit its operation, XAML allows the manufacturer to send its requirements to other Web services to cancel, compensate, or find alternative actions. XAML is an XML-based standard that will help businesses expose transactional capabilities through their Web services, and to mix and match calls to multiple Web services. XAML will enable companies engaging in B2B transactions to integrate and leverage existing transaction systems, as well as participate in new types of transactions. These interactions are called *business Web transaction processing* (BWTP). *Online transaction processing* (OLTP) is based on internal systems, but BWTP transactions may invoke low-level Web services from multiple organizations on the Web.

For example, a manufacturer may need to electronically purchase a direct material, such as a chemical product, to produce its finished goods. As the company selects the product from an electronic marketplace, it will also specify the required terms of the purchase, such as shipping availability and delivery options, payment financing, casualty insurance, and governmental compliance for safe transport. All of these interrelated requirements must be satisfied prior to a purchase transaction being finalized. This requires coordinated processing of transaction-supporting Web services between the chemical provider's inventory system and external services supplying shipping insurance, financing, and transport.

There are benefits to building Web services on a middleware platform, such as Sun's Java 2 Enterprise Edition (J2EE) or Microsoft's .NET framework. SOAP, UDDI, WSDL, and XML are the core standards needed to develop Web services. But development of a multiple-tier, enterprise-class service architecture requires a programming language platform that includes a component object model, application/server technology, portability across various platforms, and well-defined APIs for capabilities such as database access.

The Parts of Web Services

Today four core standards for Web services exist: XML, SOAP, WSDL, and the UDDI protocol. These comprise the basic capabilities necessary to build the discrete elements of a services-oriented architecture. In a distributed architecture, the uniform way of exchanging information as XML encoded data is to use SOAP, WSDL, and UDDI. Sending messages as plain XML has advantages in terms of ensuring interoperability in a heterogeneous computing platform and architecture. In the middleware design, this means trading off the costs of parsing and serializing XML to scale distributed computing on networks.

Simple Object Access Protocol

Simple Object Access Protocol (SOAP) is a messaging protocol based on XML and HTTP that is used as an application wrapper for middleware software to send messages across a network. SOAP lets services collaborate with each other over a network.

For those that want to get information from the source, there is a W3C note submission on SOAP at http://www.w3.org/TR/SOAP/. This W3C document is fairly long and technical. Submitted in 2000 to the W3C by IBM, Microsoft, UserLand, and DevelopMentor, the development of SOAP is managed by the XML Protocols Working Group in W3C.

RPC or Messaging?

Remote Procedural Call (RPC) services and the messaging services are the two primary application communication models. In an RPC model, a client invokes a remote procedure on a server, then receives a response. In a small set of servers and clients that performs tasks remotely, RPC is generally easier to set up for the simple technical requirements involving specific business functions on request. In larger systems that are exchanging data for general application communications, building messaging capabilities provides a more generic and scalable approach.

There are two way of using SOAP, based on RPC or messages:

In a communication application invoking remote procedures with XML and SOAP as the format using HTTP as the underlying communication protocol. Using an RPC service and an RPC client to invoke the remote procedure calls on the RPC server allows better error handling and passing of complex types across the network.

In a communication application that uses messages to transmit information between a client and server. This setup means the client does not have to know about a particular method on a server. Messages allow packages of data to be passed between systems using a distributed model.

A SOAP message is like an actual letter. The typical letter is sent in a paper envelope with postage and sender and recipient addresses. Likewise, a SOAP message has an envelope with recipient and sender information, and the content of the message is called the SOAP *payload*. In addition to the SOAP envelope is a set of encoding rules and a means of interaction between request and response. (See Figure 3.2.)

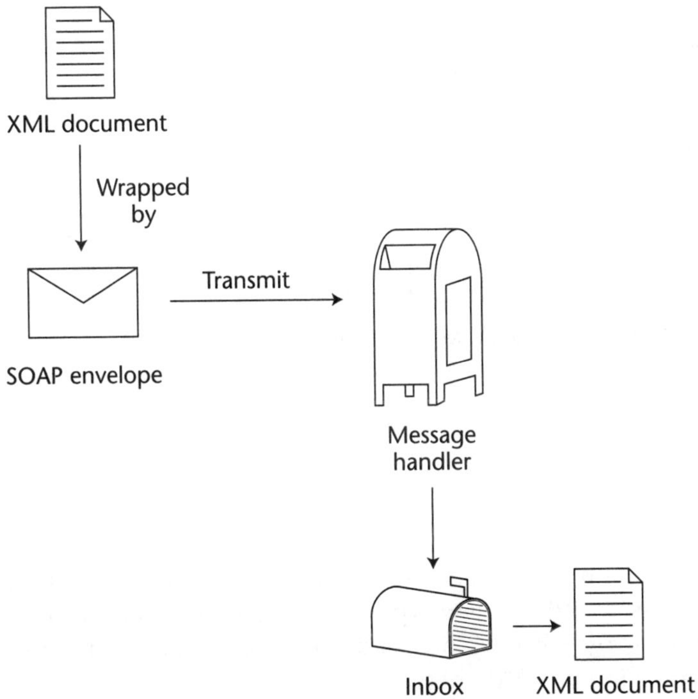

Figure 3.2 The SOAP message process.

The SOAP Envelope

The SOAP envelope has information about the SOAP payload. This includes information relating to the recipient and sender, as well as details about the message itself. For example, the header of the SOAP envelope can specify how to process the message. Before an application processes a message, the application can get overall information about a message, including how to process and interpret the message (if at all). A typical SOAP message can also include the encoding style, which assists the recipient in interpreting the message.

In Code Listing 3.1, the SOAP encoding in the envelope allows an application to determine whether it can read the contents (within the body elements). The application uses the value of the encoding style attribute. The SOAP namespace (`xmlns:SOAP`) allows the message and the SOAP message server to work together based on the same version of SOAP.

```
<SOAP:Envelope
 xmlns:SOAP="http://schemas.xmlSOAP.org/SOAP/envelope"
 SOAP:encodingStyle="http://www.fedx.com/encodings/secureEncoding"
>
<SOAP:Body>
. . . the body of the SOAP message contains the actual message
information
</SOAP:Body>
</SOAP:Envelope>
```

Code Listing 3.1 The encoding is specified with the SOAP envelope.

Encoding

SOAP allows the user to define data types simply. XML schemas can be used to specify new data types, and those new types can be represented in XML as part of a SOAP payload. By logically describing the data type in an XML schema, we can encode it into a SOAP message.

Request/Response and Invocation

SOAP has an invocation (or call) process, with defined formats for fault responses, errors, and returned results from the call. The SOAP call allows us to set the target of the call, the method to invoke, the encoding style, the parameters, and so on. Every SOAP RPC call involves the following basic steps:

1. Create the call.
2. Set the URI of the SOAP message.
3. Specify the method to invoke.
4. Specify the encoding.
5. Add any parameters to the call.
6. Connect to the SOAP service.
7. Receive and interpret the response.

ebXML and SOAP

The ebXML messaging service is a framework based on SOAP, MIME, and XML. A complete message, referred to as the *message package*, is a MIME multipart/related object. MIME types are used throughout to describe all of the contents of the message package. The message package contains two principal parts, the SOAP message container and payload containers. The SOAP message contains the ebXML SOAP extension elements routing information, trading partner information, message identification, and delivery semantics information. The payload is optional and can contain any type of information that is to be exchanged between parties. In ebXML messaging, the ebXML specification claims SOAP is used independently of HTTP, and SOAP may be used over alternative protocols such as the Send Mail Transport Protocol (SMTP). (See Chapter 7 for further details.)

Java API for XML Messaging (JAXM) was originally defined to provide a Java-centric API for B2B messaging systems, of which ebXML was the prime candidate. The focus of JAXM has also evolved to embrace SOAP. JAXM is more closely related to the other J2EE specifications than to other XML technologies. For example, JAXM uses other Java standards, such as Java Naming Directory Interface (JNDI) for naming lookup. JAXM was not intended to be solely for the use of ebXML, but ebXML became the Web services framework model under JAXM. Message passing over SOAP is not necessarily a complete solution, since SOAP is missing some key features required for e-business, primarily in the areas of security and authentication.

Universal Description, Discovery, and Integration

As mentioned earlier in the chapter, the *Universal Description, Discovery, and Integration* (UDDI) Service provides a standard way for applications to find Web services using directories. The UDDI initiative was begun by Ariba, IBM, and Microsoft in September 2000 to create a standard registry for companies to make their Web services known over the Internet. The goal is to create a standard framework for service-oriented B2B interactions and to integrate business services using the concept of standard registry services. The UDDI concept is similar to a telephone book used for online applications.

Overall, the UDDI focuses on providing businesses with a common mechanism to publish Web service information on the Internet using the XML- and SOAP-based WSDL. The UDDI model focuses on middleware connectivity. It uses XML to describe the systems that companies use to interact with one another. UDDI stores information about corporate integration profiles and capabilities in a shared directory. Other companies can access this UDDI directory as the XML standard interface.

In internal systems using UDDI, the discovery role of UDDI is not as critical as the basic directory services. Many sites developing Web services are working on private UDDI registries that also can be used by their trusted partners.

UDDI will be most valuable on the public Internet, where there are potentially thousands of Web services available and the ability to search for Web services on a global scale will become critical. Version 2 of the UDDI specification adds support for multiple languages, improved searching capabilities, and support for more complex hierarchical business organization descriptions.

The services are organized to provide business functionality similar to an online phone book. The UDDI registry system contains three types of information:

Yellow Pages. These are categories of business served by each listed company. Yellow pages will categorize companies according to U.S. government and United Nations standard industry codes, and by geographical location.

White Pages. These are listings of companies, together with contact information and business identifier numbers. White pages let companies register their names and the key services they provide. They also allow other companies to search the directory by company name.

Green Pages. These are for service deployment requirements, such as information on how to do B2B interactions with each listed company, including business processes and data format information. Green pages let companies interact with other companies listed in the registry.

UDDI is layered over SOAP and assumes that requests and responses are UDDI objects sent as SOAP messages. Using a UDDI interface, businesses connect to application services provided by external business partners.

A UDDI registry has two kinds of clients: businesses that want to publish a service (and its usage interfaces) and clients who want to obtain services and run programs on the server side.

Code Listing 3.2 is an example of using UDDI to query and retrieve information about a company (MyCompany) and its services. When placed inside the body of the SOAP envelope, this query returns information about MyCompany.

As shown in Code Listing 3.3, the result of this simple query is XML formatted information about MyCompany under the `<businessInfo>` element and its services under the `<serviceInfo>` element. This includes information about the UDDI service itself.

```
<find_business generic="1.0" xmlns="urn:uddi-org:api">
<name>MyCompany</name>
```

Code Listing 3.2 This is used inside a SOAP envelope to retrieve information about MyCompany.

```
<businessList generic="1.0
  operator="MyCompany, Inc."
  truncated="false"
  xmlns="urn:uddi-org:api">
  <businessInfos>
   <businessInfo
       businessKey="0076B468-EB27-42E5-AC09-9955CFF462A3">
    <name>MyCompany</name>
     <description xml:lang="en">
      description of MyCompany here. . .
     </description>
      <serviceInfos>
      <serviceInfo
          businessKey="0076B468-EB27-42E5-AC09-9955CFF462A3"
          serviceKey="A8E4999A-21A3-47FA-802E-EE50A88B266F">
          <name>UDDI Web Sites</name>
       </serviceInfo>
     list of more services here . . .
      </serviceInfos>
    </businessInfo>
  </businessInfos>
 </businessList>
```

Code Listing 3.3 The query result is a listing of `<businessInfo>` and `<serviceInfo>` elements registered for MyCompany.

UDDI and ebXML

UDDI has fairly broad support, led by IBM, Ariba, and Microsoft, though it is not yet an open standard like ebXML. Some have questioned whether ebXML and the UDDI initiative are trying to solve the same problems, but they are likely to end up as complementary solutions in e-commerce systems. UDDI should help accelerate the integration of systems used in marketplaces, while ebXML aims to standardize how XML is used in general business integration.

UDDI is designed to be the basis for higher-level services supported by some other standard such as ebXML. UDDI may support more complex business logic, including hierarchical support for modeling business organizations. The Web services model will need entities acting as clearinghouses for various UDDI or ebXML registry applications in a service area network. Service providers could establish themselves as the central repositories for a wide variety of applications, such as centralized security, billing, and payment management.

Web Services Definition Language

Web Services Description Language (WSDL) provides a way for service providers to describe the basic format of Web service requests over different protocols or encoding formats. WSDL is a template for how services should be described and bound by clients. In WSDL, a port is a network of endpoints, which collectively defines a service. A port is defined by associating a network address with a reusable binding. The WSDL service is defined by a set of ports.

WSDL is used to describe *what* a Web service can do, *where* it resides, and *how* to invoke it. For example, a large company has a classic problem: Various departments want to share data. However, each group has its own IT staff, computer systems, and data formats, making sharing difficult and time-consuming. Not all developers use the same development tools or programming languages, which can complicate things when developing new programmatic interfaces. A solution is to use WSDL. A developer only has to identify the departmental data to access and link to the corresponding interface, using existing development tools. This keeps services inside each department where they should be.

WSDL documents use the following elements in the definition of network services:

Types. A container for data type definitions using some type system (such as XSD)

Message. An abstract, typed definition of the data being communicated

Operation. An abstract description of an action supported by the service

Port Type. An abstract set of operations supported by one or more endpoints

Binding. A concrete protocol and data format specification for a particular port type

Port. A single endpoint defined as a combination of a binding and a network address

Service. A collection of related endpoints

WSDL is designed to be used in combination with SOAP/HTTP/MIME as the remote object invocation mechanism. UDDI registries describe numerous aspects of Web services, including the binding details of the service. WSDL fits into the subset of a UDDI service description. For example, a vendor could write a programmable interface to a shopping cart with WSDL and register it in a UDDI repository. A business customer can send a query out once a month to buy what he needs, without having to call up the customer service representative at the vendor.

A proposed extension of WSDL by Microsoft is XLANG, which specifies message exchange behavior among participating Web services supporting the automation of business processes. In XLANG, a service description based on WSDL has an extension element that describes the behavior of the service as a part of a business process. Simple WSDL services produce XLANG service behavior as providers of basic functionality for the implementation of the business process.

Who Is Using Web Services?

In the competitive Web services market, the key vendors include the usual suspects, such as Sun Microsystems, Microsoft, HP, Oracle, and IBM. Sun launched its SunOne initiative as an umbrella campaign that will house a broad range of Web services initiatives. Sun's Java 2 Enterprise Edition (J2EE) has broad vendor support as the foundation for standards-based integration. Microsoft's .NET Web services framework is designed to put more emphasis on distributed applications development. With facilities such as the UDDI registry, SOAP, and WSDL, companies can bundle software components and provide them over the Internet for other firms to use within their programs. IBM is building its Web services tools on open-source development platforms such as the Apache Web server and Linux. IBM is bringing Web services tools to market under its existing WebSphere brand of e-business software.

A common theme in all vendors is the claim and promotion of interoperability with other vendors' products. While implementing Web services with one particular vendor is easy, companies that already have a substantial investment in another vendor will not likely switch over. Most development teams have a major investment in their development tools infrastructure as well as in their legacy applications base, and will be unwilling to dump it for an expensive, one-size-fits-all life cycle management solution. Another theme is products that are fully integrated with the Web services framework, with support for multiple programming languages. These products automatically handle many common programming tasks, freeing developers to create Web applications using their language of choice.

Microsoft is basing its strategy around XML-based extensions to its current products and incorporating the products into the .NET framework. This includes Visual Studio .NET and the BizTalk server, Microsoft's B2B e-commerce server. Visual Studio .NET allows developers to wrap Web services around program logic, automatically generate corresponding WSDL, and map XML to the data stream. Microsoft Visual Studio .NET is a rapid application development tool for building Web applications and XML Web services, and it includes visual modeling and support for the Unified Modeling Language (UML). In addition, Microsoft plans to deliver its own set of applications and services over the Web under an initiative called Hailstorm. Microsoft will offer office productivity suites, Hotmail email service, Passport user-authentication services, and scheduling applications as Web services for fee or free. Microsoft is seeking a subscription model that gives it an annuity revenue stream.

IBM is focused on integrating enterprise applications. IBM's WebSphere products will use Web services to help companies that manage complex supply chains or large, dispersed internal organizations. Businesses can connect with multiple trading partners via Web services technology to automate mundane tasks. IBM released WebSphere Studio and its WebSphere Private UDDI Registry to provide a set of developer tools to create, deploy, and maintain Web services applications and to give users a secure environment for posting Web services in an extranet/intranet.

Oracle is providing support for Web services through its Oracle Dynamic Services framework, which has been available as part of Oracle's development technology. The Oracle9i Application Server can respond to SOAP requests, and a new version of the application server will include all the Oracle Dynamic Services technology.

Other than vendors, there are the business users and companies that are developing Web services. For example, Dollar Rent-A-Car Systems, Inc., a car-rental company in Tulsa, Oklahoma, uses Web services to integrate multiple services on different platforms. Using a SOAP development toolkit from Microsoft, Dollar integrated its online-booking system, which runs on a Sun server. Southwest Airlines' Web site runs on a Compaq server that uses the VMS operating system and CORBA. Despite the different platforms, a person booking a flight on Southwest.com can reserve a car from Dollar without leaving the airline's site. Dollar saves hundreds of thousands of dollars by routing customer reservations through Southwest and other airline sites.

VENDORS LEAD THE WAY IN WEB SERVICES

"Standards don't exist yet to bring together billing, catalogs, and taxonomy. The Holy Grail is to be able to plug all these pieces together, plug and play, without any integration work. Externally focused Web services may help make e-business more of a reality. Many vendors have begun to articulate this vision as well. Along with Microsoft, HP, and IBM, many other vendors—big and small—are bear watching, as the infrastructure is just beginning to take shape for e-services."

—David Smith, vice president and research area director at Gartner Group

Why Use Web Services?

Web services standards offer a way to design systems with modularity, flexibility, and platform independence. Interoperability among Web services will be a critical measure of its success. Web services offer excellent design flexibility for system architects working on internal systems, and they fit into the services-oriented architecture in which applications are designed with modular, loosely coupled interfaces that hide the complexity of the underlying systems. These services provide a common implementation, as opposed to possibly hundreds of custom interface implementations that may have been necessary in the past.

On the other hand, Web services technology is relatively new and the standards are not mature, which poses a set of challenges for developers and IT architects creating them. They are faced with an incomplete set of standards, performance constraints, and buggy developer tools. Issues from security to application compatibility need to be resolved. The quickness and simplicity of deploying interoperable Web services between vendors will be the major test.

Using the application service provider model, a company can offer hosted services to customers or suppliers using Web services technology, adding to the bottom line. This is a radical change; the business model creates new revenue streams for the software company, rather than just selling its current line of development tools and servers. Web services can underpin business models that promise new revenue opportunities. A company that takes orders for its products on the Web could provide automatic links to a shipping service, a service that provides consulting on export-law compliance, or a service that provides tax calculation. Such links could generate referral or transaction fees.

The arguments against deploying Web services include:

Slow performance due to XML processing overhead. XML parsing typically is used to decode the flow of data to a Web service, but XML parsing can be slow when large amounts of data are involved. Developers need to be judicious when deploying Web services if their application requires fast and predictable response times. The XML parsing required by Web services can slow down the speed of data delivery.

Incompatibility with Web services from different vendors. Early adopters are stumped by the lack of built-in security mechanisms in XML or SOAP, and vendors have yet to agree on a common fix. For example, it may be problematic in linking a CORBA application to one written using the latest version of Java 2 Enterprise Edition, or to Microsoft .NET.

Some technical details necessary for deployment of Web services not yet defined. For example, Web services per se are not yet suitable for handling the fault-tolerant needs of high-speed transactions, and this is dependent on the implementation in a particular vendor's application server. Web services standards such XAML will address the needs of transaction systems.

How Does Web Services Relate to ebXML?

Web services provides some of the basic application communication protocols, but we still need a standard cross-industry business framework such as ebXML messaging services to tie everything together at an architectural level. The technical architecture for ebXML provides an organizing conceptual principle for other Web services technologies. It looks at business interactions from the standpoint of business workflow, selecting and including into the architecture the objects common to many business processes, such as trading partner profiles, including location, services, and business needs. ebXML identifies and defines these objects with data attributes, along with the functions performed on those attributes. At higher levels, there are and will remain multiple approaches to solving the same problems, including ebXML, RossettaNet, or BizTalk.

Microsoft is notably absent from the consortium backing ebXML. However, the ebXML standard readily supports all major layers of the Microsoft 's Web services initiatives centered around the BizTalk/.NET, including registries (UDDI), business modeling languages (XLANG), service descriptions (WSDL), and transport/packaging/messaging (SOAP).

The core technologies in Web services are underway in standards-based, industry-wide initiatives. The next step is for companies to figure out how to assemble and augment these new technologies to ease the IT evolution and ensure business success.

Summary

Two trends are coming together in the world of e-commerce to create enormous opportunities and pressures for automation of business processes across business boundaries. One is enabling technology: the XML-based open protocols and the description and discovery standards that are growing up around SOAP. The other trend is the pressing need to truly realize the potential and promise of e-commerce by creating virtual enterprises—that is, networks of applications that automate business processes across enterprise boundaries.

In Web services, the programming interfaces are not tied to any proprietary operating system or programming language, are quite flexible, and are easier and less expensive to deploy as tools improve. Programmatic service integration based on XML, SOAP, WSDL, and UDDI will be more seamless with interoperable implementations.

SOAP, UDDI, WSDL, and XML are the beginning of a major change in the way companies work together. Web services promises an IT world with open messaging, search, and registry protocols. It will enable programmers to build software components that can automatically seek out and interact with other components built to the same standards.

On the business side, some vendors actively promote the revenue potential in Web services, along with their business users. A compelling vision is to have thousands of services available on the public Internet. However, the businesses currently developing Web services may be more concerned with private issues of their internal systems and trusted partners. The final hurdles for Web services have less to do with technology and more to do with winning over business managers to adopt the necessary collaborative practices.

On the technical side, enterprise architects and developers must make tough choices and do a lot of work to integrate Web services into their system designs. Many undefined areas remain to be mapped out, such as providing standard low-level capabilities for organizations to access securely and transact with outside systems.

In the end, the success of Web services lies with the effective use by businesses. The value of Web services lies in its capabilities for building stronger and tighter supply-chain relationships between companies.

PART

Two

ebXML Technologies

CHAPTER

4

ebXML Technical Architecture

"The work ebXML is doing to ensure interoperability will speed the job of integrators trying to make systems with disparate architectures talk to one another in B2B transactions. Obviously, a system integrator thrives on interoperability, and time to market directly impacts their business models and the ability to deliver solutions more quickly. Since ebXML is open and inclusive, integrators now have the basis to take multiple components from different vendors and put them together more quickly."

—J.P. Morgenthal, CTO for XMLSolutions, a B2B infrastructure and software vendor

AREAS COVERED IN THIS CHAPTER

- What are architecture, framework, and platform?
- What is ebXML architecture?
  - XML as the common language
  - ebXML as the unifying architecture
  - ebXML methodology
- What are the technical pieces of the architecture, such as
  - Business process model
  - Core components
  - Messaging service
  - Registry/repository
  - Collaboration protocol
  - Security
  - How it all works together
- Comparing ebXML with other B2B frameworks, such as:
  - BizTalk
  - RosettaNet

As we have seen, the ebXML architecture is built on top of existing Web services and XML. In addition to XML (and the holy trinity of Web services: SOAP, WSDL, and UDDI), the ebXML architecture leverages other Internet protocols and languages, including Hypertext Transfer Protocol (HTTP), Simple Mail Transfer Protocol (SMTP), and Transmission Control Protocol/ Internet Protocol (TCP/IP).

In this chapter, we will discuss the ebXML technical architecture, its components, and how it compares to other leading e-commerce standards. We begin by addressing the key concepts and terminology.

Architecture, Frameworks, and Platforms

What is the meaning of architecture, framework, and platform? When we are building a house, the architecture defines the overall vision and structure of the project. The framework is the skeleton for the walls and roof of the house. The platform (foundation) is the base on which framework is built.

In computer systems, we work with analogous concepts of architecture. A computing architecture defines how the technology, process, and people elements of the system are brought together.

Architecture

Software architecture defines the interfaces of the software subsystems and the rules for using them. The architecture of computer systems is essentially an approach to partition a large system into a set of subsystems. A formal architecture is more common in hardware design than software products and systems, where the process tends to be more casual and ad hoc. Many existing computer systems have grown organically over time, rather than following a formal architectural blueprint.

The architecture design of computer systems is affected by:

- The overall objectives of the system with respect to financial constraints, resource constraints, and any technical limitations.
- The tools used to construct the system, including the development protocols, languages, and operational management techniques.
- The hardware and software elements used as building blocks and their contributions of risk to system delivery.
- The degree of maintenance in terms of the ability to modify and extend the system to meet changing requirements.

Architecture evolved as a technique to manage complexity. Whether in a civil engineering structure, a piece of literature, or a computer system, a typical approach is the breakdown of the big problem into smaller and smaller problems (also called divide-and-conquer).

We can use the parts of the whole, such as systems properties, to describe the entire software architecture. The system properties of the software architecture may include:

- Elements, such as the components and parts from which systems are built
- Interactions, such as connections, connectors, glues, and relationships between the elements
- Patterns specifying the layout of the elements and their interactions, such as the number of elements, the number of connectors, order, topology, and direction
- Constraints on the patterns, such as time, cardinality, and concurrency
- Styles of architectural components from various specific architectures, for example, layered style, pipe and filter style, object-oriented style

A typical computing architecture is composed of multiple frameworks, which we discuss in detail in the next section.

Frameworks

Frameworks make up a collection of network, hardware, and software resources for managing the infrastructure. Essentially the building blocks for the architecture, frameworks define the skeleton of the functional behavior required to develop infrastructure management decisions.

The creation of business systems increasingly requires the integration of existing applications, components, and services in the context of a framework. For example, ebXML is a collection of frameworks that build on the foundations of the XML language. The frameworks for business process, messaging, registry, and components define the structure of common items across XML business data exchanges, such as the set of XML element names, attributes usage, and documents usage.

For each framework in an enterprise, off-the-shelf products and software pieces are used as components. Depending on the part of the infrastructure, these components may be specialized in a fragmented product space. Managing change and complexity is a motivator for component-based software development. A good system design is formed from parts that embody a clear separation of issues and a balanced distribution of responsibilities. A system is flexible if the islands of semantics can be encapsulated and delivered with components as the basic unit of change. As the constructed creation of semantics, both static and dynamic, a component represents a concrete abstraction. By raising the level of abstraction, components serve an important role in helping to manage complexity.

Platforms

A *platform* is a cohesive collection of software and hardware resources to build a system in less time with less effort. A platform used in a company for all computing applications and systems is often referred to an *enterprise standard*, which includes development tools and application program interfaces. The main difference between platforms and frameworks is that platforms focus on deployment of systems, and frameworks focus on development of systems. However, in the industry, there is a lot of overlap between the two terms, and we will use them interchangeably in this book.

Application program interfaces (APIs) provide transparency to internal details of the platform architecture. APIs allow application developers to write applications without intimate knowledge about the platform. One of the main reasons for calling such a platform open is the publication of the APIs. Vendors usually develop applications based on the size of the market share of a platform relative to an application, as well as ease of use, quality of the APIs, and conformation with de facto standards in the marketplace. In addition to publishing APIs, platform vendors supply developer toolkits that provide resources such as templates for interface definition. They may also provide certification services.

In the client/server model, a program (client) requests a service that another program (server) provides. A server maintains a client interface that specifies the individual services it supports. A client may only request services that are supported at the client interface. The server performs the requested service and returns the results.

Infrastructure may be viewed as a service delivery platform for client/server applications, encompassing all tangible assets such as workstations and servers as well as more abstract assets such as protocol stacks. Within such a service context, infrastructure may be modeled as a layered structure. The interfaces in each layer provide services that are accessed by a higher layer.

In an enterprise infrastructure, architecture often defines more than one platform type. Key components in the cost of ownership are developing an enterprise standard, deployment, development effort, training, and maintenance.

ebXML Architecture Overview

In this section, we describe the ebXML architecture and how it can be incorporated into existing systems. The modular ebXML architecture defines a number of frameworks focusing on business process, core components, messaging, registry, and collaboration.

The individual components of the architecture can fit with one another to build a complete system. The components in the framework can be standalone ebXML solutions, such as the registry. An ebXML system may be a single shrinkwrap desktop application or an information system involving multiple applications and platforms.

The ebXML framework serves basic functions, such as providing a common technical and business platform for trading partners. This includes defining business processes and their associated messages and content, defining company profiles, defining trading partner agreements, defining core components, and enabling the exchange of structured messages over a transport layer.

A key to understanding ebXML is to know of the role of XML as a common language. In an IT scenario where everyone speaks XML but they still have communication problems, ebXML plays an important role as a unifying architecture.

XML as the Common Language

XML solves a common problem in data interchange: how to write and use data and documents as flat files in a standard format. Flat files contain data in text format. Data is stored as a text sequence within the file.

The format and processing in a flat file system are preset and not easily adapted to changing requirements. If a data element is modified, both the business applications and parsing applications may not work properly. Each format may require a separate parser, which increases development time and cost. The data elements in the flat file are encoded in a machine-readable format. However, the format may not be human-readable. The application may be difficult to use and understand, since parsers are needed to interpret each data element.

With XML, we have a common language in a flat file format that is both human- and machine-readable for communicating among systems. As discussed in Chapter 2, a document type definition (DTD) or schema sets the semantic rules for the elements and attributes in an XML document. The language can change to meet system requirements by allowing different vocabularies and semantics in each business context. XML can be used as part of a relational database solution to communicate between different database systems as well.

Though we have a common language, a Tower of Babel may still exist in data interchange. Since different vocabularies and semantics apply to different areas of business and industry, we need to have standards. Without a shared vocabulary and semantics, two trading partners must first agree on all the technical terms of the data interchange before they can transact business, such as whether to denominate the price in U.S. dollars or Canadian dollars. As we see in the next section, ebXML offers us an XML-based solution for this problem.

ebXML as the Unifying Architecture

In a business scenario, a distributor in Shanghai wants to sell goods and services to a retailer in Beijing. The distributor calls up the retailer in Beijing, but they cannot understand each other. Regional dialects exist within China, and people from one region often cannot understand the spoken form of the language from another region. Though all the dialects are nominally the same language, there are major differences in semantics and pronunciation. The written form of the Chinese language provides a bridge among regions as the standard communication form.

By analogy, different camps with their own dialect of XML may not be able to communicate with each other. ebXML provides a bridge between these islands of semantics with a modular architectural framework, as shown in Figure 4.1. The ebXML architecture is overlaid on top of the foundation of commonly used Internet protocols and languages, such as HTTP, HTML, XML, SMTP, and TCP/IP.

A goal of ebXML is defining the technical architecture for a set of recommendations on data management based on XML for Internet communication and B2B interactions. A cornerstone of the ebXML architecture is the creation of interoperable Web services and associated components. From the strategic goals of providing standard semantics for data interchange and merging this with Internet technology, the ebXML organization derived a set of requirements and defined the technical architecture. The key design concepts for development of the ebXML architecture included standardized data infrastructure, semantic framework, and shared discovery.

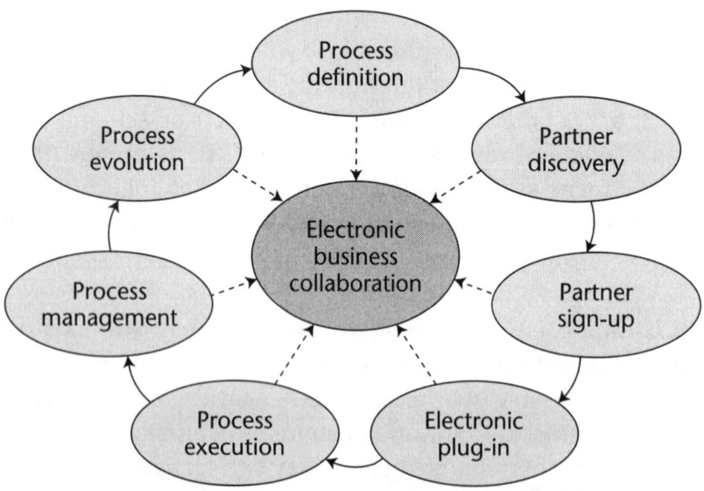

Figure 4.1 ebXML is a unifying architecture for different B2B areas.
Adapted from "ebXML Business Process Specification Schema."

First, ebXML should have a data communication infrastructure that can work between different communication systems. This infrastructure uses a standard message transport mechanism with a defined interface, packaging rules, and a predictable delivery and security model. The infrastructure acts as a business service interface that handles incoming and outgoing messages.

Second, ebXML should have a shared vocabulary and terminology library that can serve as a commercial framework. This semantic framework is a set of shared XML vocabularies and the process for defining actual message structures and definitions. This allows applications using ebXML to interoperate between different business systems in commerce. There are several pieces to this semantic framework: a *meta model* about the business process and information models, common business processes, and a set of reusable business logic based on core components.

Third, ebXML should be a way for enterprises to find each other, make agreements to be trading partners, and transact business. ebXML has a discovery mechanism that allows enterprises to find each other and agree to become trading partners. A shared repository allows businesses to register and discover each other's business services. The trading partners can use a partner profile information process for defining a system level agreement. They can also use a shared repository for company profiles, business process models, and related message structures.

The ebXML vision is expressed in a set of documents, the ebXML specification version 1.0 released in May 2001. This is a technical reference for system vendors, application developers, and architects to create software according to the published standards. The ebXML specifications may be implemented incrementally, either individually or in combinations.

In the next section, we will briefly discuss methodology and modeling in ebXML. Later in the chapter we will delve deeper into the infrastructure parts of ebXML: business process models, core components, messaging services, registry/repository, and the collaboration protocol.

Methodology

In the "Recommended Modeling Methodology" section in the *ebXML Architecture Specification*, ebXML presents business-modeling constructs called the *Business Operational View* (BOV) and *Functional Service View* (FOV), which are two concepts from the ISO Open-EDI Reference Model. Shown in Figure 4.2, the BOV addresses the business needs of trading partners, or specifically, "the semantics of business data in transactions and associated data interchanges, the architecture for business transactions, including operational conventions, agreements and arrangements, mutual obligations and requirements."

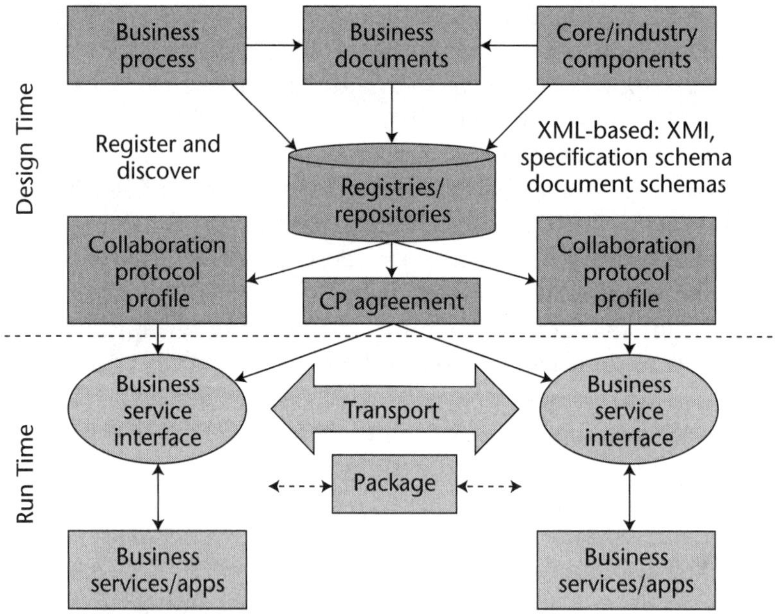

Figure 4.2 Business Operational View.
Source: "ebXML Technical Architecture Specification"

The FSV addresses the supporting services and deployment needs of ebXML technologies. Shown in Figure 4.3, this view serves as a reference model for commercial software vendors on business service interfaces, protocols, and messaging services. This includes "capabilities for implementation, discovery, deployment and run time scenarios; user interfaces; data transfer infrastructure interfaces, protocols for enabling interoperability of XML vocabulary deployments from different organizations."

In addition to the architecture views, there is a methodology in ebXML based on the Unified Modeling Language.

The *UN/CEFACT Modeling Methodology* (UMM) is a general methodology for modeling business systems applying object-oriented principles using the Unified Modeling Language (UML). It is not specific to ebXML, though it is endorsed by UN/CEFACT. The ebXML process is based on UMM and its meta model. UMM is a business process and information modeling for the e-commerce domain using the UML, developed by the Object Management Group. The meta model specifies the critical objects from the analysis and describes their relationships. The business process specification schema (BPSS) represents a subset of the information in the meta model.

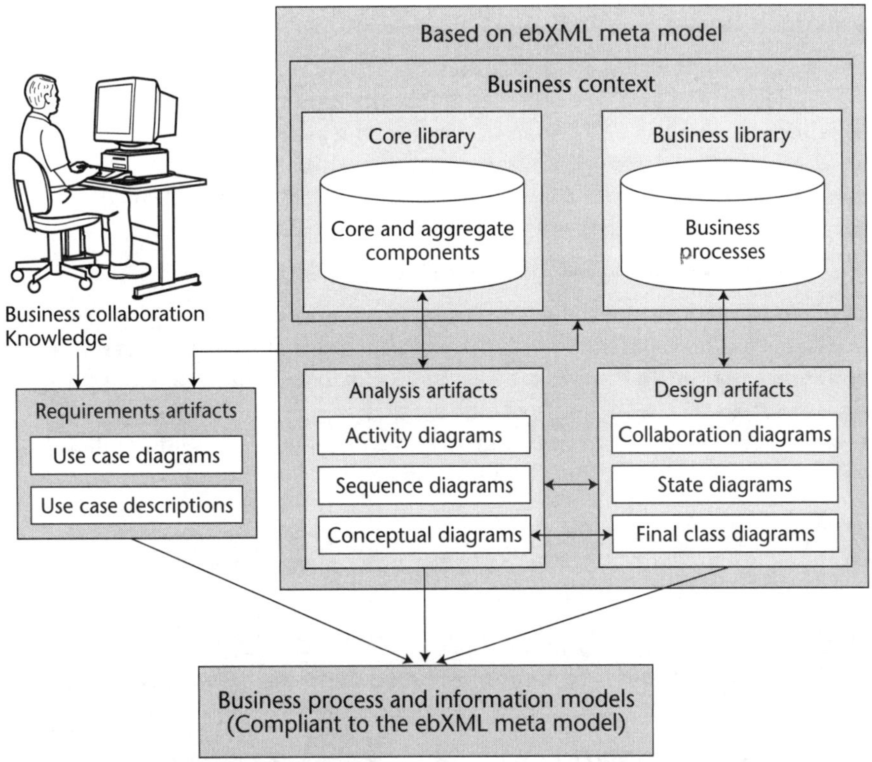

Figure 4.3 Functional Service View.
Source: "ebXML Technical Architecture Specification"

UML is the modeling language recommended by the ebXML initiative to develop business processes. This ensures that a single, consistent modeling methodology is used to create new business processes. Using a consistent modeling methodology makes it possible to compare models, thereby avoiding duplication of business processes.

In this section we will walk through a sample UMM-based process in successive phases for modeling an ebXML system, as defined in the UMM specification. The modeling techniques described are not mandatory requirements for participation in ebXML-compliant business transactions.

The core library contains data and process definitions, including relationships and cross-references, as expressed in business terminology that may be tied to an accepted industry classification scheme or taxonomy. The core library is the bridge between the specific business or industry language and the knowledge in the models in a more generalized context-neutral language.

EBXML WORKSHEETS FOR ANALYSTS

ebXML has developed worksheets that enable business analysts and non-technical business people to document the information necessary for the BPSS without a detailed UMM analysis process. The analysis worksheets draw on the catalog of common business processes and e-commerce patterns to develop a specification document that covers the essential set of data specified by the UMM meta model.

BUSINESS PROCESS ANALYSIS WORKSHEET AND GUIDELINES

A set of worksheets and guidelines for using them has been designed to assist an analyst in gathering the data necessary to describe a business process. The information can then be used to create a BPSS XML document describing the business process. The worksheets can be used as a basis for developing business process editors that can guide the user in collecting the information and automatically generate the XML business process specification.

CATALOG OF COMMON BUSINESS PROCESSES

This catalog is a preliminary cross-listing and description of business processes that may be common to several industries.

E-COMMERCE PATTERNS

These are examples and descriptions of common business patterns. The only one listed to date is for simple contract formation.

CATALOG OF CORE COMPONENTS

This is an initial catalog of core components that can be used by itself or extended to build definitions of business messages.

CATALOG OF CONTEXT DRIVERS

This is an initial catalog of the types of information describing the contexts that core components can be extended. These include such things as geographic region, industry, role, and product.

The first phase is defining requirements by describing the problem using use case diagrams and descriptions. Existing core library entries from an ebXML registry are used. Otherwise, new entries are created and registered in an ebXML registry.

The second phase is analysis to create activity and sequence diagrams that describe the business processes. Class diagrams will capture the associated business documents. The analysis phase reflects the business knowledge contained in the core library.

The design phase is the last step of standardization of the object model and the object interaction, using collaboration diagrams and state diagrams. The class view diagram from the analysis phase will be checked for consistency to align it with other models in the same industry and across others.

The implementation phase deals specifically with the procedures for creating an application of the ebXML infrastructure. A trading partner in an ebXML-compliant transaction gets copies of the ebXML specifications and subsequently downloads the core library and the business library. The trading partner can also submit its information to an ebXML registry service. The trading partner may also request information from other trading partners stored in their profile for analysis and review. The trading partner may implement ebXML by utilizing third-party applications.

The discovery and retrieval phase covers all aspects of the discovery of ebXML-related resources. A trading partner with an ebXML business service interface, the main ebXML system API, can now begin the process of discovery and retrieval. The ebXML business service interface supports requests for updates to core libraries, business libraries, and the collaboration protocol profile from another partner. This is the phase where trading partners discover the meaning of business information being requested by other trading partners.

The runtime phase covers the execution of an ebXML scenario with the actual associated ebXML transactions. ebXML messages are being exchanged between partners using the ebXML messaging service.

Similar to the modular nature of the technical infrastructure, the parts of the top-down business process analysis methodology of UMM methodology may be used independently. On the one hand, we can develop XML schemas for business documents in a bottom-up fashion strictly from core and domain components without doing any formal business process analysis. On the other hand, we can generate XML document schema from UML business process models using invented business information objects or objects from a source other than ebXML core components.

ebXML Technical Architecture in Detail

Mike Rawlins, an EDI expert and ebXML contributor, asserts that there is not one ebXML architecture but two in conventional software architecture terms. (See "Overview of ebXML Architectures" at www.metronet.com/~rawlins/ebXML2.html) One of these is the software architecture for the technical infrastructure, referred to as the *product* architecture. The other is the system analysis and development methodology architecture, referred to as the *process* architecture. However, the ebXML architecture specification does not identify two separate architectures per se.

In this book, our focus is on the software and their interaction, rather than the methodology. So we discuss the product architecture, including the business process model, the core components, messaging service, registry, and collaboration protocol, then how they are related to each other.

As shown in Figure 4.4, the main pieces of the ebXML architecture include:

Business process model. The meta model defines the deliverables needed to describe a business process; it can be expressed using UML and then recast in XML. The business process specification schema deals with the rules for the actual business process. (See Chapter 5.)

Core components. These reusable information structures are the building blocks of ebXML systems. (See Chapter 6.)

Messaging services. The messaging structure can handle any payload, including traditional EDI and encrypted payloads, over multiple communications services, such as HTTP and SMTP. (See Chapter 7.)

Registry and repository. The registry defines the extensible information model and XML-based interfaces to interact with a set of distributed ebXML compliant registries. (See Chapter 8.)

Trading partner information, also known as collaboration protocol profile (CPP) and collaboration protocol agreement (CPA). The CPP/CPA defines the capabilities of a trading partner to perform a data interchange and how this data interchange agreement can be formed between two trading partners. The CPA/CPP deals with the technical aspects of a handshake between systems prior to conducting e-business. (See Chapter 9.)

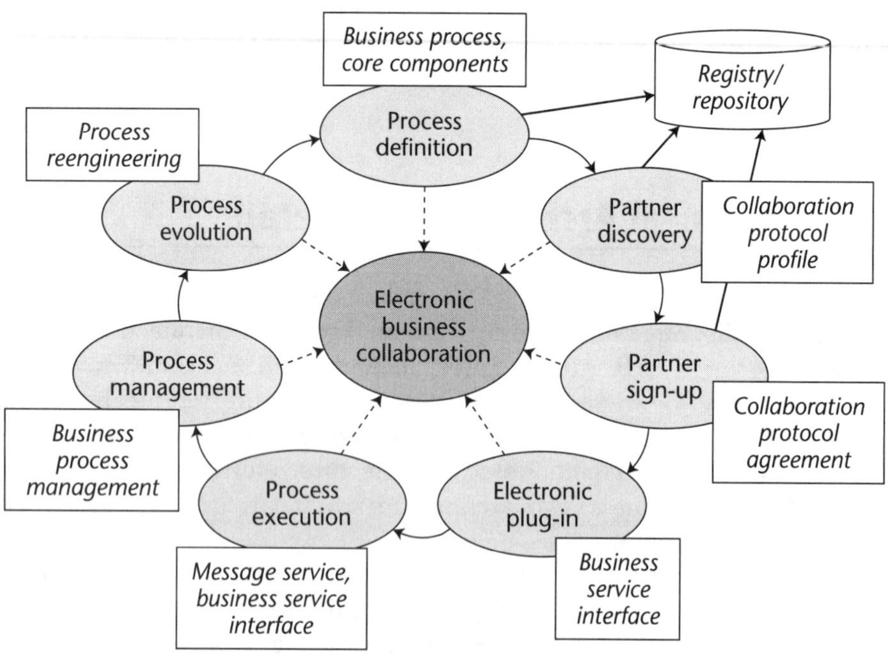

Figure 4.4 The ebXML architecture is made up of frameworks.
Adapted from "ebXML Business Process Specification Schema."

In the next section, we discuss business processes, which can be thought of as the "verbs" of e-business, because they describe actions. The business process model defines how to describe the processes. The ebXML specification allows a company to express its business processes to other companies. Using a standard for describing a business process and the information model, we can integrate business processes within a company or between companies.

Business Process

In the ebXML context, the term *business process* refers to the specific computer information used to model a real-world business process, such as purchasing a widget by a retailer from a distributor. The main goal of the ebXML business process is to standardize the semantic context, define the data interchange process, and reduce ambiguity in communication between the computer systems and people involved.

Although business practices vary from one organization to another, most activities can be broken down into common business processes. ebXML specifications standardize common business processes from the standpoint of business workflow. Business applications of one enterprise must be able to exchange structured business documents encoded in XML with applications of another enterprise, both inbound and outbound. Business applications may also need to exchange structured business documents with intermediaries such as portals and brokers. Some businesses using ebXML may not have sophisticated IT architectures. Business applications in ebXML will need to exchange structured business documents with trading partners that will print out and manually process transactions.

In more concrete terms, the ebXML business process describes how trading partners take on roles in interacting with other trading partners to exchange documents. The interaction between trading partners takes place as a sequence of business transactions. Each business transaction is expressed as an exchange of electronic business documents. Business documents, such as a purchase order, can be composed from business information objects, such as company information, shipping address, items, and item descriptions. At a lower level, business processes can be composed of core processes, and larger business information objects can be composed of smaller core components. Though we can use any methodology available to describe a business process, the ebXML specification advocates using a consistent modeling methodology based on UMM. The ebXML framework for business is very generic for information integration on different systems and interoperability on different platforms. A business process is expressible in XML syntax as a standard computer data format.

The *Business Process and Information Meta Model* (BPIMM) is a high-level information model for describing a business process in ebXML terms. It allows trading partners to capture the details for a specific business scenario, and it supports requirements, analysis, and design viewpoints that provide a set of semantics and vocabulary for each viewpoint. This model forms the basis of specification of the objects to define business process. The ebXML modeling process identifies the BPIMMs that are likely candidates for standardization into reusable components.

The *business process specification schema* is a semantic subset of the rules in the ebXML business process model that defines how an XML document can describe an organization's business transactions. It identifies such facets as the overall business process; the roles, transactions, and identification of the business documents used; document flow; legal aspects; security aspects; business-level acknowledgments; and status. Used by a software application to configure the business details of conducting e-business with another organization, the BPSS is a machine encoding of a business process and can be thought of as a view of the ebXML business process model. The BPSS is available in several representations, either in as an abstract model in UML or as a more concrete description in an XML DTD or schema.

The BPSS defines rules for business by using the concept of collaboration. Each business transaction can be implemented using a set of standard patterns. These patterns determine the exchange of messages and signals between trading partners for the transaction. To help specify the patterns, the BPSS is accompanied by a set of standard patterns with a set of modeling elements.

A major focus of ebXML is the creation of consistent standardized business processes and information models and a gradual transition to full automation of business interactions. ebXML defines a common set of business processes in a core library. Users of the ebXML infrastructure would extend this set or use their own business processes.

Business processes can be characterized in ebXML using these types of information:

- Choreography for the exchange of documents, such as the sequence of message exchanges between trading partners executing an ebXML transaction for purchasing
- References to the BPIMM or BPSS as DTDs or schemas that add structure to business data
- Definition of the roles for each participant in a business process

How can the business process model be used in conjunction with other parts of the ebXML architecture? The business process can be stored in a registry to provide the constraints for using core components in the context of data interchange. This model provides the framework for establishing collaboration protocol agreements. It also defines the domain owner of a business process and relevant contact information, as well as the business transaction rules for the set of elements required to configure an ebXML system at run time.

In addition, a specific business process defines the constraints for exchanging business data with other trading partners. The business information can be made up of reusable components from the ebXML core library. A business process document references the core components using a reference in an XML document that points to the component by the unique identifier. The document also references the appropriate business and information models defined by the BPSS DTD or schema. Each component in the core components and core library has the unique identifier. A business process document can be transported between registry services as an ebXML message. It is transported in the ebXML infrastructure between a registry and an application by the ebXML messaging service. A business process document with its unique identifier can be retrieved by a registry query.

In the next section, we present core components, which are the building blocks in the ebXML architecture.

Core Components

From a specific business document in a business process, we can refer to a *core component*, which holds a minimal set of e-business information. If the business processes are the verbs in e-business, the core components represent the nouns and adjectives. The core components are defined as shared items that are common across all businesses. A core component contains information about a real-world business concept, and users define data in core components that is meaningful to their business and would work in other business applications.

When I was a child, I had a Lego block set that I used to build houses, castles, and other interesting things. The Lego blocks are easy to work with, since the blocks have standard forms and shapes, but they can be put together to make complex objects. By analogy, a core component in ebXML can contain another core component. A core component is uniquely identifiable and can contain individual pieces of business information objects. The business process can specify any number of core components as part of a specific business document. A core component works with a registry because it is storable and retrievable using a standard ebXML registry.

Of course, we express a core component in XML syntax. A core component can be referenced as a semantic equivalent to another XML element from another XML vocabulary in a core library. A core component contains attributes and specifies the precise context or combination of contexts in which it is used. We can aggregate core components for a specific business context and identify the placement of a core component within another core component. ebXML defines an initial set of core components from which ebXML users may adopt and extend components from the ebXML core library. The information models define reusable components that can be applied in a standard way within a business context.

Similar to common business objects, core components are the basic information elements, providing an information context that allows different elements, such as party, to integrate various types of information in various industries, geographies, or even specific companies. The core components include methodologies and naming conventions. A *methodology* allows discovery of core components from existing business documents or new business processes for reuse and extending core components into domain components for use in specific industries and situations. *Naming conventions* are descriptions of the parts of a core component name, based on ISO 11179, and rules for developing the names.

The ebXML framework includes business process models that are shared and stored in a repository. This framework identifies element names that can apply across business processes and contexts, and it allows for translation into major languages. The contents of core components are independent of implementation syntax in programming languages, but they may have specific references to data structures in XML or EDI.

Messaging Service

The *messaging service* provides a standard way to exchange business messages between organizations. The message service is potentially a robust, low-cost solution in the ebXML infrastructure since it piggybacks on existing infrastructure, thereby minimizing the expensive requirement to build custom applications to support new protocols. The messaging service specification does not dictate any particular file transport mechanism, such as SMTP, HTTP, or a network protocol such as TCP/IP; instead, it is protocol-neutral for the data interchange. The ebXML messaging service provides a reliable means to exchange business messages without relying on proprietary technologies and solutions. The messaging service has security functions including identification, authentication, authorization, privacy, message signing, nonrepudiation, and logging.

An ebXML message contains two-part information structures. A message header is used for routing and delivery, and the payload section is used for actual communication among trading partners. The messaging service is a way to exchange the payload reliably and securely in B2B transactions. The payload may not be an XML business document; for example, the payload may carry information for an EDI transaction. A data interchange may have a payload that contains an array of business documents in XML or other document formats, binary images, or other related business information. Using the messaging service, we can route the payload to the appropriate internal application as well. A message has an outer-communication protocol envelope that is specific to the transport protocol and a protocol-independent message envelope. The message envelope is packaged using the commonly used Internet standard for email and document exchange called Multipurpose Internet Mail Extensions (MIME), with the multipart/related content type.

The ebXML messaging service consists of three logical parts:

- The *abstract service interface* includes the functionality for send, receive, notify, and inquire. A *send* method sends an ebXML message using the ebXML message header values for the parameters, such as sender and recipient. *Receive* receives ebXML messages. *Notify* notifies events. *Inquire* queries the status of the particular ebXML message interchange.
- The *messaging service layer* enforces the rules of engagement, using the collaboration protocol agreement and other means. It includes security and business process functions related to message delivery. The collab-oration protocol agreement defines the mutually accepted technical terms for communication used by the computer systems for each trading partner. The definition of these ground rules can take many forms, including formal collaboration protocol agreements or interactive agreements established at the time a business transaction occurs. Any violation of the ground rules results in an error condition in the data interchange system.
- The *mapping to various transport protocols* include SMTP, HTTP, and FTP. The messaging service defines formats for all messages between distributed components, including registry and user applications. It does not place any restrictions on the content of the payload. It supports one-way notification and two-way request/response and both synchronous or asynchronous message exchanges. It also supports sequencing of payloads in cases where multiple payloads or multiple messages are exchanged.

In the ebXML infrastructure, a messaging service sends and receives messages between applications and businesses. The payload of the message may contain specific instructions on how to interact with the registry interface. The messages, along with the core components, specifications, schema, and other important data, are stored and retrieved from an ebXML registry. The registry provides a set of services that enable the sharing of information.

Registry

The ebXML registry is similar in concept to UDDI in Web services, but the registry is broader in scope. An ebXML technical white paper called "Using UDDI to Find ebXML Registry/Repository" (see www.ebxml.org/specs/rrUDDI.pdf) describes a way to locate ebXML registries using UDDI.

There are two similar concepts in ebXML, the repository and the registry. They are often both called simply "registry" in the ebXML literature, rather than the more accurate term "registry/repository." Technically speaking, a *registry* stores information about items that actually reside in a *repository*. The two together can be thought of as a database. The registry and repository provide a number of key functions, including the discovery of information about each participant, such as the business processes they support, the business messages that are exchanged, and the technical configuration of the supported transport, security, and encoding protocols. Also included is a means for registering the information for discovery and retrieval, and to fulfill a mutually agreed upon business arrangement from information provided by each participant. The registry/repository stores the collaboration protocol profile and agreement, as well as the final business process definitions and a library of core components. The registry/repository gives access to specific business processes and information models to allow updates and additions over time.

Viewed separately, a *repository* provides trading partners with the process models, core components, predefined messages, model trading partner agreements, and any other objects to enable parties to exchange data electronically. A key feature in the ebXML architecture is distributed repositories, which store all of the objects needed by trading partners. The ebXML vision anticipates creation of a series of multiple distributed repositories, since a few repositories may not scale to handle the traffic. ebXML repositories store the definition and rules for the industry vocabulary and the core components. Industry repositories also contain the industry-specific components outside the ebXML core components needed for e-business with ebXML.

A *registry* serves as the index and application gateway for a repository to the outside world. A registry contains the API that governs how parties interact with the repository. The registry is an API to the database of items that supports e-business with ebXML. Items in the repository are created, updated, or deleted through requests made to the registry.

As defined by the specification, the processes supported by the registry include:

- A special collaboration protocol agreement between the registry server and registry clients
- A set of functional processes involving the registry server and registry clients
- A set of messages exchanged between a registry client and the registry server as part of a specific business process
- A set of interface mechanisms to support messages and associated query and response mechanisms
- A special collaboration protocol agreement for orchestrating the interaction between registries

- A set of functional processes for registry-to-registry interactions
- A set of error responses and conditions with remedial actions

The specific implementation of the registry/repository and actual mapping to a database is not described in the registry specification. It focuses on features that the registry must support, such as the registry interfaces and the Registry Information Model (RIM), which is the type of information that is stored about registry items. Examples of items in the registry are XML schemas of business documents, definitions of library components for business process modeling, and collaboration protocol profiles and agreements. A goal of the registry is to support a fully distributed, networked set of interacting registries that would provide transparent interaction to any registry. Security protocols may be used to offer authentication and protection for the repository when accessed by the registry.

Technically speaking, a registry is an ebXML component that maintains an interface to meta data for a registered item called the *registry entry*. Access to a registry is provided through APIs exposed by registry services for interacting with other applications such as registry clients. The registry interface serves as an application-to-registry access mechanism. A person interacting with the registry is built as a layer over a registry interface, such as a Web browser. The registry interface is designed to be independent of the underlying network protocol stack, such as HTTP or SMTP over TCP/IP.

For people interacting with a registry by using a Web browser, certain types of queries can be used to facilitate the discovery process. A user can browse and traverse the content based on the available registry classification schemes. Registry services exist to create, modify, and delete registry items and their meta data.

The ebXML registry can host anything encoded in a binary or text form and has no deep knowledge of ebXML objects. Collaboration protocol documents, schemas, core component descriptions, and other ebXML documents may be hosted by a registry.

Collaboration Protocol

The concept of a collaboration protocol originated from an IBM innovation called the trading partner agreement and its associated markup language. A *trading partner agreement* (TPA) defines the rules of engagement between entities engaging in e-business. The Trading Partner Agreement Markup Language (tpaML) streamlines the process of establishing electronic trading relationships, a process that, with earlier technologies, could take weeks or months.

In ebXML, a *collaboration protocol profile* (CPP) is a document that allows a trading partner to express the business processes and business service interface requirements in a way that can be universally understood by other trading partners. The document allows potential trading partners to publish information about their supported business processes and specific technical details about their data interchange capabilities.

The CPP is an XML document governed by a DTD (cpp-cpa-v1_0.dtd), or schema that specifies the technical details of the ability of the organization to conduct e-business in ebXML. It specifies items, such as how to locate organizational contacts and other trading partner information, the types of network and file transport protocols it uses, network addresses, and security implementations. The CPP describes the specific capabilities that a trading partner supports, as well as the service interface requirements for exchanging business documents. The CPP contains essential information about the trading partner, including contact information, industry classification, supported business processes, interface requirements, and messaging service requirements. CPP documents may contain security and other implementation-specific details. All trading partners would register their CPPs in a registry. This provides a discovery mechanism that allows trading partners to find one another and discover which business processes are supported. The CPP definition provides for clear selection of choices in cases where there may be multiple selections, such as between HTTP or SMTP transport. A CPP defines business processes supported by the trading partner, along with the roles within a business process for a trading partner. For example, two roles may be a seller and buyer within a purchasing business process.

A *collaboration protocol agreement* (CPA) serves as a formal handshake for data interchange between trading partners doing e-business using ebXML. This is in the form of a special agreement documenting the terms derived from the intersection of the CPPs of the trading partner involved in the data interchange.

The CPA represents the intersection of the CPPs of the trading partners involved in the data interchange based on mutual agreement. An XML document governed by a DTD or schema, a CPA describes the messaging service and the requirements for business processes mutually agreed to by the trading partners involved.

The CPA can be viewed as a result of narrowing subsets. The outermost scope relates to all of the capabilities that a trading partner *can* support, with a subset of what a trading partner *will* actually support. A CPA is derived through a mutual negotiation that narrows the options from the trading partners *can do* (CPP) into what the trading partner *will do* (CPA).

Trading partners may decide to register their CPAs in the registry. A CPA can be stored in and retrieved from a registry. The CPA can be used by a software application to configure the technical details of conducting e-business in ebXML. A CPA adjusts the business service interface to a set of parameters agreed to by all trading partners, defining the parameters for the business process.

A CPA is a fixed snapshot of the messaging services and the business process information from the trading partners. If any parameters contained within the accepted CPA change after the agreement has been executed, a new CPA has to be negotiated again.

Security

While specific security features are left up to the vendors and individual developers in ebXML, specifications provide some guidelines on developing ebXML security solutions. This includes using digital signatures for signing messages and authentication and authorization features for the registry.

Following is a short list of security features for an exchange of business information, used for ebXML security requirements:

Confidentiality. Only sender and receiver can interpret document contents.

Authentication of sender. The sender's identity is verified.

Authentication of receiver. The receiver's identity is verified.

Integrity. The message contents have not been altered.

Nonrepudiation of origin. The sender cannot deny having sent the message.

Nonrepudiation of receipt. The receiver cannot deny having received the message.

Archiving. A document can be reconstructed for a certain time period after its creation.

A primary solution in ebXML is using a *digital signature* to verify the identity of sender and recipient. It can be used to ensure the integrity of the message and to verify that it was sent or received. A trusted third-party intermediary can provide services for archiving, authentication, and nonrepudiation of origin and receipt. The parties to a transaction agree to use the third party to provide independent historical proof that the transaction took place at a specific time and on specific terms. The length of the time depends on the archiving and record retention needs. For example, businesses might require archiving and retrieval of important documents for a 10-year period.

Digital signatures have security and legal implications that impact e-business requirements, so new technology solutions have to address them. The digital signature enables secure transactions, ensuring the integrity and authenticity of origin for business documents.

Two new security initiatives designed for XML data are XML Signature and XML Encryption. XML Signature is a joint effort between the W3C and Internet

Engineering Task Force (IETF), and XML Encryption is a W3C effort. XML Signature both addresses the special issues and requirements that XML presents for signing operations and uses XML syntax for capturing the result. For example, in a workflow scenario where an XML document is passed between participants, each participant may wish to sign only that portion for which they are responsible. Older standards for digital signatures do not provide the syntax for doing this.

An XML document can be encrypted in its entirety and sent securely to one or more recipients, using Secure Sockets Layer (SSL) for instance. A complete XML document can be sent as one operation and then held locally, thus reducing network traffic.

Cryptography does far more than merely conceal information. Message digests confirm text integrity, digital signatures support sender authentication, and related mechanisms are used to ensure that a valid transaction cannot later be repudiated by another party. These are all essential elements of remote trading, and mechanisms for handling complete documents are now fairly well developed. Difficulty arises when digitally signing an XML document as a whole: when parts of a document need to be signed by different people, and when digital signatures are required in conjunction with selective encryption.

ebXML supports electronic transactions with digital signatures at the appropriate level. For example, security can be required at both a session layer, such as the duration of a network session in which data is exchanged, or at the document level. In addition, security level setting can be applied to a particular data interchange or a specific document as needed. For example, the application may allow unrestricted and unsecured interchanges by default. As a digital signature asserts that a certain private key has been used to authenticate something, a signer should view the item to be signed in plain text, and this may mean decrypting part of something already encrypted for other reasons.

WHAT IS A DIGITAL SIGNATURE?

A *digital signature* is an electronic identifier created by a computer. It is intended to have the same force and effect as the use of a manual signature. To do so, it must embody these attributes:

- **It must be unique to the person using it.**
- **It must be capable of verification.**
- **It must be under the sole control of the person using it.**
- **It must be linked to data in a manner that if the data is changed, the digital signature is invalidated.**

—Definition adapted from California Civil Code (adding s. 1633) (1999 CA SB 1124)

In other cases, data that is already encrypted may be encrypted further as part of a larger set, such as a series of data records used in a workflow sequence, processed by a number of different applications and different users.

In the next section, we use a concrete example of how ebXML works in a corporate environment to illustrate the abstract ideas about the architecture.

How Does ebXML Work?

Now that we understand the key elements of the ebXML specification, let's look at an example of how companies might implement ebXML to conduct business. Steps necessary for enterprises to conduct e-business in ebXML might include:

- Discover each other and the products and services they have to offer.
- Determine which shared business processes and associated document exchanges to use for obtaining products or services from each other.
- Determine the contact points and form of communication for the exchange of information.
- Agree on the contractual terms on the preceding processes and associated information.
- Exchange information and services in accordance with these agreements.

In a sample business scenario, suppose Acme Hardware is purchasing hammers and nails from Big Distributor using ebXML. First, Acme Hardware converts the existing legacy applications to conform to ebXML standards. Acme Hardware will review the contents of a registry, such as core library and registered business processes. Acme Hardware downloads the ebXML specifications, including the business process models and business scenarios, and examines them to determine which business processes best fit the needs of its business. The company may find it can only implement a subset of the business processes, and it might need to modify its existing business process to adapt to the business process defined in the specifications.

Acme Hardware can build or buy an ebXML implementation suitable for its anticipated ebXML transactions. Based on the business processes, the company has decided to build an application to support the ebXML standards. This application defines the service interfaces that other organizations can use. It also describes the input and output messages that will be given to the service. Acme Hardware has a legacy application, and it wants to leverage its investment in the system. The company creates an implementation wrapper around the legacy application to help it understand ebXML messages and exposes the legacy application as a Web service, thereby making its Web services available to other organizations.

The next step is for Acme Hardware to create and register a CPP with the registry. The information packaged in the CPP includes technical details for other organizations to use the ebXML services. Acme Hardware may contribute new business processes to the registry, or it might reference existing documents. The CPP will contain the information for a potential partner to determine the business roles for Acme Hardware and the type of communication protocols to use. The CPP will be published to the registry for other organizations to discover. If the ebXML specifications change in the future, Acme Hardware would have to reevaluate them and appropriately implement them in their application.

Now suppose Big Distributor uses a prepackaged application that is purchased from a third-party vendor but uses the standard ebXML framework. Big Distributor follows the same steps in enabling its legacy application for ebXML. The company looks in the registry for trading partners and downloads the CPP for Acme Hardware. The CPP gives enough detail on what service is provided, messages that flow in and out from its services, and how to use this particular service. Once Acme Hardware is registered, Big Distributor can look at the CPP for Acme Hardware to determine that it is compatible with the CPP and requirements for Big Distributor. Big Distributor should be able to negotiate a CPA automatically with Acme Hardware based on the CPPs. When Big Distributor wants to engage with Acme Hardware as a trading partner, both companies have to agree to the trading arrangement. This may involve an initial meeting with key employees from both companies to work out the details for a business agreement. This also impacts technical details such as the business process and infrastructure requirements as well as the messaging protocols. The organizations develop a CPA, which includes the agreed-upon technical parameters. The CPA has derived from the capabilities of both organizations described by the CPP. The CPA is mutually agreed upon by both organizations and will then serve to govern the transactions between the two organizations.

The final step is the actual transactions between the two companies involving ebXML business messages. Messages are exchanged between the two organizations by the parameters in the CPA. The messages are transported using the ebXML messaging service. After Acme Hardware orders the goods and services and the invoice is processed at Big Distributor, the next step is order fulfillment, which is the shipment and delivery from the supplier to the customer.

The ebXML infrastructure is modular, and these infrastructure components may be used somewhat independently. The elements of the infrastructure may interact with each other, but in most cases are not required to. The role of ebXML is not just to replicate the electronic versions of common paper documents such as purchase orders, invoices, and tender requests. Rather, ebXML has implementation examples from industry associations to define standard core components in the software.

Major B2B Frameworks

In Chapter 3, we discussed the ebXML framework in context with Web services. Web standards such as SOAP, UDDI, and WSDL can integrate with ebXML as a comprehensive enterprise solution. The analysis of Web services can be based on working out the requirements for an XML-based framework that can enable B2B e-commerce and enterprise application integration.

The communications model in ebXML and Web services shows both similarities, such as using SOAP as a protocol, and differences, such as the more defined framework structure for ebXML. WDSL in the Web services model is used with SOAP and HTTP to invoke the service, whereas the ebXML messaging service is used in ebXML to provide a uniform way of sending messages. One similarity is that the ebXML messaging service uses SOAP as part of its secure and reliable transport infrastructure based an underlying protocol such as HTTP. ebXML provides a standardized way to send messages to trading partners with the CPA to set the ground rules for any business transactions. The messaging services may be used completely independently, although a message header may contain a reference to a CPA. The CPA and CPP provide means to identify a specification governing how the parties do business and parameters for using the ebXML messaging service.

Comparing the definition of a service in ebXML to Web services again shows the additional structure in ebXML. WSDL is used to describe a Web service in the Web services model, while CPP is used to describe the same Web Service in the ebXML specification. WSDL provides information about a service name, parameters for that service, and the endpoint to invoke it. CPP has this and also other important parameters, such as the role of an organization in the context of a particular service, error handling, and failure recovery scenarios. The ebXML business process schema is a definition of a specific type of Web service involving a business process, rather than the generic WSDL document. ebXML identifies business processes and also the roles that an organization has to play and messages being exchanged.

UDDI is used to publish and discover Web services, whereas ebXML Registry Services can publish and discover Web services *and* provide information about, for instance, business processes, business documents, and business profiles. Both systems can be used as complementary services. UDDI can be used to inquire about businesses in the global UDDI registry, and UDDI entries can then be used in referring to ebXML Web services in the ebXML registry. The CPP, CPA, and business process documents may be stored in an ebXML registry. An ebXML registry may store any type of object, including non-XML objects. However, all communications with the registry must use the ebXML messaging service. UDDI is used in the Web services model to publish Web services to a global UDDI repository.

The other frameworks in this area are more competitive than synergistic with ebXML, and we will analyze and compare them with ebXML. The major contenders in the enterprise XML framework space are BizTalk and RosettaNet, in addition to the cross-industry ebXML initiative. Rather than delve into the details on RosettaNet and BizTalk, in the next sections, we will focus on comparing and contrasting them with ebXML.

BizTalk

The BizTalk initiative includes the BizTalk Web site (www.biztalk.org) and the BizTalk Framework to provide a set of XML guidelines for publishing XML documents and creating schema creation. The BizTalk Framework uses XML messages to integrate software for business transactions, as well using the SOAP-based envelope format for data interchanges. BizTalk leverages existing industry data models, solutions, and application infrastructure. Microsoft BizTalk Server 2000 product is a BizTalk-compliant server product on the Windows 2000 platform. The BizTalk Server product has two main components, BizTalk Messaging and Orchestration. BizTalk Messaging consists of transport, routing, data transformation, auditing, and security features. BizTalk Orchestration provides a business process modeling and workflow element. It controls and coordinates the overall application integration solution based on a defined business process model.

Comparing ebXML and BizTalk

The BizTalk initiative has been driven by the Microsoft BizTalk Server product, serving as the proving ground to evolve BizTalk and its related standards. Microsoft focuses on product development, and one measure of success is the sales of BizTalk Server. By contrast, ebXML takes a top-down approach, first defining a set of standards, then validating the standard architecture in a proof-of-concept implementation. ebXML focuses on being vendor-neutral, building on existing technologies where appropriate, such UML and SOAP.

BizTalk is suitable as an application integration solution *within* an organization. BizTalk has few open standard alternatives in internal application integration, but many substitute proprietary products are available. Microsoft is the main driver behind BizTalk and owns the standard, but various members in the technology industry also participate. BizTalk lacks a discovery protocol, but this can be addressed by technologies such as Microsoft Site Server or UDDI. An organization with a predominately Microsoft software–installed base or skill set may choose BizTalk as the alternative requiring less effort. BizTalk Server runs on the Windows 2000 platform (and other Wintel platforms), but it integrates applications on a wide range of heterogeneous platforms using XML. The dual philosophies in the BizTalk and ebXML initiatives differ here: ebXML interoperates by dictating new cross-industry standards on existing standards, and BizTalk Server interoperates by building its implementation on standard protocols such as XML, HTTP, and SOAP.

As the application integration standard *between* organizations, ebXML can integrate the business systems of multiple organizations in a dynamic market. Though overkill as a framework for application integration within a smaller company, ebXML is ideal as the integration standard between organizations that are large, loosely coupled, and widely distributed. ebXML offers ability to look up information on trading partners and form relationships. It has the capability for dynamic discovery of business information to set up business transactions. The ebXML initiative is seen as more *open* than BizTalk as a standard, since ebXML originates from two standards bodies, UN/CEFACT and OASIS. A company with trading partners on different systems and platforms would likely support ebXML for their external data interchange.

Because of the nature of the standards process, it is unlikely that either framework will become completely dominant but that interoperability will feature highly at the boundaries as time goes on.

RosettaNet

RosettaNet is a strategic initiative for e-business in the IT supply chain based on open standards for the high-tech industry. RosettaNet has a deployment history, with over 400 companies using it in their supply chain. The mission of RosettaNet initiative is developing e-business guidelines for the IT distribution channel. The guidelines are specifications of the business processes between partners in the distribution channel, called *Partner Interface Processes* (PIPs). The guidelines include specifications of the business information exchanged by interoperable software components and the sequence of the information exchange. A PIP specification consists of a business interface process captured in an information flow diagram. RosettaNet defines the data properties, messaging, transaction services, dictionaries, and framework needed for a PIP. A master dictionary is used to define the properties for products, partners, and business transactions. The RosettaNet development strategy begins by partitioning distribution business processes into categories called clusters. The clusters are then partitioned into finer-grained categories termed segments. The scope of a PIP is defined by analysis of the business processes in a segment. Based on the PIP guideline from the RosettaNet development methodology, RosettaNet-compliant software solutions are developed.

Comparing ebXML and RosettaNet

The RosettaNet e-business applications architecture, like ebXML, draws from an EDI foundation to implement interoperable computer systems on the Web. RosettaNet and ebXML differ in some ways as to their philosophy with respect to EDI. Whereas ebXML focuses on XML as the technical foundation and bases its architecture on incorporating current best-of-breed ideas, RosettaNet borrowed more architectural ideas from EDI.

In RosettaNet, the applications layer comprises service components responding to requests from other services components. Each service responds to one or more requests using a protocol. Application-specific protocols are built on top of these service protocols. Data interchange applications for e-business in RosettaNet can be categorized as follows (based on Valerie Leyland's book *Electronic Data Interchange: A Management View*):

Business-transaction-oriented data interchange. Examples are invoices, purchase orders, and delivery notes.

Information-oriented data interchange. This refers to the interchange of relatively static data that is read, updated, and retained by the recipient company, such as price catalogs and technical data.

Interactive query-response data interchange. This is the use of an interactive system, such as catalog and inventory services, where an immediate response is required.

Electronic funds transfer (EFT). This relates specifically to messages concerning the transfer of funds.

Workflow-oriented data interchange. The business interface process is treated as a workflow process that allows messages to be routed according to their state.

The RosettaNet PIP architecture has two fundamental parts: the business process model and the distributed information system design. In contrast, the ebXML architecture includes the business process model, the core components, messaging service, registry, and collaboration protocol profile and agreement.

A convergence between the two standards is likely, as RosettaNet and ebXML find common ground to interoperate. RosettaNet will integrate ebXML messaging with its framework for interoperability. RosettaNet is likely to continue adding value in business process standards for the high-technology industry, while ebXML focuses on cross-industry standards.

Summary

ebXML is ideal as a unifying set of architectural frameworks for communicating with trading partners with heterogeneous platforms. As we have seen, ebXML is built on basic design concepts of infrastructure, semantic framework, and discovery. It provides for:

- A data communication infrastructure that can interoperate between different communication systems.
- A shared vocabulary and terminology library that can serve as a commercial framework.
- A way for enterprises to find each other, make agreements to be trading partners, and transact business.

ebXML is an open forum where software engineers and organizations can create consistent, robust, and interoperable services and components. The ebXML initiative invites software vendors to design and implement commercial, off-the-shelf components. This provides the flexibility to add or remove components as needed and interface with other solutions. Depending on the budget and business requirements, the components and subcomponents may be purchased or developed in-house. Because the ebXML architecture has defined rules and interfaces for interacting with other ebXML-compliant systems, the collection of ebXML components will work with other components that are added over time, as well as the ebXML systems of current and prospective trading partners.

This chapter provided an overview of the key parts of the ebXML architecture, including the business process model, core components, messaging services, registry, and collaboration protocol profile and agreement. The following chapters will cover each of these areas in more detail:

Business process model. The meta model defines the deliverables needed to describe a business process; it can be expressed using UML and then recast in XML. The business process specification schema deals with the rules for the actual business process. (See Chapter 5.)

Core components. These reusable information structures are the building blocks of ebXML systems. (See Chapter 6.)

Messaging services. The messaging structure can handle any payload, including traditional EDI and encrypted payloads over multiple communications services, such as HTTP and SMTP. (See Chapter 7.)

Registry and repository. The registry defines the extensible information model and XML-based interfaces to interact with a set of distributed ebXML compliant registries. (See Chapter 8.)

Trading partner information, also known as collaboration protocol profile (CPP) and collaboration protocol agreement. The CPP/CPA defines the capabilities of a trading partner to perform a data interchange, and how this data interchange agreement can be formed between two trading partners. The CPA/CPP deals with the technical aspects of a handshake between systems prior to conducting e-business. (See Chapter 9.)

CHAPTER

5

The ebXML Business Process Model

"What is coming is ERP software that supports inter-enterprise business processes. The next step is to create the virtual organization, where business processes span from manufacturer through supply chain out through distribution and to the consumer."

—Baer Tierkel, Senior Vice President of Strategy, PeopleSoft

AREAS COVERED IN THIS CHAPTER:

- **What is business process in ebXML?**
  - **Business process DTD and schema**
- **What is an interchange in ebXML? (collaboration)**
  - **Interchange between two parties (binary collaboration)**
  - **Interchange between multiple parties (multiparty collaboration)**
- **Transactions in ebXML**
  - **Business document flow within a transaction**
- **The sequence of activities in an interchange (choreography)**
  - **Business states**

In the past, business process improvements have been confined largely within the four walls of an organization. At the present, new business models in B2B create opportunities for process transformation across the entire value chain. Value chain integration involves passing complex transactions and data among trading partners. However, the adoption and use of value chain integration is slowed by the lack of mature standards for transactions, data, and technology tools.

In this context, ebXML standardizes common business processes. The ebXML business process model is about the collaborative dance between trading partners. In ebXML, business workflow is defined by a standard structure for business documents passed between business partners and intermediaries, such as information portals and transaction brokers.

This chapter is based on a primary technical specification that covers this area—the business process (BP) specification (http://www.ebxml.org/specs/ebBPSS.pdf). In addition, documents in XML are defined by an external document guideline, such as the DTD or XML schema. The business documents exchanged between trading partners are governed by the rules and naming conventions in the business process DTD and schema in the appendix. This chapter describes some of the ways that documents are created and used according to these semantic rules, but does not go into the full details in the BP specification or the DTD (see the BP DTD at www.ebxml.org/specs/ebBPSS.dtd).

Business Process

In e-commerce, business documents communicate a complete thought regarding *who, what, when, where,* and *how*. These general business concepts define the business workflow and technical structure of the documents in ebXML:

- The *who* in e-business terms involves parties, either individuals or organizations, and can be associated with other parties and products.
- The *what* is usually the product, including goods and services. Goods are manufactured, shipped, stored, purchased, and inspected by parties. Services are performed by parties, and may involve additional goods and parties.
- The *when* involves events associated with the product, such as inspection, transportation, and purchase. The specific sequence of business events for a trade between two parties includes bidding, negotiation, acceptance, and agreement.
- The *where* involves the physical and virtual locations associated with the parties and products.
- The *how* is the shipping, handling, and other logistics involved in getting the product from one trading partner to another.

The ebXML business process model standardizes around fundamental concepts called collaboration and transaction. Collaboration, transaction, and related ideas communicate in the XML language with ebXML semantics how something should happen in a B2B type of workflow. They represent the system interaction and events at a technical level that model actual business trades and exchanges between businesses. In computer-facilitated e-business, the exchange of information and products happens in software applications built to ebXML specifications, referred to as the *business service interface* (BSI), that speak this technical language and support the ebXML business process model. The BSI is any type of software application interface that implements business collaborations and manages the steps in the transaction. The BSI software in the transactions enforces the ebXML semantic rules.

The *collaboration* is an interchange between parties, such as a customer and supplier negotiating a purchase of a widget. The document processing for planning, negotiating, and placing an order is standardized as an XML-based workflow using collaboration as a basis. A specific collaboration between trading partners includes one or more business transactions.

The business process in ebXML is constructed as an XML instance of the generic model. The representation of a business process document in XML allows both humans and applications to read the information.

In ebXML business processes, a transaction has a technical definition, not the common understanding of a business trading exchange between people or businesses. The *transaction* is a single step, or a basic action, in the interchange between the parties, such as the submission of a purchase order from the customer to the supplier.

For example, the collaboration involving negotiation for a widget will include some of these steps, or transactions:

- The customer inquires about the price, availability, shipping terms, and discounts on the widget.
- The supplier sends the customer the requested information.
- The customer accepts the terms or asks for more favorable terms.
- The customer submits a purchase order to the supplier for the widgets based on the negotiated terms and conditions.

In the business collaboration, trading partners perform specific roles within each business transaction. Each business transaction may also contain business document flows and business signals. Industry-specific core components can be used as templates for generating specific instances of documents.

The business transactions take place in a sequence relative to each other, called choreography, which we explain later in the chapter.

As shown in Figure 5.1, the concepts of collaboration and transaction can be expressed as a framework for business scenarios (also called use cases) between a customer and supplier. These scenarios include such activities as create long-term contract, forecast component requirements, send planning document, place order, ship order, and arrange payment.

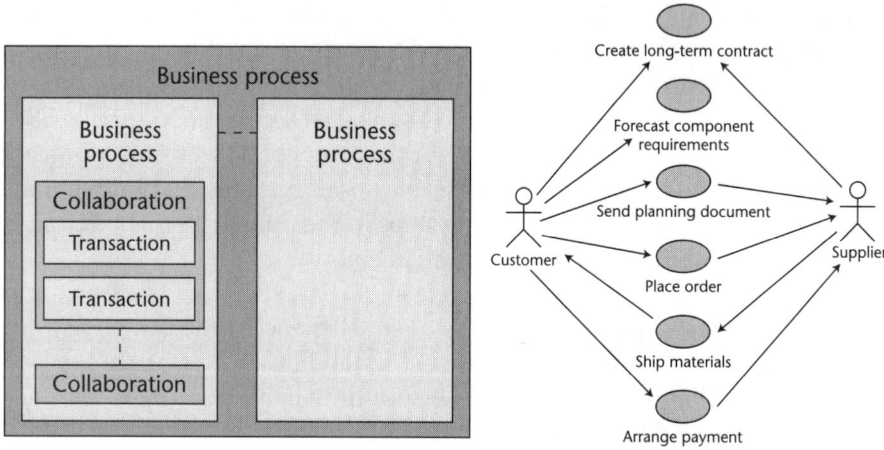

Figure 5.1 Business scenarios (use cases) are mapped to collaborations between trading partners, which are groupings of business transactions.

Source: "ebXML Business Process Specification Schema." May 2001.

The Business Process DTD and Schema

From Chapter 2, we know that XML documents are governed by a set of semantic rules. The document type definition (DTD) or XML schema defines the document semantics, such as the naming conventions for elements, attributes, and the relation between elements and the occurrence of elements.

For the exchange of business documents in ebXML, the primary rule representation is the document "ebXML Business Process Specification Schema." Any XML document will meet the requirements of the ebXML business process specification using the equivalent rules in either the DTD or the schema. Both the DTD and the schema documents are commonly referred to in the ebXML literature as simply the *business process specification schema* (BPSS).

The roadmap for ebXML business process models, the BPSS is a set of rules that define the semantics, elements, and properties necessary for collaboration between trading partners. Within these rules, the user has the flexibility to specify an infinite number of permutations of transactions and collaborations. ebXML software, such as BSI, uses the BPSS as a configuration file to specify the business process-related configuration parameters.

The BPSS does not have to be developed using the full UMM process. With a business process editor that supports the Business Process Analysis Worksheets, it can be automatically generated.

Using the BPSS

The business process framework in ebXML is used in context with other ebXML frameworks. This intent is expressed in the architecture design in Figure 5.2, where the ebXML software packages (business service interface and business application) use the BPSS as a configuration file to implement the data interchange between trading partners.

The BPSS, along with other ebXML documents such as the collaboration protocol profile and core components, specifies a complete environment for business collaboration. The BPSS in XML format, with related business documents and core components, is stored in a central location in the registry/repository. The registry serves as a central database and directory in the ebXML architecture, providing the storage and retrieval for an ebXML document from the trading partners. The business service interface (BSI) is any ebXML software with an application interface supporting the business process specification and schema.

The trading partners have to agree upon a collaboration protocol agreement (CPA) in order to transact business. Each partner plays one or more roles in the collaboration. The collaboration protocol profile and agreement serve as the configuration for the initial handshake and exchange of documents between trading partners. (See Chapter 9 for details on the collaboration protocol profile and agreement.)

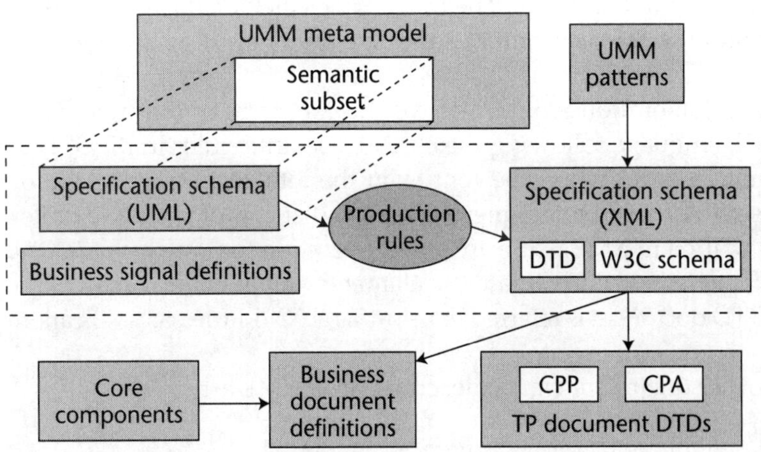

Figure 5.2 The relationship between business process, collaboration profile, and core components in ebXML.
Source: "ebXML Business Process Specification Schema." May 2001.

The following sections describe in more detail the concepts of business collaboration, business transaction, business document flow, and choreography, which is the precise sequence of events.

Collaboration: Interchange in ebXML

In e-commerce, the exchange of information usually involves two or more parties. In ebXML, the communication and exchange of documents between business partners is in the context of the business collaboration.

Any interchange between parties using ebXML semantics is an ebXML business collaboration. The grand idea is that all document processing for e-commerce is standardized using the business process framework in ebXML. The document information is written in XML and follows the semantic rules defined in the BPSS DTD or schema. This should provide some justification for the pedantic terminology we will use in this chapter to describe basic document exchange between companies.

The business collaboration includes a set of transactions. Depending on the number of parties, a business collaboration falls into either a binary collaboration (two parties) or multiparty collaboration (three or more parties).

For example, in a trading relationship between a retailer and distributor, the binary collaboration includes the contract negotiation for a large-volume order between the retailer and distributor. The transactions include the retailer sending a purchase order to the distributor or the distributor sending an invoice to the retailer.

Typically the collaboration would involve the exchange of multiple document in the XML language following the ebXML semantic rules in BP DTD or schema. A purchase order would be sent from the retailer to the distributor, with a purchase order acknowledgment from the distributor back to retailer. This would be written in XML using an XML generation tool, such as an XML editor. An XML parser would validate the elements and attributes against the BP DTD. (The DTD document is referred to below as ebXMLProcessSpecification-v1.00.dtd)

A purchase order document can be described in ebXML as:

```
<BusinessDocument name="Purchase Order"/>
```

Another purchase order acknowledgment document can be described in ebXML as:

```
<BusinessDocument name="PO Acknowledgement"/>
```

With the prolog, the expanded document would be:

```
<?xml version="1.0" encoding="UTF-8"?>
<!DOCTYPE ProcessSpecification SYSTEM "ebXMLProcessSpecification-
v1.00.dtd">
<ProcessSpecification name="Simple" version="1.1"
uuid="[1234-5678-901234]">
<BusinessDocument name="PO Acknowledgement"/>
```

In the following sections, we discuss data interchange between two parties (binary collaboration) and multiple parties (multiparty collaboration). In the code examples, we use code snippets to provide a condensed treatment rather than the full XML documents (with prolog, and so on).

Interchange between Two Parties (Binary Collaboration)

The *binary collaboration* is an interchange in ebXML between two parties using ebXML semantics. There are defined roles for the parties and a number of steps defined by the transactions. The idea is that multiple documents for a specific business process would be governed by ebXML rules, such as the document processing for planning, negotiating, and placing an order.

The parties have so-called authorized roles because they are authorized to participate in the collaboration. For each activity, one of two roles is assigned to be the requesting role and the other to be the responding role.

For example, Code Listing 5.1 defines a binary collaboration called `New Order`. A buyer in an initiating role and seller in a responding role create an order in a transaction. Typically this would happen where the buyer has taken the order information and sent it to the seller along with the following XML information for processing. Using software that supports ebXML, the computer would interpret this binary collaboration and its transaction and process the new order. The prolog and the rest of the order information are not included in the example for conciseness.

```
<BinaryCollaboration name="New Order">
<InitiatingRole name="buyer"/>
<RespondingRole name="seller"/>
<!--Transaction: buyer to create an order with seller -->
<BusinessTransactionActivity
 name="Create Order"
 businessTransaction="Create Order"
 fromAuthorizedRole="buyer"
 toAuthorizedRole="seller"/>
</BinaryCollaboration>
```

Code Listing 5.1 This new order is initiated by the buyer and responded to by the seller.

The transactions are defined by the `<BusinessTransactionActivity>` element, with attributes defining the name of the business transaction, the authorized roles for the sender (from) and recipient (to). The number of attributes and attribute values for `<BusinessTransactionActivity>` would vary based on the type of transaction and the transaction information.

Two parties can engage in multiple business transactions within a binary collaboration. Many data interchanges between two parties involve more than one transaction. It is possible to incorporate all of the transactions in a given collaboration or break them up into different collaborations over a period of time. To put it another way, collaborations are a way to group transactions between parties, and we can group transactions to reflect our preferences.

For example, Code Listing 5.2 defines a binary collaboration called `Fulfillment` with a buyer in the initiating role and seller in the responding role. The two transactions in the collaboration are (1) creating an order and (2) notification of shipment. Again, the prolog and the rest of the order information are not included in the example for conciseness.

In this example, the transactions are defined by the two `<BusinessTransactionActivity>` elements and their attributes, which define the names of two business transactions (`Create Order` and `Notify Shipment`) and the authorized roles for the sender (from) and recipient (to). If necessary, additional transactions can be added to this binary collaboration to complete the entire data interchange between the buyer and seller.

In the next section, we discuss the interchange between multiple parties, which is a logical extension of the concept of binary collaboration.

```
<BinaryCollaboration name="Fulfillment">
<InitiatingRole name="buyer"/>
<RespondingRole name="seller"/>
<!--Transaction: buyer to create an order with seller -->
<BusinessTransactionActivity name="Create Order"
 businessTransaction="Create Order"
 fromAuthorizedRole="buyer"
 toAuthorizedRole="seller"/>
<!--Transaction: buyer to notify seller in case of advance shipment -->
<BusinessTransactionActivity name="Notify Shipment"
 businessTransaction="Notify of advance shipment"
 fromAuthorizedRole="buyer" toAuthorizedRole="seller"/>
</BinaryCollaboration>
```

Code Listing 5.2 The fulfillment transactions are initiated by the buyer and responded to by the seller.

Interchange Between Multiple Parties (Multiparty Collaboration)

Multiparty collaboration is the interchange between multiple groups in ebXML using ebXML semantics. It can be viewed as a combination of several binary collaborations. Multiparty collaborations occur between three or more roles and can be created from binary collaborations. If roles A, B, and C collaborate and all parties interact with each other, there will be a separate binary collaboration between A and B, one between B and C, and one between A and C. The multiparty collaboration will be the sum of all the binary collaborations in the transaction.

A multiparty collaboration consists of a number of business partner roles. We could define all possible exchanges between all of the parties; however, doing so would involve a lot of work. Alternatively, we can specify a multiparty collaboration by defining all the two-party collaborations in which its business partners play different roles.

Roles are used to define situations where the named parties act in transactions. Similar to a popular TV show where actors play different roles in successive comedy sketches, such as *Saturday Night Live*, the participants in ebXML collaboration play different roles at different places in the ebXML program. The intent of this feature is to provide flexibility in defining the possible interactions between a fixed set of players.

Specified by the `Performs` element, each role performs one authorized role in one or more binary collaborations. For example, in Code Listing 5.3 we can specify a multiple-party exchange between the customer, retailer, and drop ship vendor using two binary collaborations.

- In the multiple-party document exchange called `DropShip`, the customer will play the initiating role as the buyer.
- In the two-party document exchange called `New Order`, the customer will play an initiating role as the buyer and the retailer will play a responding role as the seller.
- In the two-party document exchange called `Fulfillment`, the retailer will play will play an initiating role as the buyer and the drop ship vendor will play a responding role as the seller.

```
<MultiPartyCollaboration name="DropShip">
<!--Role: customer to play buyer in New Order collaboration -->
<BusinessPartnerRole name="Customer">
<Performs initiatingRole='//binaryCollaboration[@name="New Order"]
```

Code Listing 5.3 This collaboration happens with customer, retailer, and drop ship vendor playing buyer and seller roles at different points in the transactions. *(continues)*

```
/InitiatingRole[@name="buyer"]'/>
</BusinessPartnerRole>
<!--Role: retailer to play seller in New Order collaboration-->
<!--Role: retailer to play buyer in Fulfillment collaboration-->
<BusinessPartnerRole name="Retailer">
<Performs respondingRole='//binaryCollaboration[@name="New Order"]
/RespondingRole[@name="seller"]'/>
<Performs initiatingRole='//binaryCollaboration[@name="Fulfillment"
/InitiatingRole[@name="buyer"]'/>
</BusinessPartnerRole>
<!--Role: vendor to play seller in Fulfillment collaboration-->
<BusinessPartnerRole name="DropShip Vendor">
<Performs respondingRole='//binaryCollaboration[@name="Fulfillment"
/RespondingRole[@name="seller"]'/>
</BusinessPartnerRole>
</MultiPartyCollaboration>
```

Code Listing 5.3 This collaboration happens with customer, retailer, and drop ship vendor playing buyer and seller roles at different points in the transactions. *(continued)*
Source: "ebXML Business Process Specification Schema." May 2001.

In this example, the `Performs` element links together the business partner (customer, retailer, or drop ship vendor) and the authorized role (buyer or seller). This allows us to roll up two binary collaborations into a single multi-party collaboration, along with their transactions.

We have three trading partners (drop ship vendor, customer, and retailer) that can communicate with each other using XML documents following ebXML semantics. The customer can access the retailer's Web site and place an order for the widget as an XML document. The back-end systems that fulfill the order would process and send the XML document to the drop ship vendor, which would process the order and send the products to the customer. The software applications that run the supply chain would manage the process using XML documents sent between each business as a basis of communication. The XML parsers in the software would use the BPSS to validate the XML documents, ensuring that they all use the same names and the same definitions for elements and attributes.

The worlds of collaborations and transactions are tightly coupled in ebXML, since collaborations are the way to group together transactions between two or more parties. In the next section we explore transactions in more detail.

Transactions

In commerce, a transaction often refers to any trade or exchange between people or businesses. ebXML defines *transaction* more narrowly as a single logical step in an data interchange between partners. The collaboration is the more general concept, which is analogous to a conversation or session between trading partners, such as a customer negotiating a purchase with a vendor. A transaction is analogous to a single task in the conversation, such as any of these tasks that make up the collaboration: recording item sales, processing refunds, recording coupons, handling voids, verifying checks before accepting them as tender, or settling the amount to be paid to the customer.

A transaction is the basic unit of work in a trading arrangement between two business partners. As an atomic unit, the transaction cannot be broken down into separate transactions. The transaction is conducted between parties playing roles. In a two-party exchange, there are two opposite roles—requesting and responding.

For example, a business transaction for a purchase order can be described simply as:

```
<BusinessTransaction name="PO">
. . .
</BusinessTransaction>
```

A transaction always results in a success or failure. If the transaction is a success, it may become a legally binding contract, such as denoted by the `isLegallyBinding` attribute in the `BusinessTransactionActivity` element. If the transaction is a failure, it is rolled back to the previous condition before the transaction happened. Any claims in the proposed agreement in the transaction are also null and void.

Transactions in ebXML are particularly useful because we can ensure that important documents are sent and received as intended. If a purchase order or invoice gets lost in the communication, we know about it and can take appropriate steps. This is important in the design to ensure timely and precise delivery of documents.

In the next section, we present the flow of business documents in the context of a transaction.

Business Document Flow

Business document flow is the exchange of documents between parties within a transaction in ebXML. Optional business signals in the transaction can be used to convey the meaning of acknowledgments and related matters. Documents are defined by other ebXML specifications, such as the core component specifications, or using an XML DTD or schema.

Business document flows between the requesting and responding roles takes place within a transaction, as shown in Figure 5.3.

A requesting business activity is described as:

```
<RequestingBusinessActivity name="something">
```

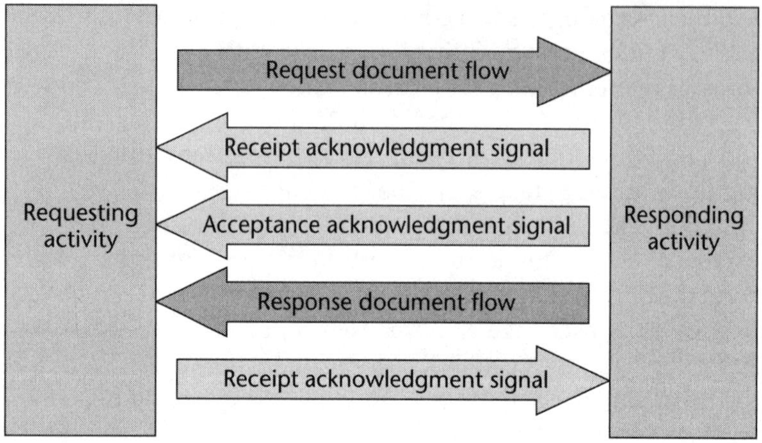

Figure 5.3 The document flow and business signals between two parties and their sequence within a transaction.

A requesting document contained by a document envelope is associated with the requesting business activity. A document for a purchase order is described as:

```
<DocumentEnvelope BusinessDocument="Purchase Order"/>
```

An optional responding document may also be associated with the responding business activity, depending on whether the transaction is set up for one-way notification or two-way conversation.

Transactions include one or more business document flows, and transactions can be used to group together the individual business document flows between parties. Document flows may also include attached document envelopes containing business documents. This structure is shown for a purchase order transaction in Code Listing 5.4.

```
<BusinessTransaction name="PO">
<RequestingBusinessActivity name="sendingPO">
<DocumentEnvelope BusinessDocument="PurchaseOrder"/>
</RequestingBusinessActivity>
<RespondingBusinessActivity name="acknowledgePO">
<DocumentEnvelope BusinessDocument="POAcknowledgement"/>
</DocumentEnvelope>
</RespondingBusinessActivity>
</BusinessTransaction>
```

Code Listing 5.4 Business transaction with requesting and responding business activity and attached purchase order documents for purchase order and acknowledgment.

In a transaction activity, binary collaboration roles are assigned to the transaction. For example, in a transaction between a buyer and a seller, the systems participate in document flows between the requesting activity and the responding activity.

In the requesting role, the buyer has to initiate the request document flow, but the response document flow from the seller is optional. The buyer can define in the transaction whether a response document is required. The buyer may define that completing a contract or agreement requires both a request and response document flow. The buyer may also define that a notification on price changes only needs a request document flow.

Code Listing 5.5 is an example of a simple notification about delivery terms and conditions with a document flowing from the buyer to the seller.

In the responding role, the seller can use business signals to acknowledge the receipt and acceptance of documents. These acknowledgments are application-level documents that signal the current state of the business transaction. Business documents can vary in structure, but business signals always have the same structure.

In this example, there is a time limit on the transaction. The buyer and seller have 5 days from the start of the transaction to complete it. (`P2D` means Period=2 Days; `P3D` means Period=3 Days; `P5D` means Period=5 Days. These periods are all measured from original sending of request. This is from the W3C Schema syntax adopted from the ISO 8601 standard.)

In the transaction, the buyer specifies whether the seller has to send a receipt acknowledgment or acceptance acknowledgment signal. The receipt acknowledgment signal indicates that a message has been properly received. The acceptance acknowledgment signal indicates that the received message has been accepted for business processing.

The transactions are rolled back if the recipient fails to send either signal by the specified time-out period. Coding Listing 5.6 is a purchase order transaction called "PO" with receipt and acceptance acknowledgment.

```
<BusinessTransaction name="delivery notification" timeToPerform="P5D">
<Documentation>
timeToPerform = Period: 5 days from start of transaction
</Documentation>
<RequestingBusinessActivity name="SendingNotice">
<DocumentEnvelope BusinessDocument name="NoticeNotes"/>
</RequestingBusinessActivity>
<RespondingBusinessActivity name="ReceivingNotice">
</RespondingBusinessActivity>
</BusinessTransaction>
```

Code Listing 5.5 Delivery notification transaction with a requesting and responding business document flow.

```
<BusinessTransaction name="PO">
<RequestingBusinessActivity name=""
 isNonRepudiationRequired="true"
 timeToAcknowledgeReceipt="P2D"
 timeToAcknowledgeAcceptance="P3D">
<DocumentEnvelope BusinessDocument="Purchase Order"/>
</RequestingBusinessActivity>
<RespondingBusinessActivity name=""
 isNonRepudiationRequired="true"
 timeToAcknowledgeReceipt="P5D">
<DocumentEnvelope isPositiveResponse="true"
 BusinessDocument="PO Acknowledgement"/>
</DocumentEnvelope>
</RespondingBusinessActivity>
</BusinessTransaction>
```

Code Listing 5.6 A transaction with a request that requires both receipt and acceptance acknowledgment, and the response that requires receipt acknowledgment.

A document envelope sent by one role and received by the other represents a document flow. The document envelope represents the flow of documents between the activities. The document envelope is associated with one requesting activity and one responding activity.

Document envelopes have names, with one required envelope for a requesting activity and optional envelopes for a responding activity. Each envelope carries exactly one primary document. An envelope can have one or more optional attachments, all related to the primary document. The document and its attachments in a transaction are packaged in the payload in the message structure.

For example in Code Listing 5.7, suppose in a business transaction the buyer sends one request to create a purchase order with an attachment `"Delivery- Notes"`. There are two possible responses, a success and a failure. The request/response document flows between the sender and recipient. The business documents are attached in the transaction. The response document envelopes for the purchase order transaction are `"ebXML1.0/PO Acknowledgement"` and `"ebXML1.0/PO Rejection"`. In the actual execution of the purchase order transaction only one of the defined possible responses will be sent.

```
<BusinessDocument name="Purchase Order"/>
<BusinessDocument name="PO Acknowledgement"/>
<BusinessDocument name="PO Rejection"/>
```

Code Listing 5.7 A business transaction for a purchase order, with attached documents. *(continues)*

```
<BusinessDocument name="Delivery Instructions"/>
<BusinessTransaction name="Create Order">
<RequestingBusinessActivity name="">
<DocumentEnvelope isPositiveResponse="true"
 BusinessDocument="ebXML1.0/PO Acknowledgement">
<Attachment
 name="DeliveryNotes"
 mimeType="XML"
 BusinessDocument="ebXML1.0/Delivery Instructions"
 specification=""
 isConfidential="true"
 isTamperProof="true"
 isAuthenticated="true">
</Attachment>
</DocumentEnvelope>
</RequestingBusinessActivity>
<RespondingBusinessActivity name=""
<DocumentEnvelope
 BusinessDocument="ebXML1.0/PO Acknowledgement"/>
</DocumentEnvelope>
<DocumentEnvelope isPositiveResponse="false"
 BusinessDocument="ebXML1.0/PO Rejection"/>
</DocumentEnvelope>
</RespondingBusinessActivity>
</BusinessTransaction>
```

Code Listing 5.7 A business transaction for a purchase order, with attached documents. *(continued)*

Choreography: A Sequence of Activities in the Interchange

In a movie or a play, a choreographer works with the actors to make sure that certain actions happen in the order they are supposed to. The actors rehearse the script over and over following the choreographed actions. By analogy, in a data interchange the application has to follow a predictated sequence of events, according to the choreography of the business activities. The choreography is specified in terms of business states and transitions between those business states (see Figure 5.4). The business transaction choreography describes the ordering and transitions between business transactions within a binary collaboration.

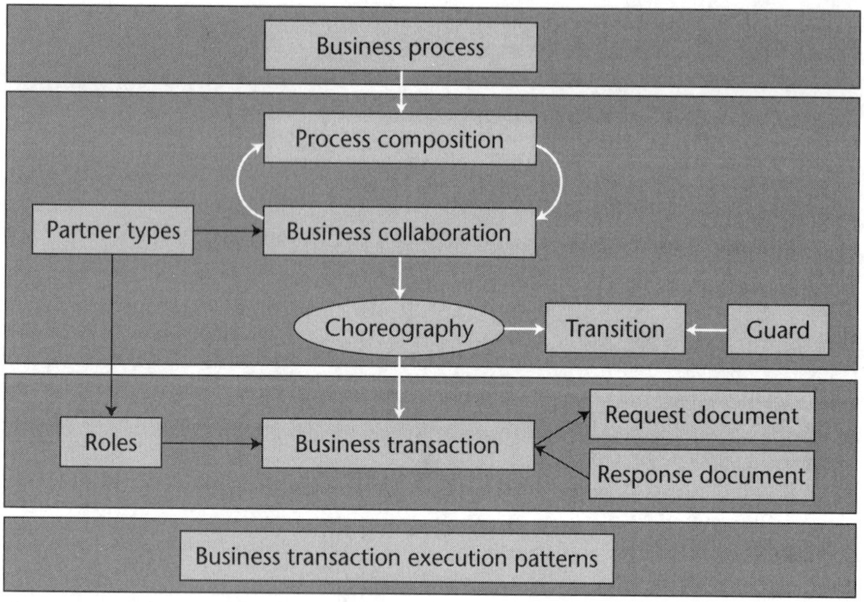

Figure 5.4 The choreography includes concepts such as start state, completion state, activities, synchronizations, transitions between activities, and guards on the transitions.
Source: "ebXML Business Process Specification Schema." May 2001.

Business States

A number of business states are used for coordinating the sequence of business activities in a data interchange. The business states include a start state, a completion state of either success or failure, a fork state, and a join state:

Start. The starting state for a binary collaboration. A binary collaboration should have at least one starting activity. If none is defined, then all activities are considered allowable entry points.

Success. A completion state that defines the successful conclusion of a binary collaboration as a transition from an activity.

Failure. A completion state that defines the unsuccessful conclusion of a binary collaboration as a transition from an activity.

Fork. A state with one inbound transition and multiple outbound transitions. All activities pointed to by the outbound transitions are assumed to happen in parallel.

Join. A business state where an activity is waiting for the completion of one or more other activities. A join is the point where forked activities join up again.

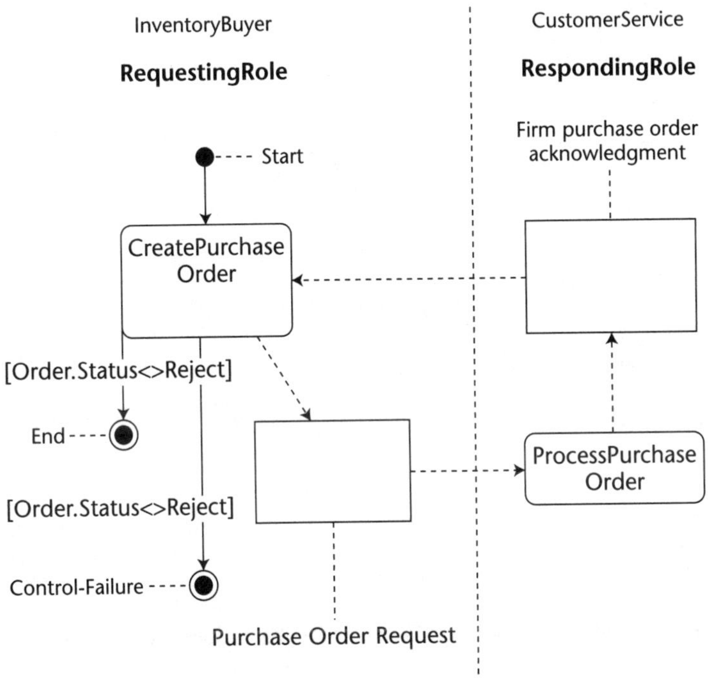

Figure 5.5 The states for creating a purchase order.

In the choreography, transitions allow us to move from business states to business states. Transitions can be gated by guards. Guards can refer to a number of items in the document: the status of the document envelope, the type of document, the content of the document, or continuation conditions on the state before the transition. An example of the purchase order process expressed using business states is shown in Figure 5.5.

One way of using choreography is that different paths can be taken depending on the outcome of the transaction. For example, in this fulfillment binary collaboration between buyer and seller, the choreography dictates the create order as the start state and the completion state (with success or failure as the outcome). There is the notify shipment transition between the state and completion states. The two possible outcomes of this collaboration are success and failure for the fulfillment and notification of the order. (See Code Listing 5.8.)

```
<BinaryCollaboration name="Fulfillment">
<InitiatingRole name="buyer"/>
<RespondingRole name="seller"/>
<BusinessTransactionActivity name="Create Order"
```

Coding Listing 5.8 Fulfillment collaboration shows use of transitions between states. *(continues)*

```
  businessTransaction="Create Order"
  fromAuthorizedRole="buyer"
  toAuthorizedRole="seller"/>
 <BusinessTransactionActivity
  name="Notify shipment"
  businessTransaction="Notify of advance shipment"
  fromAuthorizedRole="buyer"
  toAuthorizedRole="seller"/>
 <!-- Choreography: specifying Start, Transition, and Completion -->
 <Start toBusinessState="Create Order"/><Transition
  fromBusinessState="Create Order"
  toBusinessState="Notify shipment"/>
 <Success
  fromBusinessState="Notify shipment"
  conditionGuard="Success"/
 <Failure
  fromBusinessState="Notify shipment"
  conditionGuard="BusinessFailure"/>
 </BinaryCollaboration>
```

Coding Listing 5.8 Fulfillment collaboration shows use of transitions between states. *(continued)*

Summary

Supply chain applications provide standard communication tools to enhance the collaboration among trading partners so that business processes are streamlined and more effective. The new business models rely heavily on standards, improved applications, and process reengineering. Business processes will be optimized to achieve the next level of processing efficiency and speed, as well as more advanced capabilities.

The ebXML business process model provides a solid foundation for describing business services such as purchasing, shipping, and ordering. This model standardizes around fundamental concepts called collaboration (an exchange between two or more parties) and transaction (a basic action between two parties). In a given collaboration between trading partners, business transactions take place.

The concepts of collaboration and transaction provide a framework for business scenarios between a customer and a supplier. The document processing for planning, negotiating, and placing an order is standardized as an XML-based workflow using collaboration as a basis, and industry-specific core components are used as templates for generating specific instances of documents.

The business process specification schema (BPSS) is the guidebook of rules for this collaborative dance between partners. Within these rules, the user has the flexibility to specify an infinite number of specific transactions and collaborations. The BPSS provides the semantics, elements, and attributes to define business collaborations.

Business documents may be assembled from core components, as we will describe in Chapter 6.

CHAPTER

6

Using Core Components

"A Core Component captures information about a real world business concept, and relationships between that concept and other business concepts. A Core Component can be either an individual piece of business information, or a family of business information pieces. It is core because it occurs in many different areas of industry/business information exchange."

—Definition from ebXML "Core Component and Business Process Document Overview"

AREAS COVERED IN THIS CHAPTER:

- What is a core component?
- Basic object concepts
- Definition of terms
- Identifying core components
- Methodology
- How to use core components
- What is context?
- Different types of context
- Constraint language
- Example of using context
- How to use document assembly
- Assembly rules
- Example of using document assembly

Object technology is a critical enabler for ebXML core components. The methodology is language-independent in that it does not depend on the features of any particular object language. It assumes that objects provide the fundamental building blocks of all business models. ebXML builds on the object concept by extending it to a model called a core component, which is the basic building block for ebXML software. In this chapter, we define what a core component is, how to use it, and how it relates to other parts of ebXML. This chapter is based on information in the ebXML core component bible, the *Core Components Technical Specification version 1.5* (www.ebxml.org/specs/). For simplicity, we will use the term *schema* to refer to any one of the various dialects of XML schemas and DTDs.

What Is a Core Component?

Before we tackle defining core components, we must first look at a few basic concepts concerning objects. The central activity of working with objects is not programming but representation. A software object represents an important real-world concept in object modeling. The software object reflects the information and behavior in the real-world object. The business object software represents the essential elements of a business in objects. Hence, we can reproduce the behavior of the business by causing the objects to act out their roles within the model.

Basic Object Concepts

Most businesses work with companies from many other industries, which may have their own business practices. Typically the same set of practices for procurement, payment, and shipping applies each time we do business with a company. Most businesses base their practices on simple conventions that are widely accepted, such as the purchase order, invoice, and other forms. These conventions and shared documents are the basis for an abstract model to represent a business and its processes, for example, business objects.

- An object is a model of a real-world business concept and relationships between that concept and other business concepts. An object can be either an individual piece of business information or packaged as a family of business information pieces. For example, the ordering information for a product contains details about the order itself, such as payment, delivery, and references to external business agreements. Some parts of the order document are the same across all industries, while other details, such as the product type, are different for each industry. Specific business data in the document, such as product identification using SKUs, are the same across different industries.

- Business objects represent real-world business concepts in a particular business domain, such as sales order, address, or currency. The design of a specific model would capture real-world concepts such as the information and exchange requirements, identifying the sequence, timing, and purpose of each exchange.

Objects come in many different varieties called *classes*. A class is simply a generic definition for similar objects, which are called *instances* of that class. Classes specify what their instance objects can know and do. For example, a business design can require a customer class that defines the structure and behavior of customer objects.

Objects are defined by classes and contain *methods* and variables. Methods are named sequences of computer instructions that allow the object to carry out actions. Although similar to functions or procedures in programming languages, methods are defined in the context of a specific class. *Variables*, also known as attributes, are named locations where data can be stored. They are similar to variables in programming languages, but they can contain references to other objects, as well as basic data types as numbers, dates, and text.

A class defines the available methods and variables. An instance of the class holds the values associated with its variables. These values can change over time, either through interactions with other objects or through user action.

Though closely related, objects and components are *not* the same thing, but closely related ideas. A *component* is a software building block that contains a defined set of business information.

The *composite object* is a business object that contains other objects, called *component objects*. A composite object is created by references to component objects in its variables. When a composite object needs to interact with its components, it looks up their current location in the appropriate variables and sends them messages. Composite objects contain references to their component objects and do not contain the objects themselves. Hence, an object can appear as a component in any number of composite objects.

Definition of Terms

A child can use Lego blocks to construct numerous things. The blocks are easy to work with, since they have standard forms and shapes, but they can be put together to make complex objects. By analogy, a core component in ebXML can contain another core component, and can be used as a building block to create more complex and interesting objects.

A *core component* is a basic, reusable building block that contains information representing a business concept. Some examples of core components for parts of a purchase order are "Date of Purchase Order," "Sales Tax," and "Total Amount." In general, core components are used in many different domains, industries, and business processes. In the ebXML environment, core components are the building blocks for XML semantics and business vocabulary that are used in messages and documents. They are reused many times for specific business purposes and are a way to apply object models to structured information in XML. From the basic structure of elements and attributes in XML documents, we need to put together standard objects in the software architecture. An application would generate XML documents containing core components for procurement, payment, and shipping for a particular industry. Users can select core components from a registry to assemble into their documents and messages. The core library in the registry contains a dictionary of business terms, so that businesses can share core components for business transactions.

The basic parts in ebXML are (1) attributes and elements, (2) core components, (3) document/messages, and (4) syntax. In the English language, this is analogous to (1) letters and words, (2) sentences, (3) paragraphs/chapters, and (4) grammar in XML attributes. Elements (letters and words) are put together into core components (sentences), which are grouped into documents/messages (paragraphs/chapters) following rules set by syntax in an ebXML DTD (grammar). The syntax in a DTD dictates the order and structure of the XML attributes by the use of rules and special characters, just as in grammar we have commas, periods, spacing, and so on. The ebXML core component is the semantic equivalent of the segment concept in EDI, with the additional object-oriented innovations of context and assembly.

A *domain component* is specific to an individual industry area and is only used within that domain. It may be reused by another domain if it is found to be appropriate and adequate, and it then becomes a core or common component. If the component is appropriate for common use in the industry, it may be adapted as a core component by an industry association.

Within this chapter, *context* has a specific meaning in relation to core components. A core component is independent of context by itself, or context-free. However, using core components in ebXML involves incorporating context. Context is a way to classify different business situations in using core components. With business contexts, we can use generic *context-free* core components and make contextual changes needed to support the business process at run time. A new business information name exists for each context-specific reuse of a common component. A *business information entity* (BIE) is a core component used in a real business situation that is the result of using core components within a specific business context. If a core component is analogous to an object class, then BIEs are specific instances of the class.

Components can be aggregated into documents. An *aggregated component* is made up of several components. They can be generic and used across several industries, and they can be reused for a specific business purpose, defined by a set of context information. A new business information name is used for each context-specific reuse of an aggregated component. Aggregated components can also be specific to a business domain. A document becomes more domain-specific and context-specific as it is aggregated from its constituent components, which form documents or partial documents in a business process. The components become more useful when assembled to meet the business process requirements. Figure 6.1 shows the relationship between core components, context, and aggregated components.

An *aggregate core component* (ACC) is a set of information representing a business concept, such as a purchase order. Each ACC has its own unique semantic definition and can contain one of the following:

- Two or more basic core components
- At least one basic core component plus one or more aggregated core components

An aggregated business information entity (ABIE) is an aggregated core component used in a specified business context. If an aggregated core component is analogous to an object class, then ABIEs are specific instances of the class.

Repository meta data concerns core components, such as context classification and business information entities, along with business message descriptions. This information about relationships between the objects helps standardize reuse.

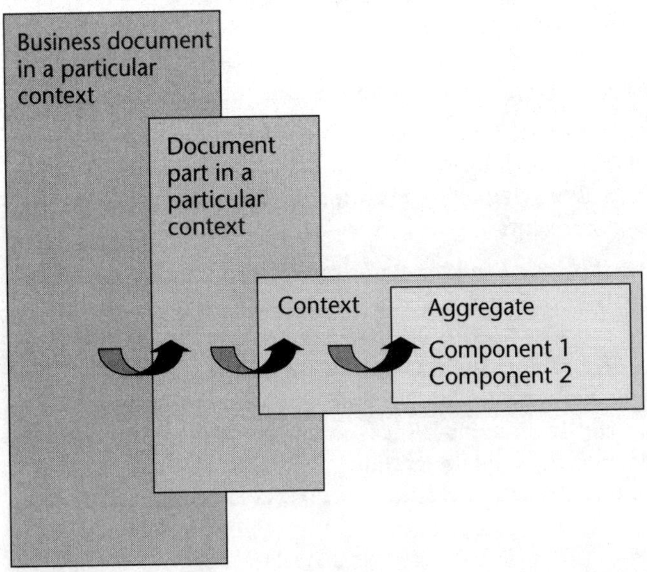

Figure 6.1 Relating core components, context, and aggregated components.
Source: "Core Component and Business Process Document Overview." May 2001.

Identifying Core Components

A core component is uniquely identifiable. The business process can specify several core components as part of a business document. A core component identifier can define a party in multiple contexts. For example, the same core component identifier would apply to the airline passenger, buyer of the gift, shipper of the package, and guest at the hotel. Each company stores the common identifier in the repository, which is related to its specific industry terminology, such as passenger, buyer, shipper, and guest.

TOOLS AND REFERENCES

Following is a short list of the essential references and tools for core components provided by ebXML for the business and technical analyst. (See www.ebxml.org to download copies of these documents.)

- ***Context and the Re-usability of Core Components v. 1.04.*** **The document contains context definitions, the sources of classification value lists, and a pictorial model of core component and context descriptor relationships.**
- ***Catalog of Context Drivers v. 1.04.*** **This document provides a catalog of context drivers. It describes the categories of business context descriptors that have been identified as the most critical for facilitating the reuse of core components and business process models.**
- ***Document Assembly and Context Rules v. 1.04.*** **This describes the procedures and schemas for assembling documents using contextually driven core components. The business information is what must be represented by the core components. Context drivers are derived from information contained in both the business process and the CPP and CPA documents.**
- ***Core Components Dictionary.*** **This document is divided into sections. Each section begins with the information on the applicable category and core component type. The sections also contain additional information for the listed core components.**
- ***Core Components Editor and Browser.*** **Core components capture the essence of reusable data definitions. To be usable, core components must be instantiated in a context. These tools help analysts browse existing core components and integrate them to define the format of the XML messages exchanged between trading partners and to properly define and apply the context rules. Some of these tools may also provide direct interfaces to ebXML registry implementations.**

Let's look at an example of how to use core component identifiers in a purchasing process. A manufacturer (seller) uses ebXML software for an e-business process that allows other businesses to purchase its products. A distributor (buyer) sends this list of information in a purchase order to the manufacturer:

- Company name and details for buyer
- Purchase order number
- Date of order
- Order details (model, size, color)
- Subtotal amount before taxes
- Total amount

We want to have standard core components for the business process that can be reused and are nonspecific to the two companies. We build a set of core components by abstracting from the information in the purchase order, such as in Table 6.1. The unique ID (UID) is used for each core component. Table 6.1 is simplified as a high-level abstraction for illustration purposes, and not as the actual model in a software system. The core components would vary in syntax based on the context of the business process. For instance, if the buyer and seller are European, the total amount can be expressed in euros. If the buyer and seller are American, the total amount can be in U.S. dollars. Otherwise, the amount would have to be denominated in both currencies for the transaction.

UID, UUID, URN, URI

There are many ways to represent the complete address and route for locating resources across electronic networks:

- **A unique ID (UID) is used for ebXML core components.**
- **Universal Unique Identifier (UUID) is used in the ebXML registry.**
- **A Uniform Resource Name (URN) is a naming convention for permanent unique addresses for resources over a network.**
- **A Uniform Resource Identifier (URI) is a schema that allows resources to be uniquely named using UUIDs.**

Table 6.1 Core Components for a Sample Purchase Order

CORE COMPONENT UID	CORE COMPONENT NAME	DESCRIPTION
001	Name and details for buyer	The party name and details, including a unique identifier for the business.
002	Purchase order number	The purchase order number, a unique identifier used to track the order.
003	Date of order	The date of the order. The value can be expressed in ISO-8601, the international time and date standard notation, YYYY-MM-DD.
004	Order details	The product attributes for the order, such as model, size, color, and quantity, is expressed as a string format. This value can be in English, Spanish, Chinese, or other languages.
005	Sales tax	The sales tax levied by federal, state, and local governments. The value can be expressed in different currencies, such as U.S. dollars or euros.
006	Subtotal amount	The subtotal amount of the invoice. The value can be expressed in different currencies, such as U.S. dollars or euros. (Note: In a more formal modeling process, we would include a qualifier for currency code.)
007	Total amount	The total amount of the invoice. The value can be expressed in U.S. dollars or euros.

Using Core Components

This section covers the processes for deploying core components. The XML message structure is defined and governed by a standard XML DTD or schema.

However, use of core components and context occurs before using a DTD to create an XML message. Instead of examining the DTD for syntax and interoperable semantics, we have to look at the semantic models per se.

These are recommended steps from the *Core Components Specification,* as shown in Figure 6.2. These steps assume we have *existing* core component definitions that have already been discovered and published by standards groups. When selecting a business process, registry searches are made according to the requirements of the trading partners. The core components and context rules are useful in determining the best possible match in the registry. The comparison can be automated and serve as a feature implemented in the repository.

Step 1: Find a Business Process That Meets the Requirements

The user searches in the registry on all available published business processes (BPSS). If the business process is found, it is configured with the trading partner profiles and agreements. Using the Catalog of Common Business Processes (CCBP) makes finding interoperable business processes much easier. If no existing business process can be found, the process is modeled as core components and published to the registry.

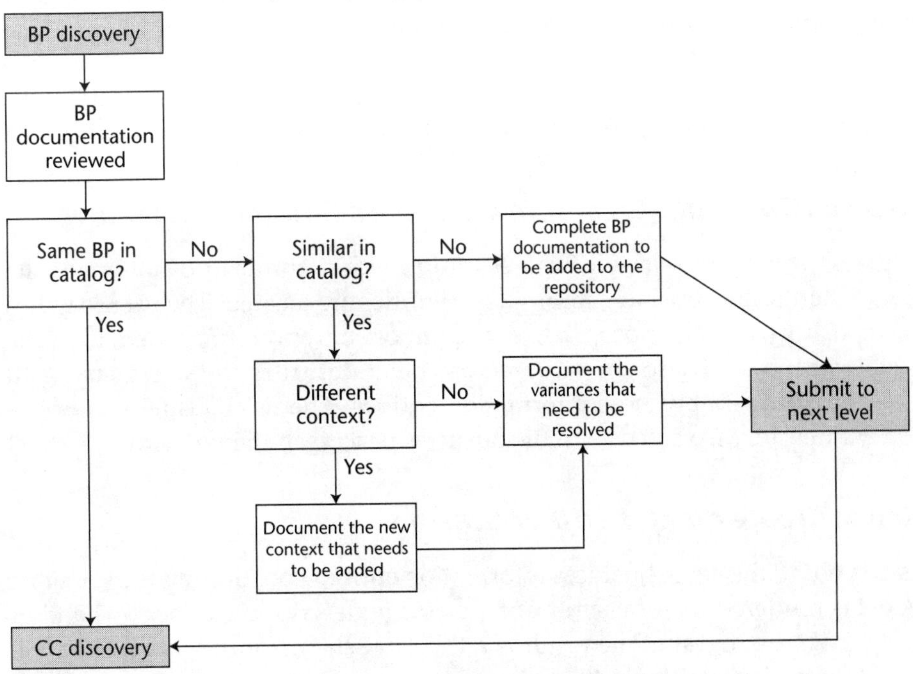

Figure 6.2 Flowchart showing how to use core components.
Source: "Core Components Specification Documentation." February 2002.

Step 2: Identify Contexts

The user identifies the business process selected using the registry browser and identifies other relevant context. The registry provides information on the specified context:

- Geopolitical context
- Business process context
- Industry context
- Product context
- Official constraints context
- Partner role context
- Supporting role context
- System capabilities context

Step 3: View and Select the Core Components and Associated Business Information Entities in the Registry

Business information entities are core components used in a real business situation, the result of using core components within a specific business context. After the context is identified, the registry provides a matching list of business information entities with the context information. The registry should also return partial matches to ensure that business information entities cover the right business data and meet all user needs. The user selects a set of the business information entities for inclusion in the business process.

Step 3b (Optional): Create New Business Information Entities

In cases where the selected business information entities do not cover the requirements, new business information entities are created. The user searches the repository for the appropriate core components and refines them to fit the business process. These are captured as constraint rules in the registry with the newly defined business information entities. The new business information entities are associated with the business process in the repository.

Step 4: Create an XML DTD or Schema

As this point, the set of business information entities constituting the semantic model is rendered into the syntax of a message description, either by hand or by a software program. The result is a DTD or schema representing the business information entities in the repository.

Context

Context is the circumstance in which something will happen; it is used to interpret the intent of the action. For example, when someone is entering your home, your response is very different depending on whether it is a stranger breaking in or a family member returning from work. In more technical terms, the context of a core component modifies the usage and behavior. In essence, the same core component information is used in *all* the business processes. However, the additional contextual information fulfills the unique requirements of a *specific* business process. The context of a business process may modify the way the business information is used. For example, we use context to describe that "business process = procurement" and "geographical = European Union". The context tells us how a basic set of information in a core component is adapted for use in a specific business situation.

For further clarification, let's look at how the geographical context is applied to a sample purchasing order information. As shown in Table 6.2, in the core components for date of order, the date information differs depending on whether the components are used in North America or Europe: January 2, 2002 can be expressed as 02-01-2002 (DD-MM-YYYY) in Europe, as 01-02-2002 (MM-DD-YYYY) in North America, or as 2002-01-02 (YYYY-MM-DD) in ISO 8601 format. In addition, core component elements and attributes can be expressed in any language. Many businesses use English as the common language for commerce, though doing so is not a requirement.

Table 6.2 Context Applied to a Sample Purchase Order

UID	NAME	DESCRIPTION	GEOGRAPHICAL CONTEXT = NORTH AMERICA	GEOGRAPHICAL CONTEXT = EUROPE
003	Date of order	The date of the order	Expressed in ISO-8601 format of YYYY-MM-DD. Element name is `<Date format= "ISO-8601">` Example: `<Date format= "ISO-8601"> 2002-01-02</Date>`	Expressed in EU format of DD-MM-YYYY. Element name is `<Date format= "EU">` Example: `<Date format= "EU">02-01-2002 </Date>`

Overview of Context

A promise of ebXML is the reuse of the business processes and methodologies across businesses and industries. If everyone defines their own information in their format, they would not be able to interoperate. Whenever an interchange takes place between trading partners, data is exchanged in the form of business messages. That data exists in a particular business context in ebXML. The context can be specified by a set of categories and their associated values. The core components have no context independent of their use. With context, we can express the full semantic meaning for the core component used in a business process. This way we can describe semantic meanings for core components when they are used in a specific business process in a specific context. The business information entity resulting from the process of combining core components with context is a reusable software component. This software can be used as the basis of a syntax-specific document, such as a business message description, an EDI message, an XML DTD, or a schema.

There are some possible scenarios in the real-world problems of document design involving semantics and context:

Same data, different names. In this case, multiple sets of business vocabularies refer to the same data with two or more different names, To solve, we can use mapping and translation tools and code conversions to get the semantic equivalents between vocabularies.

Same data, different structural positions. The same piece of data may be located structurally in different places in equivalent messages with the same meaning.

Same data, different processes. Differences in business processes may result in the same data being expressed in various ways.

Same data, different culture. Different cultures may format and structure data differently from other cultures involved in international trade.

In each case, trading partners can describe data needs for each interoperable business process in the form of assembly and context rules. These are made available in a repository or sent directly to prospective trading partners. In its simplest form, this is the abstract idea of the core components and context morphed into concrete XML-based software. The following sections address the context categories and rules in detail.

Context Categories

As mentioned earlier in the chapter, a list of categories is used in describing the particular business context within which a business process exists. These include business process, geopolitical, product, partner and supporting role, official constraints, industry, and system capabilities. The context allows one or more data values to be associated with any business message or component. A context describing process is called *process context* and one describing a process-independent context is called *property context*.

Let's look closer at each context category.

Business Process

How will the business process be conducted? We have to understand the semantic context for interpreting the business process. The business process context is based on the list of core business processes. To make the business process interoperate across businesses and industries the Catalog of Common Business Processes is used as a reference. Business process specifies the values for only process-type, not property-type, contexts.

Geopolitical

Where will the business process be conducted? Will the core component information be used across international boundaries? This context covers semantic context for geographical factors that influence business vocabulary, such as the currency, as shown in Table 6.3. A single set of business data is often structured differently in various parts of the world because of cultural differences in business practices. One example is the location and address data structure. However, a trading partner will probably only be capable of processing a small number of the possible structural variations.

Table 6.3 Geopolitical Context Applied to a Sample Purchase Order

UID	NAME	DESCRIPTION	GEOGRAPHICAL CONTEXT = NORTH AMERICA	GEOGRAPHICAL CONTEXT = EUROPE
007	Total amount	The total amount of the invoice.	Expressed in U.S. dollars; uses a period as a decimal indicator. Element name is `<Total>` Example: `<Total symbol="$" currency="USD"> 99.99</Total>`	Expressed in euros; uses a comma to separate major and minor currency values. Element name is `<Total>` Example: `<Total symbol="E" currency="EUR"> 109,99</Total>`

The regional classification uses the following structure: Global, Continent, Economic Region, Country, and Region. At any level of the hierarchy, a value may be a single value, a named aggregate, or a cross-border value. Country attribute uses ISO 3166.1 for values. Region uses ISO 3166.2. For example, the following basic, single-value hierarchy of recommended values is based on the common ISO 3166 Country Codes:

```
Europe :: Eastern Europe :: AL - ALBANIA, AM - ARMENIA
```

In Table 6.3, in the core component for total amount, the price information is expressed differently in Europe (euros) than in North America (U.S. dollars).

Product

What are the goods or services concerned in the collaboration? The product context covers semantic context involving the purchasing and handling of goods or services, such as the buying of hammers and nails or the selling of technical consulting services. Product context specifies the values for both process-type and property-type product contexts. According to the *Core Components Technical Specification*, some of recommended sources for product classifications are:

- United Nations Standard Product and Service Code (UN/S1PSC) [Custodian: United Nations]
- Standard International Trade Classification (SITC Rev. 3) [Custodian: United Nations Statistics Division (UNSD)]
- The Harmonized Commodity Description and Coding System (HS) [Custodian: WTO]
- Classification of the Purposes of Nonprofit Institutions Serving Households (COPI) [Custodian: UNSD]

Partner and Supporting Role

What are the roles in the business process played by the user and the trading partners? What other significant parties will be using the data in the messages and what are their roles? Role context covers semantic context related to the role of the partners engaged in the interchange, as defined in the ebXML business process bible, *Business Process Specification*. This context category only exists as a property-type context because role is tied to the formal identification of the business process. Role context identifies the trading partners according to their role within the business process. The values will need to be on the level of buyer, seller, shipper, insurer, and so forth, rather than on the level of sender or receiver. Supporting role context covers the business vocabulary related to non-partner roles, such as data required by a third-party shipper in an order response going from seller to buyer. This can be used to describe third-party actors who may be important to the business process but are not active in it.

Official Constraints

Are there any legal restrictions or governmental requirements on the business process, such as hazardous materials information required by law when shipping goods? Official constraints describes semantic context for official standards, legal or regulatory requirements, contractual or business agreements, and similar official circumstances. There are at least two values for the process-type and property-type official constraints context—the legal classification and the official constraint itself. These values may represent a hierarchical structure. The list of official constraints context includes:

- Regulatory and legislative, such as customs and international trade regulations
- Standards, such as ISO and mil specs (military specifications)
- Guidelines, such as best practices and unofficial standards
- Conventions and treaties
- Contractual and trading partner agreement

Industry

What are the relevant trading partner industries? Industry context covers semantic context related to the industry or industries of the trading partners, such as product identification schemes used in different industries. An industry is an organization or group of organizations involved in a particular commercial and institutional activity. According to the *Core Components Technical Specification*, some of recommended sources for industry classifications are:

- International Standard Industrial Classification (ISIC) Custodian: UNSD
- United Nations Standard Product and Service Code (UN/SPSC) Custodian: United Nations. Top-level Segment (digits 1 and 2) used to define industry.

System Capabilities

Are there any major restrictions from legacy systems? Which type of system is it? The system context identifies a system or class of systems. Its purpose is to address the limitations of legacy systems, such as an existing back-end system that uses financial data or shipping address in a certain format. The system context requires at least two values: the system ID and the system name. In addition, other values may be needed to uniquely identify a specific system. For example, to identify the system of a trading partner, we can use a standard classification scheme like DUNS and the internal name for the system as a way to refer to the system.

Context Rules

Context allows a trading partner to express its data structure needs using context rules. The rules can transform semantic equivalent information between different data formats. With fixed semantics and syntax in XML, a problem is that data fields are provided in a description of the document structure for all of the data at every stage of the process. Anything that cannot be included at every point across the business process is made optional.

Using context rules, we can produce individualized formats for each trading partner based on their individual business practices and data structures. The context rules consist of two parts: a language for assembling an aggregated component and a language for refining the assembly. The latter involves adding business process semantics, as well as restricting and extending the semantic model. The dual languages allow a simpler two-step process: first processing the standard component/entity assembly, then refining the software assembly for actual use. This process is similar to how EDI standards and message implementation guides work. Both languages allow simple commands to dictate how core components will be used, how they will be named, and how they relate to each other. Context rules can dictate action on core components with specific context values to produce business information entities.

Furthermore, context rules can express conditional relationships involving core components and context. For example, using context rules, we can express this conditional statement to assemble and modify the core components to produce the appropriate business information entity: "If the geopolitical context has a value of Europe, and the industry context value has a value of automotive..."

Using the constraint languages, we can express action involving the conditional, possibly expressed as a programming algorithm: "If the geopolitical context is Europe and industry is automotive, then take the core component called Address and use associated rules to provide the correct names and format for the data fields." When we do business in Europe with a trading partner in the automotive industry, then a specific context value for that process will trigger this rule, providing a set of business semantics expressed as business information entities.

The business information entity is a model that has no relationship to a specific syntax. A business information entity can be expressed in multiple syntax, such as the XML vocabularies for different industries. This activity of associating a business information entity with a specific syntax is called *syntax binding*.

Example of Using Context Rules

Context rules can solve interoperability problems in supply chain scenarios where small suppliers are selling into more than one industry vertical. The large buyers at the top of the supply chain dominate industry verticals. Typically, large buyers have highly automated back-office systems and the smaller suppliers do not. Because industries view things from their own perspective, they organize data differently, and they often use classifications specific to their industry. Smaller suppliers often produce goods and services for many different industries. Hence, a niche market manufacturer may sell a product used in making planes, cars, and other widgets, each of which is a separate industry vertical. Since each industry vertical has different names for the same things and different data formats, the business has difficulty handling all the data variations in processing orders and interfacing with other companies. It takes longer for data to travel up and down the supply chain, inventories are higher, and the supply chain loses efficiency.

Code Listing 6.1 shows a purchase order that uses context rules to define data formats. The context rules are used to adjust for address and other core component information in the purchase order for different industries. The ebXML DTD called contextrules.dtd in the specification governs the semantics and syntax in the XML document. We use context rules to process the purchase orders received by our small manufacturer for different standard vocabularies.

In the United States, the state is included in the buyer address information, as well as the floor and suite number.

```
<Taxonomy context="Industry"
ref="http://ebxml.org/classification/industry/aviation"/>
<Condition test="$Geopolitical='United States'">
<Action applyTo="//Buyer/Address">
<Occurs>
<Element>
<Name>State</Name>
</Element>
</Occurs>
<Add after="@id='joe'">
<CreateGroup type="choice">
<Element>
<Name>Floor</Name>
```

```
<Type>string</Type>
</Element>
<Element>
<Name>Suite</Name>
<Type>string</Type>
</Element>
</CreateGroup>
</Add>
```

For the automotive industry, the purchase order information includes an element called `TaxIdentifier`.

```
<Condition test="$Industry='Automotive'">
<Occurs>
<Element>
<Name>TaxIdentifier</Name>
</Element>
</Occurs>
</Condition>
```

For the aerospace industry in California, the address information includes a `Zip` element, and it is located only once in the header.

```
<Condition
  test="$Geopolitical='California' and $Industry='Aerospace'">
<Occurs>
<Element>
<Name>ZIP</Name>
</Element>
</Occurs>
</Condition>
```

In XML, either an entirely new document type must be described or a field must be made optional that might be better required at some other point in the process. To have precise validation, each transaction needs a separate document description. If we want the simplicity of a single document type, then the trade-off is validation capability in XML. This is solved through the application of context. Hence, a company can run ebXML software using Code Listing 6.1 and produce specific documents from core components in the purchasing process for each customer by industry context, geographical context, and so on.

```
<?xml version="1.0"?>
<!DOCTYPE ContextRules SYSTEM "contextrules.dtd">
<ContextRules id="Purchase_Order_Context">
<Rule apply="hierarchical">
```

Code Listing 6.1 Context rules for a purchase order.

```
<Taxonomy context="Geopolitical"
ref="http://ebxml.org/classification/ISO3166"/>
<!--Industry Context: aviation  -->
<Taxonomy context="Industry"
ref="http://ebxml.org/classification/industry/aviation"/>
<Condition test="$Geopolitical='United States'">
<Action applyTo="//Buyer/Address">
<Occurs>
<Element>
<Name>State</Name>
</Element>
</Occurs>
<Add after="@id='manufacturer'">
<CreateGroup type="choice">
<Element>
<Name>Floor</Name>
<Type>string</Type>
</Element>
<Element>
<Name>Suite</Name>
<Type>string</Type>
</Element>
</CreateGroup>
</Add>
<Condition
test="$Geopolitical='California' and $Industry='Aerospace'">
<Occurs>
<Element>
<Name>ZIP</Name>
</Element>
</Occurs>
</Condition>
</Action>
</Condition>
<!--Industry Context: automotive  -->
<Taxonomy context="Industry"
ref="http://ebxml.org/classification/Industry/Automotive"/>
<Condition test="$Industry='Automotive'">
<Occurs>
<Element>
<Name>TaxIdentifier</Name>
</Element>
</Occurs>
</Condition>
</Rule>
</ContextRules>
```

Code Listing 6.1 Context rules for a purchase order. *(continued)*

We can specify the needed data and options within a single document type using context rules and tie them to a specific transaction or point within the business process. We have the structural advantage of smaller and more specific documents with a single base document type. This process traces a data element back through the context rules and assembly rules to a specific core component.

Assembly

A future vision is that an open market for business components will emerge, and we will make the transition from scratch-built systems to software by assembly. We could just snap software components from multiple vendors together, and they will fit perfectly. If this becomes a reality, we will not need a methodology for software by assembly. We will simply need a few instructions, such as insert tab A in slot B, and so forth. Any incompatibilities among the components would be worked out among themselves. However, in the foreseeable future, we deal with manual assembly, compatibility issues, workarounds, custom components, and a host of other issues. This will require a systematic methodology, even in the age of software by assembly.

The assembly process is that the assembly rules are applied, resulting in a schema or DTD modeling the relevant information. Context rules then adapt the schema to the contexts for the trading partners. The output is a customized schema that has all of the information for the interaction, using standard core components for interoperability.

Schema annotations (meta data) must be made available at the core component level to specify bindings to system resources, such as ERP systems, EDI gateways, and Web forms. These annotations reference standard core components but are trading-partner-specific. The schema annotations tell the runtime integration engine how to marry these standard core components with the implementation details of the systems in each company. We can use the context and contextual modification mechanisms to keep the information sets common to all industries. This keeps business processes and business information reusable.

Example of Document Assembly

In Code Listing 6.2, we assemble a document from elements such as name, address, building name, street name, city, and zip code. This is a purchase order with a buyer and seller, and it has two parts, the order and the receipt. Because the core component that exists as the basis of any vocabulary can be traced back through this chain, the base semantic of any field or message structure can be determined. By mapping each piece of data in each document structure back to its core and then comparing the two, equivalence can be automatically determined and a mapping can be derived for use by a transformation engine. This mapping process is automated by semantic identification documents, which describe how a document was created from assembly and context rules. Assembly and context rules create a specific industry vocabulary from a set of core components. Tracing back to the core component can identify the semantics in the data.

```
<?xml version="1.0"?>
<!DOCTYPE Assembly SYSTEM "assembly.dtd">
<Assembly version="1.0">
<Assemble name="PurchaseOrder" id="PO">
<CreateGroup>
<CreateElement location="UUID" id="Buyer">
<Name>Buyer</Name>
<Type>PartyType</Type>
<CreateGroup>
<UseElement name="Name">
</UseElement>
<UseElement name="Address">
<CreateGroup id="manufacturer">
<CreateGroup type="choice">
<UseElement name="BuildingName">
</UseElement>
<UseElement name="BuildingNumber">
</UseElement>
</CreateGroup>
<UseElement name="StreetName">
</UseElement>
<UseElement name="City">
</UseElement>
<UseElement name="State">
</UseElement>
<UseElement name="ZIP">
</UseElement>
<UseElement name="Country">
</UseElement>
</CreateGroup>
</UseElement>
</CreateGroup>
<Condition test="$Geopolitical='United States'">
<Rename from="address" to="addressUS"/>
<Rename from="Place" to="City"/>
<Rename from="address/County" to="State"/>
<Rename from="address/PostalCode" to="ZIP"/>
</Condition>
```

Code Listing 6.2 Document assembly for a purchase order. *(continues)*

```
</CreateElement>
<CreateElement id="Seller" location="UUID">
<Name>Seller</Name>
<Type>PartyType</Type>
</CreateElement>
</CreateGroup>
<CreateElement location="UUID" id="Item">
<Name>Item</Name>
<Type>ItemType</Type>
<MinOccurs>1</MinOccurs>
<MaxOccurs>unbounded</MaxOccurs>
</CreateElement>
</Assemble>
<Assemble name="PurchaseOrderReceipt" id="POR">
<CreateGroup>
<CreateElement idref="Seller">
</CreateElement>
<CreateElement idref="Buyer">
</CreateElement>
</CreateGroup>
<CreateElement idref="Item">
</CreateElement>
<CreateElement location="UUID" id="Ack">
<Name>Acknowledgment</Name>
<Type>AckType></Type>
</CreateElement>
</Assemble>
</Assembly>
```

Code Listing 6.2 Document assembly for a purchase order. *(continued)*

A single item of data can be used in multiple transactions within a single business process. It can also be used in two related business processes. A single message structure can be used to support these different processes or related transactions. For example, an Order may be used to request a purchase order (`OrderRequest`), to place an order (`Order`), and to change an order (`ChangeOrder`). These three transactions require a nearly identical set of data but are different in use and context. These differences result from something related to a specific point in the business process.

Summary

Core components are basic, reusable building blocks in ebXML. From a specific business document in a business process, we can refer to a core component, which holds a minimal set of e-business information. If the business processes are the verbs in e-business terms, the core components represent the nouns and adjectives. Core components appear in many different circumstances of business information and in many different areas of business. A core component can be used across several business sectors, but it also can become context-specific to a business domain, such as an individual industry area. A core component works with a registry, since it is storable and retrievable using a standard ebXML registry. A central core component library serves as a reference document for common business practices across industry business processes. Similar to Lego blocks with standard forms and shapes, a core component in ebXML can contain another core component. It is uniquely identifiable and can contain individual pieces of business information objects.

Context rules in ebXML allow us to express the relationship between specific business context and how semantics are applied to the core components to produce business information entities. Using context rules, we can produce individualized formats for each trading partner, based on their individual business practices and data structures. The context rules consist of two parts: a language for assembling an aggregated component and a language for refining the assembly. The latter involves adding business process semantics and restricting and extending the semantic model. The dual languages allow a simpler two-step process, first processing the standard software assembly, then refining the software assembly for actual use.

The ebXML framework includes business process models that are shared and stored in a repository. This framework identifies element names that can apply across business processes and contexts, and it allows for translation into major languages. The contents of core components are independent of implementation syntax in programming languages but may have specific references to data structures in XML or EDI. In this chapter, we discuss core components and how to use them in context. In the next chapter, we discuss the ebXML messaging functionality, which is designed to incorporate existing Web standards such as HTTP and SOAP.

CHAPTER

7

ebXML Message Services

"The ebXML Message Service defines robust, yet basic, functionality to transfer messages between trading parties using various existing communication protocols. The ebXML Message Service is structured to allow for messaging reliability, persistence, security, and extensibility."

—"ebXML Messaging Service Specification"

AREAS COVERED IN THIS CHAPTER

- Basic concept of messaging
  - RPC versus messaging
  - XML messaging
  - What is SOAP?
- What is ebXML message service?
  - Overview
  - Design criteria
  - Architecture
- How to format messages
  - Message package
  - Header container
  - ebXML SOAP extensions
  - Payload container
- How to handle messages
  - Reliable messaging
  - Security

XML messaging enables various forms of interbusiness electronic communication. Within XML messaging, a Web service technology called Simple Object Access Protocol (SOAP) has widespread industry support and is used in many XML standards. SOAP was developed by Microsoft and its partners as a technical standard for XML messaging and remote procedure call to enable the exchange of information over the World Wide Web. The ebXML messaging service is the messaging framework of the ebXML infrastructure and builds on a SOAP foundation with added ebXML syntax extensions. ebXML supports messaging using common communication protocols, such as Hypertext Transfer Protocol (HTTP) and Simple Mail Transfer Protocol (SMTP). The framework provides general design principles about message enveloping and header document schema used to transfer messages over a generic communication protocol.

This chapter is based on information in the ebXML messaging service bible, the "Messaging Service Specification version 1.0" found at www.ebxml.org/specs/ebMS.pdf. For simplicity, we will use the term *schema* in discussions to refer to any one of the various dialects of XML schemas and DTDs.

Messaging Basics

We begin with the basic concepts in messaging. A *message* is a collection of data fields sent or received between software applications. A message contains a header and payload. The *header* stores control information about the message. The *payload* is the actual content of the message. A *messaging system* uses messages to communicate with different systems in order to perform computer operations. For example, messaging systems include message-oriented middleware (MOM) products such as IBM MQSeries, Tibco Rendezvous, and the Java Message Service (JMS) provider. An email system is a specific messaging system that is designed for people. Messaging systems are like email for applications, and, in fact, they share many features. Messaging can be either synchronous or asynchronous. *Synchronous* messaging is coordinated real-time both ways. *Asynchronous* messaging involves communication between parties independently, and each side is responsible only for one-way communication. A communication is called *message-oriented* because the system sends and receives messages to perform operations.

RPC versus Messaging

There are two architectural styles for application communication over the network: using remote procedure calls or messages. A *remote procedure call* (RPC) is a programming function that invokes a system or application process on a remote system. Using RPCs, the client (the "calling" application) has to know the procedure to invoke and the parameters for the procedure. The client waits while the application on the server completes the procedure. Using messages, the sender can be agnostic about what is happening on the recipient side. The sender creates a message of a specific format known to both the client and server, and he sends it to the server over the network. The sender is dependent on the message format but independent of the server and the server-side procedures. The communication can be asynchronous, which means the sender can send a request and not wait for the response. The client can continue to operate even if the server is unavailable, as in the case of disruption in the server or communication channel. This architectural design is called *loosely coupled*, since there is no or little dependency between the client and server.

With RPC, one party sends a request to a remote application, where it is processed, and the result is sent back in a response message. The two main RPC protocols currently in use are the Microsoft Distributed Common Object Management (DCOM) and CORBA Internet Inter-ORB Protocol (IIOP) defined by the Object Management Group (OMG). In general, the Object Request Broker (ORB) software that implements these protocols tries to make low-level communication aspects as transparent as possible to the programmer.

Traditional RPC, such as Microsoft DCOM and CORBA IIOP, are not well-suited to the actual Web services deployment environment because they were primarily designed for use in business applications within the enterprise. There are possible solutions, such as tunneling to pass firewalls and bridges to link cross-vendor implementations. However, they can be hard to implement and cause loss of performance and functionality for higher-level services, such as transaction management and security. Traditional RPC mechanisms are most powerful and useful in the context of a central group of servers housed in one location, running the same operating system and using an ORB product from a single vendor. However, in an open Internet environment, the advantages of CORBA and DCOM are lost among complexity and flexibility issues.

Communication in B2B e-commerce often occurs on the Internet with the client of one company talking to a server from another company. These corporate partners can find common ground in a simple messaging format, compared to the quagmire in a programmatic procedural interface. These companies may prefer the asynchronous communication model, where the communication systems are independent of each other. By doing so, these companies can sidestep issues of server availability and communication disruptions.

The communication model based on messages is flexible, compared to a model based on remote procedure calls. The message-oriented approach enjoys advantages such as loose-coupling, simple message routing, easy format transformation, and options in using binary attachments and multiple messages. On the other hand, this approach requires more effort in development than using remote procedure calls. Message communication involves software for writing message on the client side and software to process messages on the server side.

A trend in messaging is the growth of the Internet as the medium for inter-enterprise business communications. However, for a variety of reasons including the lack of standard interfaces and security issues, the applications integration technology that worked within the enterprise has been unsuccessful beyond the boundaries of the corporate network infrastructure. Lack of a standard interface means that business applications in one enterprise often are incompatible with the applications of its partners, suppliers, and customers, due to proprietary interfaces or differences in version and configuration. Security issues include enterprise firewalls that will not allow direct access to the enterprise's computing resources from the Internet. *Business-quality messaging* describes the set of requirements that a business should expect of a messaging service used to exchange business information with partners, suppliers, and customers.

In sum, many business applications were not designed for the Internet or for inter-enterprise messaging. The first step for an interoperable message framework is to incorporate basic standards such as XML and SOAP for a common interface.

XML in Messaging

The XML language is a flexible data formatting language for the messages. Both the client and the server have to use a standard messaging format. XML solves a common problem in data interchange, which is defining how to write and use data and documents as flat files in a standard format. With XML, we have a common language in a flat file format that is both human- and machine-readable for communicating between systems. A DTD or schema sets the semantic rules for the elements and attributes in an XML document. The language has flexibility to adapt to system requirements by allowing different vocabularies and semantics in each business context. The parties using or exchanging an XML document can validate using a DTD that their copies of XML documents follow the same common rules.

The true power of XML to improve business processes is evident when multiple documents all use the same public data format. A single software application can process the set of a document, and a single screen layout can display it. If the format is publicly available, anyone can generate a document that can be processed by the software or displayed in the screen layout.

Even with a common language, a Tower of Babel can exist with proliferating standards. A number of emerging standards exist designed to deliver business information over the Internet in a secure and reliable manner. However, each existing standard addresses the requirements for business-quality messaging differently, resulting in different standards that do not interoperate. Businesses that must use more than one standard vocabulary have to deploy multiple solutions to meet their business needs. In addition, the messaging frameworks are often designed around a transaction vocabulary for a specific industry vertical. Most are not designed for the broader context of an open, nonproprietary messaging infrastructure. Later in this chapter, we will see that the messaging framework in ebXML defines the XML- and SOAP-based structures. This supports messaging service features such as messaging reliability, persistence, security, and extensibility. The ebXML infrastructure can be used for the secure, reliable exchange of information. It is independent of transaction vocabulary, encoding, and the choice of vendor solution.

In sum, messaging can be based on open standard protocols such as HTTP, SMTP, or SOAP, as well as proprietary standards. SOAP is a standard based on a technical specification produced by Microsoft, DevelopMentor, and UserLand Software. SOAP is a means for exchanging XML over the World Wide Web. The SOAP standard is also applicable for EDI-style document exchange.

SOAP Basics

Don Box, one of the founders of SOAP, concisely states "the guiding principle behind SOAP was to invent no new technology." The SOAP mechanism is platform-independent, language-neutral, and nonintrusive. It has minimal impact on existing applications, and investments in legacy systems can be leveraged for Internet-based systems.

SOAP is the one of the most widely accepted XML messaging standards, so other SOAP-compliant messaging systems are fairly common. In addition, SOAP supports message or remote procedure call communications, a feature differentiating SOAP from other messaging standards. However, SOAP requires other supporting standards to provide full functionality. For example, because SOAP does not include any header elements, this feature is defined in the ebXML messaging service on top of SOAP. This implies that all parties must understand both SOAP and ebXML. In addition, different SOAP implementations may not interoperate. Despite a stable specification, SOAP software is still changing rapidly in the marketplace.

The SOAP design is a minimalist approach and assumes as little as possible about the underlying implementation of the communicating systems. SOAP uses standard Internet protocols, such as HTTP; in fact, it can be viewed as the combination of HTTP and XML, with other standards such as namespaces and schemas. SOAP puts XML data into the payload of the HTTP message. This information can consist of a request or response with parameters to invoke application logic on the receiving side. The SOAP request/response model can be a protocol for RPC. The basic HTTP request/response model fits the needs of an RPC system, and the use of the HTTP POST method allows any kind of data to be sent.

SOAP is far more limited in scope than distributed object protocols such as Microsoft DCOM and CORBA IIOP. According to the SOAP 1.1 specification, several features, such as distributed garbage collection, are clearly designated as *not* being part of SOAP in the design goals. On the contrary, major goals were simplicity and extensibility. In the context of ebXML, extensibility by using extension headers is very important: A lot of functionality has to be provided by other protocols or systems that are layered on top of SOAP. In addition, the *SOAP Messages with Attachments* specification addresses the packaging requirement of attachments. SOAP does not define the transactions, business process, and security aspects. These features are left to higher-level frameworks, such as ebXML.

According to the SOAP specification, the SOAP 1.1 protocol consists of three parts:

- The SOAP envelope, describing the general structure of the message (header and body), intermediaries, processing party, and optional or mandatory nature
- A set of encoding rules to define a serialization mechanism using typed XML data
- A convention to represent RPCs, possibly over HTTP

Now let's discuss SOAP in greater detail. First we will look at the core concept in SOAP, which is the message structure for the request or response. Then we will examine the basic architecture for SOAP interaction.

SOAP Message Structure

Figure 7.1 describes the general SOAP message structure, which includes the HTTP header, the SOAP envelope, the SOAP header, and the SOAP body.

To illustrate, let's walk through a sample SOAP message used for a stock quote. The HTTP header is at the beginning of the message and used by the HTTP server software to handle the SOAP message. The first line contains the POST method for sending the request, the URI that is the target of the request, and the HTTP version. The value `/StockQuote` for the URI tells us where the application on the server is located.

```
POST /StockQuote HTTP/1.1
```

The next line is the target host for the message:

```
Host: www.stockquoteserver.com
```

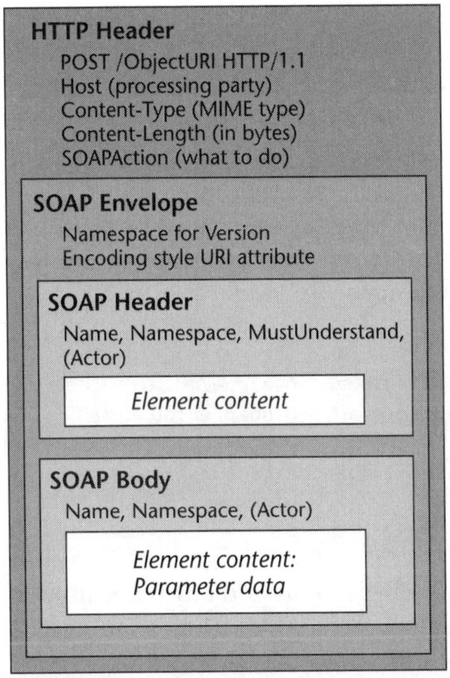

Figure 7.1 Example of Basic SOAP message structure.
Adapted from SOAP v1.1 Specification (www.w3.org/TR/SOAP)

The next line is the content type (must be text/xml) of the SOAP message payload, the character set (UTF-8):

```
Content-Type: text/xml; charset="utf-8"
```

The next line is the content length of the payload in bytes:

```
Content-Length: nnnn
```

The last line in the HTTP header is the "SOAPAction," which tells the SOAP application what to do. The value is composed of a URI, a # sign, and an identifier that must equal the first element of the SOAP body.

```
SOAPAction: "Some-URI#GetLastTradePrice"
```

The next part of the message is the SOAP envelope `SOAP-ENV: Envelope`, also called the SOAP message payload, and is expressed in XML. The XML structure contains several specific tags and attributes, which are identified by the `SOAP-ENV` namespace prefix. This namespace is defined in the first attribute of the SOAP envelope itself, which also functions as a kind of version indicator. The encodingStyle URI points to a link where the encoding rules are defined. The SOAP envelope consists of an optional SOAP header and the SOAP body. The SOAP header may contain any user-defined elements. Header elements in a SOAP document can be labeled as mustUnderstand, meaning that the server that processes the message must understand that type of header element or it must reject the message by generating SOAP faults. Faults occur when processing a message, and they may be caused by an unrecognized header field, a message that cannot be authenticated, or errors that occur when invoking a method to process a message.

```
<SOAP-ENV:Envelope
xmlns:SOAP-ENV="http://schemas.xmlsoap.org/soap/envelope/"
SOAP-ENV:encodingStyle="http://schemas.xmlsoap.org/soap/encoding/"/>
<SOAP-ENV:Header>
<t:Transaction xmlns:t="Some-URI" SOAP-ENV:mustUnderstand="1">
</t:Transaction>
</SOAP-ENV:Header>
```

A namespace prefix (t) is assigned, since all elements and attributes used in a SOAP message must be qualified by a namespace. SOAP 1.1 also introduced the concept of intermediaries, or applications where a SOAP message passes through before going to its final destination. In the message, these intermediaries are represented by actor attributes (goes after the mustUnderstand attribute, not shown in the example here). This way, it can be indicated if certain information is intended for a particular intermediary.

The last part of the SOAP message is the required SOAP body SOAP-ENV:Body, which contains the data that have to be passed to the service. The first element, GetLastTradePrice, is the name of the method, and it contains the XML data as input for the method.

```
<SOAP-ENV:Body>
<m:GetLastTradePrice xmlns:m="Some-URI">
<symbol>DEF</symbol>
</m:GetLastTradePrice>
</SOAP-ENV:Body>
</SOAP-ENV:Envelope>
```

The SOAP request/response model maps onto HTTP requests and responses. The response to this request has a similar structure. There is the HTTP header and a SOAP envelope with a header and a body.

Encoding Rules

SOAP can be seen as the sum of HTTP and XML. A SOAP message is simply the HTTP request or response in which the payload data are in XML format.

Since RPC parameter data can be in some object structure, the data have to be converted to XML format using SOAP encoding rules. SOAP defines a serialization mechanism for the body of a SOAP message. The resulting XML schema represents the structure of the object data to be passed. The encoding rules describe a standard method to do this, including using "Element Normal Form," where all values are represented as elements. SOAP uses many of the XML schema constructs and adds a few more constructs, such as arrays. SOAP is called *payload-neutral*, which means it does not impose any limitations on or make any assumption about the contents.

SOAP Transport Architecture and Mechanism

Figure 7.2 is an overview of a sample SOAP architecture and the interaction between a client and a Web service. The SOAP transport architecture and mechanism is based on a Web service application, but it is also applicable for data and document interchange.

For example, suppose a customer wants to use a purchase order Web service that is exposed on the application server of another company. It issues a command, which is passed to the API that provides access to the SOAP processor. This API serializes the call using a schema provided by the other party and sends the result as an XML document to the XML parser in the SOAP processor. After the document is checked to see that it is well formed, the order document is packaged as a SOAP request and sent over HTTP to the other party. Assume the message arrives at its intended destination. After smoothly passing any firewalls between the two companies, the request arrives at the receiving party's SOAP processor. The message is parsed and checked to ensure it is well formed and valid. The SOAP application does additional verifications, including identifying the message parts that are addressed to it. The application must check if all mandatory parts with `mustUnderstand="1"` are supported, or it must respond with a fault message. The application processes the order and generates a result. A response process is started, this time transferring the result back in a response message. The application that invoked the service receives the result.

SOAP provides a message-based interface that allows loosely coupled enterprises with different applications, languages, and platforms to communicate. The platform or programming language of the receiving application and its implementation should not pose a middleware integration issue because the XML data can be parsed by any system. The design and implementation of the server-side programs executing the request should not pose a middleware integration issue to the application client. The SOAP processors can be standalone, special-purpose applications, or they might be integrated into another system, such as a Web server or the ebXML message service handler.

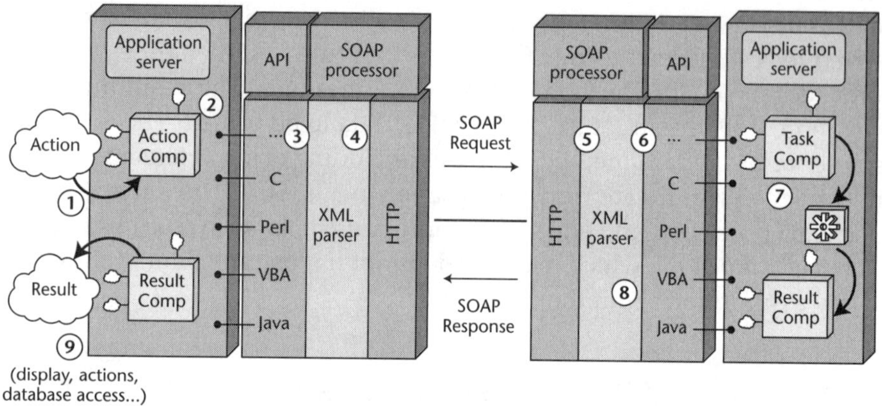

Figure 7.2 A sample SOAP architecture.
Source: Techmetrix.com

SOAP Messages with Attachments

A major disadvantage of SOAP 1.1 is its inability to transfer non-XML data. Related attachments often have to accompany a message, such as a scanned image of a physical document. These attachments can be of various types, such as a binary format.

SOAP Messages with Attachments (SwA) is a short specification submitted as a W3C Note by Hewlett-Packard and Microsoft. An extension to SOAP 1.1, SwA describes a standard way to associate one or more attachments in any format with a SOAP message. The resulting SOAP message package is a multipart MIME structure, which consists of a root body part containing one primary SOAP 1.1 message, with a MIME content type equal to `text/xml` and one or more referenced parts containing the attachment(s), for which the `"Content-Type"` can be any media type. The root and its parts are separated by MIME boundaries. The SwA specification describes a method to refer to the MIME attachments from the primary SOAP 1.1 message by using the URI references in an `href` attribute. It also describes the resolution process for these absolute or relative URIs. These references contain the `Content-ID` or `Content-Location` header of the referenced MIME part. The specification recommends *Content-ID* for more robust error detection. The SwA specification is not limited to a specific protocol; it explicitly describes how to use HTTP and assumes SMTP can be implemented.

SOAP explicitly avoids inventing anything new but, rather, describes how existing technologies (SOAP, MIME, HTTP, SMTP71) can be used in a standard way to associate attachments with a SOAP message. To the SOAP processor, the MIME structure is part of the transport protocol layer. The SOAP processor must treat the primary SOAP part as the message itself. A SOAP processor can process the primary SOAP message according to SOAP 1.1, and based on the message processing semantics, it can determine whether or not resolving the URI is necessary.

For more information on issues related to MIME, consult http://www.ietf.org/rfc for RFC2387 (MIME Multipart/Related Content-type), RFC2045 (MIME Part One: Format of Internet Message Bodies), and related documents.

SOAP as a Standard

One reason why SOAP has been widely adopted in the marketplace may be that it has been submitted to the W3C as a Note. According to the W3C Web site: "A W3C Note is a dated, public record of an idea, comment, or document" (see www.w3.org/Consortium/Process-20010208/tr). This submission has two consequences. First, no further revisions of SOAP will be issued. From a developer's viewpoint, this means that SOAP-based implementations can be built on a stable specification. Second, SOAP is generally expected to be the basis for the W3C XML Protocol Activity (abbreviated as XP), which should encompass all similar initiatives and become the final standard for XML-based messaging systems. According to the XML Protocol Charter (www.w3.org/2000/09/XML-Protocol-Charter): "The Working Group shall start by developing a requirements document, and then evaluate the technical solutions proposed in the SOAP/1.1 submission against these requirements. If in this process the Working Group finds solutions that are agreed to be improvements over solutions suggested by SOAP 1.1, those improved solutions should be used."

The advantages of SOAP as opposed to traditional RPC are its simplicity, its extensibility, and its ability to pass through firewalls. Earlier in the specification development, debates occurred regarding the merits of SOAP versus ebXML message service. However, the broad consensus was that convergence between the two standards would be the direction for ebXML. In the next section, we see that the ebXML message service takes advantage of the extensible transport foundation formed by the minimal framework in SOAP.

ebXML Message Service

ebXML provides a standard framework for inter-enterprise business communications with partners, suppliers, and customers. The *ebXML Message Service Specification* is an open standard specification designed for the secure, reliable exchange of e-business information. The messaging framework in ebXML defines the XML and SOAP-based structures to support messaging service features such as messaging reliability, persistence, security, and extensibility.

Overview

A complete message is called the *message package*, which is a Multipurpose Internet Mail Extensions (MIME) object. MIME types, such as "multipart/related," describe the contents of the message package. The message package contains two principal parts: the required SOAP message container and optional payload containers. The SOAP message contains the SOAP extension elements for ebXML, such as routing information, trading partner information, message identification, and delivery semantics information. Payloads are optional and can contain any type of information that is to be exchanged between parties. The ebXML message service has a manifest for each message. The *manifest* contains references to each of the payload objects, along with schema location and version information about the payload.

The separate version tracking of inner and outer layers permits the ebXML message service to be payload-neutral. An older version of the ebXML message service software can still route messages with newer version numbers; you don't have to upgrade the message service software. The payload objects are not affected when the message service is versioned. Potential version issues exist in standards with the payload inside the message envelope and headers. This limits the flexibility of these standards in a broader context where uniform versioning is unrealistic.

Design Criteria

According to the *Messaging Service Specification*, the design goals for the ebXML message service are to:

- Leverage existing standards wherever possible
- Be simple to implement
- Support enterprises of all sizes
- Support a wide variety of communication protocols (HTTP, SMTP, FTP, etc.)
- Support payloads of any type (XML, EDI transactions, binary data, etc.)
- Support reliable messaging
- Ensure security

These design criteria are obviously the result of the organization behind the standard. As in SOAP, the intention in ebXML is not to reinvent the wheel and leverage from other standards and technologies when possible. The ebXML message service leverages de facto public standards wherever possible. With the version 0.98 draft of the *Message Service Specification* published in March of 2001, the ebXML message service is defined as a set of layered extensions on the SOAP 1.1 and SwA specifications. The message service provides the necessary extensions for security and reliability. These features are not addressed by the SOAP 1.1 specification. Using these de facto standards leverages existing application code and simplifies development and integration. In this aspect, ebXML converges with the work of the W3C XML Protocol Core (XMLP) Working Group.

In sum, standard bodies rather than software vendors back ebXML. Hence, there is no real deep desire to build or refine software implementation details. This heavy lifting is left to software vendors, and the focus is on defining an architectural framework for interoperability. The only implementation efforts within ebXML have been to create basic trials for the viability of the specifications. A special project team was established within ebXML to provide for proof-of-concept (POC) implementations of the specifications as a means of ensuring their viability. The ebXML message service has received more attention in the POC as one of the earliest specifications made available for public review. The architecture is central to this principle, as we see in the next section.

Architecture

The ebXML message service provides the message exchange functionality within the ebXML infrastructure. The message service provides the messaging interface for the registry/repository and its clients. In addition, the collaboration protocol agreement (CPA) may be used to provide a run-time configuration mechanism for the message service. This allows two message services to interoperate in ebXML using the configuration from the same CPA.

The ebXML message service was designed to work within the overall context of the ebXML initiative. However, the ebXML technical architecture is modular, and the message service can be used independently of ebXML. Software vendors can easily integrate message service functionality into their existing enterprise solutions. The Java API for XML Messaging (JAXM) provides the message service implementation that can be used to integrate message service functionality into an application or product. The message service yields an interoperable mechanism that can be easily implemented and used for a variety of applications. The message service has been designed to be as simple as possible. As a pragmatic issue, complex specifications are difficult to correctly implement and integrate. This can lead to interoperability issues between different vendor solutions.

Architectural Levels

The message service has three logical architectural levels between the business application and the network protocols: (1) the message service interface, (2) the message service handler, and (3) the transport interface. Figure 7.3 shows the relationships between these functional modules within the message service architecture in ebXML.

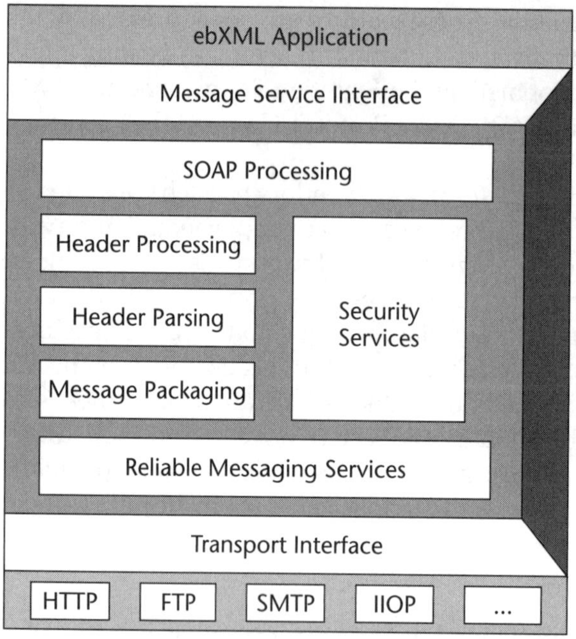

Figure 7.3 Relationship between ebXML message service handler components.
Source: "ebXML Messaging Service Specification"

What are the basic building blocks of the messaging system? At the center is a software system that handles all the messages. This is equivalent to the mail server in email systems. It is the central nervous system of the messaging service. The *message service handler* (MSH) has basic services, such as header processing, header parsing, security services, reliable messaging services, message packing, and error handling.

Header processing. Header processing is usually one of the first operations performed in the message upon its receipt by the message handler. This type of processing involves examining the header fields of incoming messages and performing some operations.

Header parsing. This involves extracting or transforming information from a received SOAP header or body element into a form that is suitable for processing by the message handler.

Security services. These services include digital signature creation and verification, authentication, and authorization. Security services may be used by other components of the message handler, including the header processing and header parsing components.

Reliable messaging services. These services handle the delivery and acknowledgment of messages, including handling for persistence, retry, error notification, and acknowledgment of messages requiring reliable delivery.

Message packaging. This is the final enveloping of an ebXML message, including SOAP header, body elements, and payload, into its SOAP container.

Error Handling. This component handles the reporting of errors encountered during the processing of a message by the message handler.

The *message service interface* (MSI) is an application interface for business applications to invoke message handler functionality for sending and receiving messages. Similar to ODBC, JDBC, and other abstract service interfaces, it exposes the message handler functionality as a defined set of APIs for business application developers. The MSI is the interface layer between the business application and the message handler. The message handler can also use MSI to access functionality within business applications that have sent or received messages.

The *transport interface* is designed to send messages over a variety of network and application-level communication protocols. The transport interface transforms ebXML-specific data to other forms carried by network services and protocols. This involves a complete exchange between two parties, piggybacking on top of existing protocols in the network stack. This depends on the application and the existing network configuration, which includes HTTP, FTP, and SMTP at the application level and TCP and SNA/LU6.2 at the network level.

Formatting Messages

An ebXML message has to be formatted according to the *ebXML Message Service Specification* and must conform to the MIME syntax, format, and encoding rules. The definition of the XML elements are provided by an XML schema, which extends SOAP to define the ebXML message header, trace header, manifest, status, and acknowledgment.

In Figure 7.4, the packaging involves putting an ebXML message, with its outer SOAP header, body elements, and payload, into its SwA envelope and communication protocol envelope. The header container contains one SOAP 1.1–compliant message. The SOAP message is an XML document that consists of the SOAP envelope element. This is the root element of the XML document representing the SOAP message.

The SOAP envelope element consists of one SOAP header element and one SOAP body element. The header element is a way to add features to a SOAP message, including the ebXML-specific header elements. The SOAP body element is a container for ebXML MSH control data and information related to the payload parts of the message.

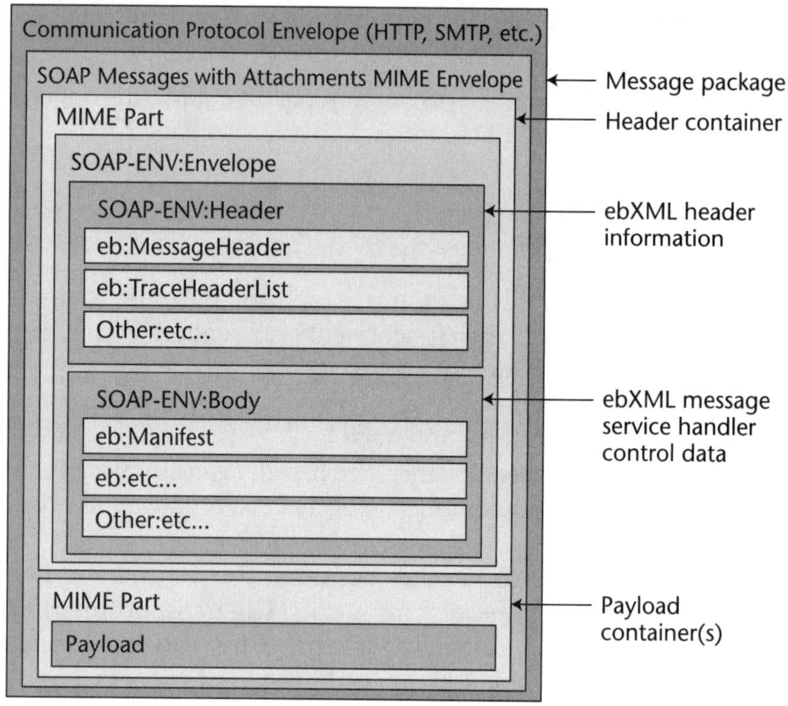

Figure 7.4 The General structure and composition of an ebXML message.
Source: "ebXML Messaging Service Specification"

The payload containers hold payloads for business applications. The ebXML messaging framework does not limit the structure or content of application payloads. Payloads can be simple plaintext objects or complex nested multipart objects.

Message Package

An ebXML *message package* consists of a MIME/multipart message envelope and its contents, structured in compliance with the SwA specification. The packaging involves the enveloping of an ebXML message, including SOAP header, body elements, and payload, into its SwA MIME envelope.

The `Content-Type` MIME header contains a `type` attribute with the value set to `text/xml` for all ebXML message packages, as shown in the following code snippet:

```
Content-Type: multipart/related;
type="text/xml";boundary="boundaryValue";start=messagepackage-123@foo.com
```

For error detection, the ebXML specification recommends that the root part contains a `Content-ID` MIME header and the `start` parameter is present in addition to the required parameters for the Multipart/Related media type, as shown in this code snippet:

```
Content-ID: <ebhandler@foo.com>
```

The following examples show the communication protocol envelopes for an ebXML message sent in Internet transport systems as defined in email and Web formats. For example, this is a sample SMTP header for an ebXML message to be sent in an email format:

```
From: tom@foo.com
To: scott@foo.com
Date: Fri, 17 Aug 2001 19:32:11 EST
MIME-Version: 1.0
SOAPAction: ebXML
Content-type: multipart/related; boundary="BoundarY"; type="text/xml";
start=" <tom@foo.com>"
```

All ebXML message parts that follow the ebXML message envelope, including the MIME boundary string, constitute the HTTP entity body. This encompasses the SOAP envelope and the constituent ebXML parts and attachments, including the trailing MIME boundary strings. The identity of the ebXML MSH, such as the servlet "ebhandler," may be part of the HTTP `POST` request. The Internet Engineering Task Force (IETF) defines HTTP methods, such as `GET` and `POST`. `GET` is used for sending static Web pages. `POST` is used for building applications, because it can transmit arbitrary data values in html form elements. For example, this is the HTTP header for a sample ebXML message:

```
POST /servlet/ebhandler HTTP/1.1
Host: www2.foo.com
SOAPAction: ebXML
Content-type: multipart/related; boundary="BoundarY"; type="text/xml";
start=" <ebhandler@foo.com>"
```

The message has to be formatted according to the ebXML *Message Service Specification* and the HTTP-specific MIME canonical form before transmission over HTTP. (See http://www.ietf.org/rfc2616.txt for MIME formatting.) Since the HTTP protocol supports 8-bit and binary data, a message can be encoded for transmission over HTTP. The rules for creating an ebXML-compliant HTTP message specify that all MIME headers in the message envelope are part of the HTTP header, including the Content-Type: Multipart/Related MIME header. The required `SOAPAction` HTTP header field is in the HTTP header and has a value of `ebXML`.

Header Container

The SOAP header is an optional element in the SOAP specification, but it is very important in ebXML messages. This is part of the extensibility design goal in SOAP. SOAP headers offer a flexible way to extend a message with certain characteristics, such as ebXML features.

The root part of the message package is the header container, which is a MIME body part that consists of one SOAP message. The MIME `Content-Type` header in the header container is required to have the value `text/xml`. The `Content-Type` header may have a `charset` attribute that identifies the character set used to create the SOAP message. For example:

```
Content-Type: text/xml; charset="UTF-8
```

In the code snippet, we find the SOAP envelope, header, and body in the header container. The outermost element is `SOAP-ENV:Envelope`. `SOAP-ENV:Header` carries meta data about the SOAP message. `SOAP-ENV:Body` contains the message payload.

```
Content-ID: messagepackage-123@foo.com
Content-Type: text/xml; charset="UTF-8"
<SOAP-ENV:Envelope
    xmlns:SOAP-ENV="http://schemas.xmlsoap.org/soap/envelope/">
  <SOAP-ENV:Header>
    ...
  </SOAP-ENV:Header>
  <SOAP-ENV:Body>
    ...
  </SOAP-ENV:Body>
</SOAP-ENV:Envelope>
```

By default, SOAP headers are optional, so an application can ignore such a header if it is not recognized. However, an important attribute here is `mustUnderstand`. If this attribute has a value of 1, the header is mandatory, so the receiving application must return an error message if it does not recognize it. For example, in this ebXML message header, the SOAP header is required:

```
<eb:MessageHeader SOAP-ENV:mustUnderstand="1" eb:version="1.0">
```

The SOAP envelope contains the complete ebXML header. Any deviation from the message semantics that is essential for correct processing will be noticed and will probably produce erroneous results.

Header Processing

Header processing could include the creation of the SOAP header elements for the message and checking all the header fields necessary to process the message, such as the To element to ensure this is the proper destination for the message. The MSH can use input from many sources, including data from the application passed through the message service interface and the CPA that associated with the message. In addition, the input for the MSH can be information generated from digital signatures, timestamps, and unique identifiers.

ebXML SOAP Extensions

The ebXML message service defines header and body element extensions within the envelope. Separate ebXML extension elements are used where different software components are likely to be used to generate ebXML SOAP extension elements. Carrying ebXML headers in SOAP messages does not mean that ebXML overrides existing semantics of SOAP, but rather that the semantics of ebXML over SOAP maps directly onto SOAP semantics.

SOAP Header Extensions

The ebXML message service provides the security and reliability features that are not provided in SOAP and XML. The ebXML message service is defined as layered extensions to the foundation of the SOAP specification and SwA specification, which defines how a SOAP message can be carried within the MIME model. The SOAP request/response model is specifically suited for RPC systems, although more general messaging systems can also be built on top. RPC-style communication basically means that requests and responses are exchanged in pairs between two applications.

The ebXML message header, part of the SOAP envelope header, is not to be confused with the SOAP header. An ebXML message extends the SOAP message with the principal extension elements. According to the *ebXML Messaging Service Specification*, the SOAP header extensions for ebXML are these XML elements:

MessageHeader. (required) This element contains routing information for the message (To/From, etc.), as well as other context information about the message. The ebXML message header element is a subelement of the SOAP header element and is required in all ebXML messages. The `MessageHeader` element has two required attributes—`mustUnderstand` and `Version`—and the optional id attribute.

TraceHeaderList. (optional) This element contains entries that identify the message handler that sent and should receive the message.

ErrorList. (optional) This element contains a list of the errors that are being reported against a previous message. The `ErrorList` element is only used if reporting an error on a previous message.

Signature. (optional) This element contains a digital signature.

Acknowledgment. (optional) This element acknowledges from the receiving message handler to the sending MSH that a previous message has been received.

Via. (optional) This element conveys information to the next message handler that receives the message.

SOAP Body Extensions

The SOAP body element is within the SOAP envelope element and contains the elements for the manifest, status, and delivery receipt. It has a namespace qualifier that matches the SOAP envelope namespace declaration for the namespace "http://schemas.xmlsoap.org/soap/envelope/". According to the *ebXML Messaging Service Specification*, the SOAP body extensions for ebXML are these XML elements:

Manifest. (optional) This element points to any data present either in the payload container or accessible via the URI.

StatusRequest. (optional) This element identifies a message whose status is being requested.

StatusResponse. (optional) This element is the response by an MSH to a request on the status of a message that was previously received.

DeliveryReceipt. (optional) This element is a delivery receipt from the recipient (To) of a message, to let the sender (From) of the message know the message was received.

Payload Container

As mentioned, the payload can be a simple plaintext object or a complex nested multipart object. ebXML does not define the structure or content of application payloads. The specification of the structure and composition of payload objects are defined by the organization that defines the business process or information exchange. The SOAP payload is part of the SOAP envelope and should not to be confused with the ebXML payload. The ebXML payload is contained with the SOAP payload container.

The ebXML message service is payload-neutral, meaning that any kind of information can be reliably routed. This information can include XML documents, binary data, or EDI messages. Businesses can incorporate ebXML technology to leverage their existing infrastructure. The ebXML message service meets these goals by defining a MIME packaging scheme and an XML message header structure that can envelope XML documents or other forms of business information.

The following fragment represents an example of a payload container. If the message package contains an application payload, it is enclosed within a payload container. The payload is the invoice information.

```
Content-ID: <host.foo.com>
Content-Type: application/xml
<Invoice>
<Invoicedata>
. . .
</Invoicedata>
</Invoice>
```

The contents of each payload container are identified by the ebXML message manifest element within the SOAP body.

The ebXML message service has a MIME packaging scheme that separates routing information in the header from the business information in the payload. The message payload may be encrypted for security. The designated recipient has the key to decrypt the message and process the contents. This separation of header and payload becomes even more important when a third party is involved in the transaction. For example, suppose a sealed confidential document is sent to a lawyer handling documents on behalf of a client. The encrypted information in the payload is separated from the routing information in the header. Hence, the lawyer does not read the encrypted confidential information when routing the message to the final recipient. This enables a simplified and highly efficient processing by a third party involved in handling the message. The third party need not understand or even process the contents of the message payload.

In the previous section, we covered the ebXML message format. In the next section we cover how to handle messages once they are sent or received by a message handler.

Handling Messages

The ebXML message service specification has a message structure and protocol that is independent of the underlying transport protocol, such as SMTP, FTP, HTTP, or any other protocol capable of exchanging MIME data. Thus, businesses can choose the best available way to use a standard message structure for the transfer of messages with their partners, suppliers, and customers. This feature enables the messaging service to be integrated with the enterprise applications rather than with each transport protocol. Transport protocol adapters can be plugged into the ebXML message service implementation.

Since the ebXML message service is based on existing standards, such as SOAP, XML, SMTP, and HTTP, companies can build new applications on existing email and document exchange systems, such as Microsoft Exchange or UNIX sendmail.

As mentioned previously in the chapter, the message service handler is designed to serve as the "carrier" of ebXML messages over a variety of network and application-level communication protocols. MSH functionality includes features such as header processing, header parsing, security services, reliable messaging, messaging packing, and SOAP processing.

The *message transfer agent* (MTA) is a software application that sends and receives mail messages with other message transfer agents on behalf of mail user agents. MTAs can serve as mail hubs and can typically service hundreds or more mail user agents. For example, an MTA can be existing mail servers, such as Microsoft Exchange Server or UNIX sendmail.

The *mail user agent* (MUA) is an electronic mail program used to construct electronic mail messages and communicate with an MTA to send and retrieve mail messages. For example, MUAs can be commercial mail clients, such as Microsoft Outlook or UNIX elm. MUAs are responsible for constructing electronic mail messages in accordance with the *Internet Electronic Mail Specifications*.

Mentioned earlier in the chapter, the message service interface is an abstract service interface that business applications use to interact with the MSH to send and receive messages and which the MSH uses to interface with applications that handle received messages.

Reliable Messaging

An important feature in a communication system with their partners, suppliers, and customers is quality of service. The message delivery should be secure, reliable, and timely. Unfortunately, reliability is not an inherent feature for Internet protocols, such as HTTP and SMTP. Businesses cannot effectively exchange information with a degree of certainty that the messages they send have been received, or vice versa. Reliability is specifically addressed in the ebXML messaging service for exchange of business information via the Internet.

The ebXML reliable messaging protocol provides for the following:

- One and only one copy of the message will be delivered to the receiving application. This is for any given message by the sending application to the ebXML message service.
- A positive acknowledgment will be sent from the receiving service to the sending service. This ensures the message has been received and stored persistently.
- If an acknowledgment is not received, the sending service will either retry delivery or notify the sending application.

The ebXML messaging service uses positive acknowledgment and persistent storage to guarantee reliable message delivery. The message service will save the message in persistent storage before sending a message. The receiving service will save the message in persistent storage after the message has been received. In addition, the receiving service sends an acknowledgment message to the sending service. After the sending service receives the acknowledgment, it may delete the message from persistent storage. If the sending service does not receive acknowledgment, it can send the message again or notify the sending application that the message was unable to be delivered.

The entire messaging operation is asynchronous—that is, multiple message transmissions can happen at once. A message service does not have to wait for the response before engaging in other operations, such as sending additional messages. If the sending message service does not receive acknowledgment, it tries a recovery sequence. The sending service will send the message again and wait for acknowledgment. This cycle is repeated a number of times. The number of retries and retry interval can be configured based on requirements.

The ebXML message service does not place any requirements on the reliability of the underlying transport service. The underlying transport need not guarantee transmission or acknowledge transmission, so almost any available transport can be used. This permits the ebXML message service to be used with high-end application servers, Web servers, or even email. This gives businesses a choice of solutions that are interoperable and fit their existing infrastructure and IT budgets.

To ensure smooth operation in a message handler implementation, a messaging client should be able to check on the status of the message handler receiving the message. The message handler is required to supports two services for reliable messaging: message status request and ping/pong. Otherwise, the message handler receiving the message has to return a SOAP error message (fault).

Message Status Request

The message status request service is a way for a messaging client to check the status regarding a specific message from the message handler. It is a request/response mechanism between the messaging client and message handler. The messaging client sends the message status request message to a message handler, and it responds with a message status response message. A message handler responds to message status requests for messages that have been sent, and the message ID is archived. The message is then sent to the recipient specified in the header. The recipient receives the message status request message and generates a message status response message.

Ping/Pong Services

The concept of a ping/pong service is for a message client to check if the message handler is receiving any messages at all. The sample scenarios between two message handlers can be:

MSH1: "Are you there?"

MSH2: "Yes, I am."

The ping/pong service is a simple, but optional, service for the message handler. A message handler sends a ping message to a message handler, and the receiving message handler responds with a pong message. There are benefits of implementing this option, such as helping with troubleshooting and as a simple way to check if the message handler and the server are "alive." The absence of a pong response to a ping request does not mean that there is a communication failure, however. It is possible that the receiving message handler did not choose to implement ping/pong. On the other hand, receiving a pong message does mean there is an established communication link between the message handlers.

Any message service used for business purposes must tolerate faults in the network, the software, or the hosts on which the services are run. To guarantee message delivery, the ebXML message service must have error recovery, retry logic, and duplicate detection.

Lost Messages

A message is lost when a receiving message handler does not receive a response to a message. What is to be done in this situation? If an acknowledgment message has not been received, the sending message handler should send the original message again up to the maximum number of times as specified in the message parameter. After these attempts, the message handler may notify the application and system administrator of the failure to receive an acknowledgment.

Duplicate Message Handling

A duplicate message contains the same header, body, and payload as an earlier message that was sent. The sender should send the identical message if no acknowledgment message is received. When the recipient receives a duplicate message, it should respond with a message identical to the first message sent. The recipient should not forward the message a second time to the application/process. For example, suppose Acme Hardware Company wants to order 100 boxes of hammers from Big Distributor, Inc. It sends a purchase order to Big Distributor, and Big Distributor sends an acknowledgment message back to let Acme Hardware know that it received the purchase order. Big Distributor also passes the order on to its order-processing application. Unfortunately, the acknowledgment of the purchase order never got to Acme Hardware. Since Acme Hardware never got the acknowledgment, it sends the order again. Due to high Internet traffic, the message did not arrive again. Acme Hardware still has not received an acknowledgment for this message, so it tries to send it yet again. This time, Big Distributor does receive it and realizes that it is the same message that it has already processed. Since it is a duplicate, Big Distributor doesn't pass it on to its purchase-order-processing application, but it does send another acknowledgment message, which is finally received by Acme Hardware.

Failed Message Delivery

If a message cannot be delivered, the message handler should send a delivery failure notification to the sender. The delivery failure notification message identifies who detected the problem, who created the undelivered message, and contains a warning or error message.

Error Reporting and Handling

How does one message handler report errors it detects in a message to another message handler? The error reporting and handling in the ebXML message service is considered a layer of processing above the SOAP processor layer. This means the message handler is an application-level handler of a message from the perspective of the SOAP processor. The SOAP processor can generate SOAP fault messages if it is unable to process the message. A sending message handler is required to be prepared to accept and process these SOAP faults. A SOAP fault may also be generated and returned to the sender of a SOAP message.

Security

A security assessment balances the inherent risks and the value of the assets at risk with using resources for countermeasures. No technology is an adequate substitute to the effective application of security management policies and practices. Good business practice in this case is just as important as advanced technology. We should minimize risks that are introduced when doing business electronically via the Internet. The ebXML message service can face certain security risks, such as:

- Unauthorized access
- Data integrity and/or confidentiality attacks (e.g. through man-in-the-middle attacks)
- Denial-of-service, spoofing, and bombing attacks

The ebXML specifications provide general guidance rather than specific implementation techniques for security management policies and practices. These security risks may be addressed by the application of the countermeasures described in the *ebXML Message Service Specification*. The specification describes a set of profiles, or combinations of selected countermeasures, that have been selected to address key risks based upon commonly available technologies. Each of the specified profiles includes a description of the risks. ebXML security uses open standards and widely available techniques, such as XML signatures, cryptography, and secure transmission protocols.

The W3C/IETF XML Signature standard is the basis for enabling a digital signature in an ebXML message. This enables the recipient of a digitally signed ebXML message to authenticate its source and verify the integrity of the message. The W3C/IETF XML Signature standard provides a wide variety of public key infrastructure (PKI) environments used with the message service.

The payload of an ebXML message can be encrypted and digitally signed using popular MIME-based cryptographic standards such as S/MIME and PGP/MIME. The intended recipient can access and verify the authenticity and integrity of contents of the message. A variety of network protocol security standards such as SSL and IPSEC may be used to provide confidentiality, authentication, and message integrity. This enhances the security countermeasures defined in the *ebXML Message Service Specification*. Emerging security standards, such as Security Assertion Markup Language (SAML), may also be used with the message service through extension of the SOAP envelope. SAML is a standard being developed by the OASIS Security Services Technical Committee to enable the exchange of security assertions between enterprises.

From a security perspective, the message handler has three major functions: authentication, authorization, and encryption. First, the message handler will authenticate messages against a security database or directory based on the security control information in the message. Second, the message handler will authorize operations that can be performed based on the message type and the access level of the principle. Third, the message handler may have to encrypt sent messages and decrypt received messages based on a defined encryption algorithm, such as public key encryption.

Persistent Digital Signature

An XML signature is used to bind the header and body to the payload or data that relates to the message. An XML signature can selectively sign portions of an XML document, permitting the document to be augmented with new element content added, while preserving the validity of the signature. A signed message may be acknowledged with a delivery receipt acknowledgment message that itself is digitally signed. The acknowledgment message has to contain a digital signature reference of the original message within the acknowledgment. An example of a digital signature "ds:Signature" for a message is in the following code snippet:

```
<ds:Signature xmlns:ds="http://www.w3.org/2000/09/xmldsig#">
<ds:SignedInfo>
<ds:CanonicalizationMethod Algorithm="http://www.w3.org/TR/2000/CR-xml-
c14n-20001026"/>
<ds:SignatureMethod Algorithm="http://www.w3.org/2000/09/xmldsig#dsa-
sha1"/>
<ds:Reference URI="">
<Transforms>
<Transform Algorithm="http://www.w3.org/TR/1999/REC-xpath-19991116">
<XPath xmlns:dsig="http://www.w3.org/2000/09/xmldsig#">
not(ancestor-or-self::eb:TraceHeaderList or ancestor-or-self::eb:Via)
</XPath>
</Transform>
</Transforms>
<ds:DigestMethod Algorithm="http://www.w3.org/2000/09/xmldsig#dsa-sha1"/>
<ds:DigestValue>...</ds:DigestValue>
</ds:Reference>
<ds:Reference URI="cid://. . ./">
<ds:DigestMethod Algorithm="http://www.w3.org/2000/09/xmldsig#dsa-sha1"/>
<ds:DigestValue>...</ds:DigestValue>
</ds:Reference>
</ds:SignedInfo>
<ds:SignatureValue>...</ds:SignatureValue>
<ds:KeyInfo>...</ds:KeyInfo>
</ds:Signature>
```

Summary

SOAP has widespread industry support and a simple design, and it is used in other XML standards. ebXML messaging is built on a SOAP foundation on which ebXML extensions are added. The messaging framework defines the XML- and SOAP-based structures to support messaging service features such as messaging reliability, persistence, security, and extensibility. The most popular communication protocols, such as HTTP and SMTP, are supported within the framework. In addition, SOAP provides general design principles about message enveloping and header document schema used to transfer ebXML messages over a generic communication protocol. The message service has been designed to be transport- and network-protocol-neutral.

XML messaging systems are more prevalent in enterprise deployments, but with different XML messaging standards, this becomes a Tower of Babel. There is hope that ebXML message services will become the unifying transport framework, replacing existing means such as EDIINT AS1 and AS2 for point-to-point EDI over the Internet. On the other hand, the ebXML message services offer a coexistence alternative with EDI. As a protocol-neutral and content-agnostic framework, the messaging service can transport traditional EDI payloads as well as XML documents.

Reliable messaging means that message handlers can reliably exchange messages that are sent, resulting in the recipient receiving the message once and only once. In ebXML, reliable messaging is the result of an MSH responding to a received message with an acknowledgment message and archiving messages and message ID in persistent storage. In this context, persistent storage is a method of storing data that does not lose information after a system failure or interruption. The end-user software must supply basic header information and the optional payload. The message service will accept this information and prepare a well-formed message and route it appropriately. If an error occurs, recovery will be attempted. If the error is unrecoverable, the end-user application must then handle the error in a business-specific way.

Enterprise applications will leverage the ebXML message service through customized software, which requires software vendors to add message service functionality to their existing software packages. End-user software can range from large-scale applications to small business accounting packages.

In this chapter, we covered the message service that provides the messaging component of the infrastructure for a heterogeneous, distributed environment. The messaging service incorporates the necessary logic to achieve the level of reliability in any business, large or small. In the next chapter, we explore the registry/repository functionality for storing and retrieving ebXML-related documents.

CHAPTER

8

Using the ebXML Registry Services

"[We] develop specifications to achieve interoperable registries and repositories, with an interface that enables submission, query and retrieval on the contents of the registry and repository. Further, [we] seek to develop specifications that serve a wide range of uses, covering the spectrum from general purpose document registries to real-time business-to-business registries. Additionally, as part of its specification development work, [we] explore and promote various emerging models for distributed and cooperating registries."

—Charter of the ebXML Registry Technical Committee in OASIS

AREAS COVERED IN THIS CHAPTER

- Who uses the registry?
- Business semantics and the registry
  - Meta data and shared context
  - Shared semantic discovery
  - Directory model
  - Registry model
- What is the ebXML registry?
  - How the registry works
  - Registry/client communications
  - Classification system
  - UUID as a unique identifier
  - Managing objects in a registry
  - Searching for registry entries
  - Registry security

The ebXML registry is central to the ebXML architecture. The registry manages and maintains the shared information as objects in a repository. Repositories provide trading partners with the shared business semantics, such as business process models, core components, messages, trading partner agreements, schemas, and other objects that enable data interchange between companies. The ebXML registry is an interface for accessing and discovering shared business semantics. In this chapter, we will explore who uses the registry, the business semantic model, and the registry functionality. This includes registry classification, registry client/server communications, searching for registry objects, and managing registry objects.

This chapter is based on information in the primary ebXML registry reference documents, including the "ebXML Registry Service Specification" and the "ebXML Registry Information Model." For simplicity, we will use the term *schema* in discussions to refer to any one of the various dialects of XML schemas and DTDs.

Who Uses the ebXML Registry?

ebXML registry users from any business of any size, in any industry, at any location, offering any kind of service can build data interchange services using the ebXML registry. Companies may also be registered by third parties, called *registrars*, such as marketplaces, exchanges, Internet service providers, and application service providers. The registry is an access point for Web service types and service specifications that can be shared with other businesses. A complete registry system with a scalable architecture will likely depend on registrars that can implement and host distributed repositories. The individual industries or companies can populate and update the hosted repositories at the registrars.

The ebXML vision includes creation of a series of multiple distributed registries or repositories, since one or even a few repositories may not scale sufficiently to handle anticipated message traffic. The participants in an existing marketplace are part of that particular ecosystem. They conform to the technology infrastructure of the marketplace. There are hundreds of marketplaces today, many of which use different application technology. A supplier in one vertical marketplace may not be able to easily participate in a horizontal marketplace that was implemented using a different standard. A registry will help businesses in different marketplaces determine which potential trading partners use the same technology. This encourages Web services that translate from one technology to another, which in turn helps to unify businesses and marketplaces through the use of a common set of specifications for discovery, description, and integration of business semantics.

A sampling of companies that use the registry includes:

Large organizations. This includes Fortune 500, Global 2000, large manufacturers, international financial institutions, and healthcare providers.

Small and medium enterprises. This includes regional distributors, services and consulting firms, local retailers of goods and services, and restaurants and hospitality companies.

Independent software vendors and integrators. This includes ERP vendors, networking companies, Big-5 consulting firms, and local software houses.

Marketplace creators. This includes net market makers, horizontal marketplaces, and corporate exchanges.

Industry and standards organizations. This includes IT standards bodies and industry vertical organizations and associations.

Business Semantics and the Registry

Registries help businesses take advantage of Web services by extending their reach and reducing time to market. Businesses will have a means to describe their services, business semantics, and business processes in an open environment on the global Internet. Potential trading partners will quickly discover and interact with each other using applications. This lowers the barriers to rapid participation in the global Internet economy. It allows businesses to organize their portfolio of services in a controlled environment.

The power of ebXML lies in its ability to express the business semantics for a shared set of trading processes at a high level (such as what constitutes a returned product) and low level (such as which part numbers are valid). In particular, ebXML specifies the common protocols and agreements these processes can use to exchange messages across differing software systems and platforms.

To understand the value of a registry, we have to first understand business semantics, shared context, and shared semantic discovery. Many technologies assume that as if by magic, business can automatically interoperate with technology alone. However, various complex problems in business semantics must be solved. The essence of business semantic problems can be characterized in this dialogue between two trading partners:

Partner 1: "Do you have widgets?"

Partner 2: "No, our store is closed. But we get new shipments on Monday."

Partner 1: "I'll buy 100 units in black."

Partner 2: "What's a widget?"

Partner 1: "Here's 100 dollars."

Partner 2: "Is that in U.S. dollars or Canadian?"

On the surface, communication seems to be happening, but without the true meaning being communicated. For systems to interoperate for a data interchange, we have to agree on the meaning, as dictated by a business vocabulary and a shared context for the messages in the communication.

As we covered in Chapter 2, the business requirements for application and document exchange on the Internet include (1) the meta data to denote the logical structure and (2) the shared context for specifying the meta data rules.

Meta Data and Shared Context

As mentioned in Chapter 2, meta data is data about data, or information about information. Meta data makes it possible to find data and associate data with a description. It should be used with shared context to fully express its meaning. *Shared context* is a formal description of the rules meta data must follow.

For example, a shared context applies to a particular type of document and serves as an agreement between the sender and the recipient of the document. The sender agrees that the document conforms to the shared context. The recipient agrees to interpret the document according to the shared context. Two companies would agree to a shared context for documents being exchanged so both parties have a common understanding of semantics.

In e-commerce, there are multiple data-interchange enabling technologies, such as the Internet, XML, and Web services, but a lack of shared context and means to enable it. The parties have to explicitly agree on the overall structure and usage context of the meta data. This is addressed in ebXML with core components, which provide meta data for "price," and define whether we are dealing with U.S. or Canadian dollars. Using core components, we can use meta data to describe explicitly a piece of business information. This is also the case in using DTD and schemas for describing XML documents for the business process, messaging, and other context.

Is Web services a framework in which any two arbitrary applications can interact? XML provides shared languages, but not a shared vocabulary. The Web services stack pushes this shared semantics problem into higher layers without solving it. People cannot create perfectly transparent descriptions, and they simply will not try without economic incentive. Are Web services the way to automate remote transactions, such as the Web for online publishing? Web services can do for applications what the Web did for publishing—but only if Web services adopt the contextless Web model, which means loosely coupled passing of structured documents. The documents will not be limited to a predefined set of methods and tags, and the recipients of the data will be other applications, rather than human beings.

By itself, XML can interoperate at the language level, but it does not create shared context. Context refers to the things that a Web service needs to know about the service consumer to provide a customized, personalized experience. This includes the identity, the location, and any business vocabulary associated with the industry. When aggregating a number of services to create a composite business service, all the services need to share this context.

Web services has the issues of how to share context and interoperate at the semantic level. Web services provide a simple way for organizations to discover each other and exchange information. Web services simplify some of the issues of developing low-cost, widespread B2B applications in an industry. Web services examples that work are based on an existing relationship and the shared semantics. By themselves, Web services are the plumbing technology in the background. Web services may simplify the gritty details, after the semantic level agreements are worked out—for example, using a context-sensitive XML editor to manually define the Web service interfaces and generating the interface using a toolkit. Web services are sold not only as improved plumbing, but also as the way to create software, seamlessly and automatically, connecting any two business processes or applications as if by magic.

But how does the developer associate these new Web service interfaces with existing applications and services? And how does he or she assemble multiple discrete Web services into a composite business service? Where are the guidelines to put all of these Web services technologies and standards into perspective? How should information about the identity of each user be maintained? The challenge in Web services technology is lack of standards for Web sites to share context. Interoperable vendor implementations are subject to these challenging questions. Without shared context, the vision of seamless assembly and integration of distributed, heterogeneous Web services is a distant dream.

The foundation for e-business includes a shared semantic registry. A service has to be able to share context with other services. A new set of standard vocabularies is needed to represent all the components of shared context and to define open, vendor-neutral Web services to support the infrastructure. This includes (1) a standard XML vocabulary to represent corporate and service identity components, (2) a standard XML framework that enables policies to govern access and control to corporate information, and (3) a standard XML vocabulary that enables context descriptions. Without standards or conventions for representing this context, every site maintains identity and history information in a proprietary format. With shared context, the vision of transparent, dynamic interaction of widely distributed, heterogeneous Web services can be a reality. A proprietary solution from a single vendor lacks the cross-industry consensus and support to be really open and interoperable. This issue of shared context must be solved using a public standards-based solution.

Shared Semantic Discovery

The issues of shared semantic discovery is characterized in this dialogue between two trading partners:

Partner 1: "I want to do business with you. So that we can agree on the definition of terms, let me use the business vocabulary in the guidelines stored in this registry."

Partner 2: "I have looked up the business vocabulary in the guidelines in the registry. Let's talk about your purchase."

Partner 1: "I want 100 units of widgets at $1 each, shipped tomorrow."

Partner 2: "OK. Let me look up what widget means. . . ."

Without artificial intelligence, the description and discovery of Web services is going to require traditional human intelligence. When people are involved, there will be the possibility of context errors. With a shared semantic discovery model, shown in Figure 8.1, the use of a reference context in a registry addresses such errors, providing the key to resolving ambiguity. A shared context standard has to be both industry-specific and industry-wide. Industries with complicated supply chains will benefit from the simplicity of dynamic systems integration. Industries with intense vendor relationships will enjoy

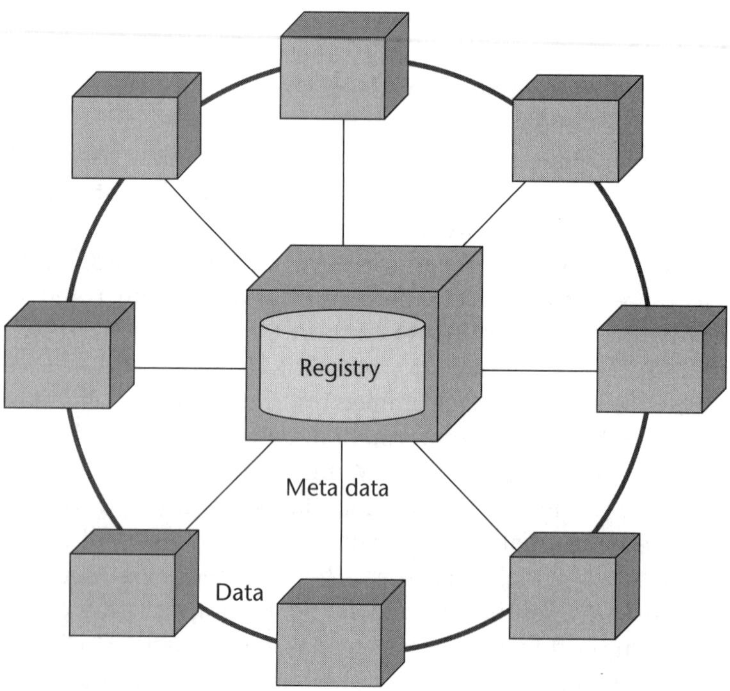

Figure 8.1 Meta data is stored in a registry for shared semantic discovery.

increased access to systems and business information. Industries with dynamic systems will leverage the value of a single source for information.

A common type of Internet registry, the Internet search engine, can help us understand the registry functionality. Internet search engines are large databases, directories, and registries that we use as an index to Web sites on the Internet. They are giant databases of URLs and keywords associated with them. The focus of Internet search engines is to allow a human using a Web browser to search for and find relevant Web sites. Search engines serve up URLs and HTML documents for Web browsers. These engines get populated by employing Web crawlers that go out and find Web sites. They store URLs and any keywords and other data that could be used to index the sites. Another way to have a listing published in a search engine is via a business deal with the company running the search engine. We can pay for a listing and positioning in the search engine, and we can earn the right for a listing if we advertise with a search engine or an affiliate company.

In general, a registry works with not just the location for Web sites, but also more general information types for applications, such as application properties. The search engines store only Web site location, not email addresses, XML schemas, or business documents. The locations have only one document type in HTML, not XML documents. The search engines are meant for Web browsers, rather than invoking applications. With a registry, we have complete control over describing, categorizing, and registering the business and service information that is published. A registry can also use more specific applications and can access the registry using messages. And the programs can register themselves with minimal human intervention using messages and client-side APIs for accessing registries. The registry has structured data, compared to the unstructured text and documents in a search engine. A query against the registry can only retrieve data stored within the registry. Traditional search engines could use the registry as a source when compiling their responses and results.

With a protocol and an interface describing a service, the next step is registration and discovery by a registry. Businesses can publish their Web services in a registry so that others can discover these services. For example, a registry can have business names, mailing addresses, contact names, phone numbers, Web services offered by businesses, and meta data describing the interfaces of Web services. A registry enables a business to (1) describe its business and its services, (2) discover other businesses that offer desired services, and (3) integrate with these other businesses. Today organizations may find it difficult to locate a business that offers services that best fit their needs. The registry makes it possible for organizations to quickly discover the right business. Once an organization finds a potential business partner, there is a standard mechanism to conduct e-business with this partner.

Two similar models for shared discovery on the Internet include the *directory model* and the *registry model*. The directory model is geared toward solving problems of single-login and searching for users and hosts. As we'll see in the next sections, the directory and registry models are designed to do different things. A specific-purpose registry, such as UDDI, is intended to manage descriptions of Web service types, business organizations, and the Web services the businesses offer.

Directory Model

The Internet still lacks a comprehensive directory service. Though most sites run some kind of local service, there is no global framework capable of tying them together into a uniform service throughout the Internet.

Lightweight Directory Access Protocol (LDAP) is an extensible, general-purpose directory that is most often used to manage users and resources. It uses proven Internet technology, such as the Domain Name System (DNS) and URLs and pieces of other services, such as X.500 and WHOIS++, SOLO. The main constraint during the search process is resource efficiency. If only one or a few servers are involved, it is not unreasonable to contact them all with the search request. For wider searches, this approach is not feasible. For example, suppose a user wants to search for a friend named "Jane Smith." One approach would be to extend the search to every directory server in the edu domain. However, this domain contained over a million hosts. Contacting them all would leave our user waiting for a long time for the results. If there are many such queries, the network and server resources consumed would be a major problem.

Using LDAP, a client's first step is to look up edu in the DNS, asking for directory exchange records. It may return several records, but assume it chooses the one providing an LDAP service for the edu domain, ldap://hostname. The client contacts the LDAP port on hostname and sends it an LDAP subtree search of the edu domain for an entry with a person, a locality, and a name of Jane Smith. The LDAP server consults the index it has collected and finds that there are two possible services where the client should continue the search—one at Stanford University and another at University of Nevada. The corresponding directory exchange referrals, which it returns to the client, are dx://stanford.edu and dx://nevada.edu. The client may present these referrals to the user, or it may follow them automatically. Choosing the latter, it looks up stanford.edu and nevada.edu in the DNS, asking for directory exchange records. For each set of directory exchange records returned, the client chooses one corresponding to a protocol it understands. In our example, the chosen records might be ldap://stanford.edu and ldap://nevada.edu. The client contacts each directory through the protocol and continues its search, retrieving the results.

A registry implementation could be built using an LDAP directory, rather than relational databases, as long as it conforms to the specified behavior.

Registry Model

As mentioned, Web services are self-contained, modular business applications that have open, Internet standards-based interfaces and communicate directly with other Web services via standards-based technologies. These standards-based communications allow Web services to be accessed by customers, suppliers, and partners independent of hardware, operating system, or even programming environment. The result is that businesses can expose their current and future business applications as Web services, which can be easily discovered and used by external partners. Web services offer improved time-to-integration and lower overall cost-of-ownership as compared to EDI and nonstandard B2B solutions.

The dynamic discovery of businesses and their services is a key step in Web services. E-commerce requires seamless access to information about trading partners and the ability to integrate with them. However, there are myriad ways to describe products and Web services. Without a shared standard or infrastructure for e-commerce participants, how can we find services and work with potential trading partners? In the enterprise, large, complex IT infrastructures have a number of services that need shared context for semantics. Marketplaces, businesses, and directory providers are working on these communication and transaction problems, with distinct and divergent approaches centered on their requirements. The result is broad diversity in approach, content, and architecture.

There are numerous standards for distributed Internet registries, each having its own information models and APIs. A few of these registries are the ebXML registry, the OASIS registry at xml.org for finding XML schemas, Universal Description, Discovery and Integration (UDDI), and Web Services Description Language (WSDL). The ebXML registry is broader in scope compared to UDDI because it addresses business semantics in a more fundamental manner. An ebXML technical white paper called *Using UDDI to find ebXML Registry/Repository* (see http://www.ebxml.org/specs/rrUDDI.pdf) describes a way to locate ebXML registries using UDDI. Because each registry has its interfaces to access content, porting Web service applications from one Web services registry to another is a challenge. Java API for XML Registries (JAXR) provides a standard and uniform interface for accessing these registries right from within the Java application. JAXR APIs provide an abstract registry layer for Java code to access both UDDI and ebXML registries.

A common analogy used for UDDI is a phone book for Web services. The information provided in a UDDI registry consists of three components: white pages, which include address and contact information; yellow pages, which contain standard industrial categories; and green pages, which contain the technical information about services that are exposed by the business. Green pages include references to specifications for Web services, as well as support for other discovery mechanisms. The UDDI specification defines an XML-based data model and a set of SOAP APIs to access and manipulate that data model. The SOAP APIs define the behavior for a UDDI registry.

UDDI makes it possible for organizations to programmatically describe their services and business processes and their preferred methods for conducting business. UDDI can simplify the effort of integrating disparate business processes.

WSDL lets a provider describe a service in XML, but it does not solve the shared context problem. A provider can't describe critical business aspects of its services, such as price or contractual requirements. To get a particular provider's WSDL document, you must know where to find it. UDDI is meant to aggregate WSDL documents. But UDDI does nothing more than register existing capabilities; it does not create shared semantics. These kinds of advanced discovery features require further collaboration and design work between buyers and sellers. As the UDDI technical white paper says, "The ability to locate parties that can provide a specific product or service at a given price or within a specific geographic boundary in a given timeframe is not directly covered by the UDDI specifications." After using XML to create a description in WSDL and registering it with UDDI, two arbitrary entities do not automatically interoperate. An organization looking for a Web service may not be able to specify its needs clearly enough that its inquiry will match the descriptions in the UDDI database. Shared context has to come from somewhere. Defining the business semantic problem at higher layers is doomed to fail, since the problem exists in the higher layers as well. There will be a layer that contains the ambiguity of two-party communication. Creating a semantic ontology rich enough to express a large subset of possible interests while sufficiently restricted to ensure interoperability between any arbitrary parties is difficult. This issue exists no matter how a language is described.

WSDL and UDDI are attempts to provide a framework for rigorous business descriptions, but there is no third party to judge the accuracy of the contents. If WSDL and UDDI work for services that can be described without shared context, they will be limited to a subset of problems that do not require human interpretation and business semantics, such as calculating shipping costs and looking up zip codes.

An ebXML registry and repository enables the storing and sharing of business semantic information between parties to allow e-business collaboration. The ebXML registry and repository can be used to store BPSS, CPP, and CPA documents, UML models, and documents that may be needed to support e-business collaboration. Standards such as ebXML and UDDI allow Web services to form the central piece of e-business collaboration. UDDI registries serving as business directories can be used to discover services published in UDDI registries. They can point to ebXML registries for ebXML-related services. The ebXML standard addresses the demands of e-business collaborations on Web services by going beyond service description, service publication, and discovery by providing a framework for establishing the business context and addressing issues such as the following:

- What business process is this Web service interaction part of?
- What are the roles of the various parties involved?
- What are the XML documents exchanged for in the business interactions?
- Who are the parties involved?
- What are the environmental requirements of this business collaboration (in order to succeed)?
- Do negotiation patterns exist for collaborating parties, after service discovery?

What Is the ebXML Registry?

In a marketplace populated by computer companies with proprietary hardware, operating systems, databases, and applications, ebXML gives business users and IT groups control over their lives. The ebXML registry is not bound to a database product or a single hardware vendor, and it is designed to interoperate on all kinds of computers.

An ebXML registry serves as the index and application gateway for a repository to the outside world, and it contains the API that governs how parties interact with the repository. The registry can also be viewed as an API to the database of items that supports e-business with ebXML. Items in the repository are created, updated, or deleted through requests made to the registry.

As defined by the specification, the processes supported by the registry includes:

- A special collaboration protocol agreement between the registry server and registry clients
- A set of functional processes involving the registry server and registry clients
- A set of messages exchanged between a registry client and the registry server as part of a specific business process
- A set of interface mechanisms to support messages and associated query and response mechanisms

- A special collaboration protocol agreement for orchestrating the interaction between registries
- A set of functional processes for registry-to-registry interactions
- A set of error responses and conditions with remedial actions

The ebXML registry serves as a database for sharing of relevant company information for ebXML business transactions, such as corporate capabilities, business process, technical blueprints, order forms, invoices, and so on. The registry makes this information available so that organizations can engage in business process integration to facilitate partnerships and transactions. The registry manages and maintains the shared information as objects in a repository. The registry provides a stable, persistent store of submitted content, which includes XML schema and documents, process descriptions, core components, context descriptions, UML models, information about parties, and even software components. This can be represented as a software stack of services, as shown in Figure 8.2. In the ebXML architecture, businesses could query many repositories with ebXML-compliant registries. The *ebXML registry client* is a client application that interacts with the registry, accessing registry services through defined registry interfaces.

As mentioned in Chapter 4, a registry is an ebXML component that maintains an interface to meta data for a registered item called the *registry entry*. A registry entry submission includes a registry entry list with the objects for submission. The registry entries can reference other objects already registered. Each registry entry has a number of attributes, which include:

Association. Defines the relationship between a registry entry and other objects.

Auditable event. Generates an audit trail for the registry entry, including tracking content associated with registered users.

Classification. Categorizes registry entries, and provide flexibility for variations for classification systems based on industries or markets.

Classification node. Defines a branch in the tree structure for the classification system, and a classification associates the registry entry with the classification node.

External identifier. Identifies the registered item, such as a UCC code.

External link. Offers a way for an object to reference Internet resources outside the registry, such as a schema with an URN that refers to another schema.

Organization. Defines the submitting organization for the registry entry, including references to the parent organization.

Package. Offers a way of grouping registry entries together for managing the group.

APIs that are exposed by registry services for interacting with other applications, such as registry clients, provide access to a registry. In this way, the registry interface serves as an application-to-registry access mechanism. A person interacting with the registry is built as a layer over a registry interface, such as a Web browser. The registry interface is designed to be independent of the underlying network protocol stack, such as HTTP or SMTP over TCP/IP.

The *Registry Information Model* (RIM) provides a high-level blueprint for meta data in the ebXML registry. This can be represented as a software stack of services, as in Figure 8.2, or as a service pyramid, as in Figure 8.3. The elements of the information model represent meta data about the content, not the content itself in the repository. The registry information model defines what types of objects are stored and organized in the registry. The information model is a roadmap to the type of meta data and the relationships between meta data. The registry information model may be mapped to a relational database schema, object database schema, or some other physical schema. For example, a trading partner might use the ebXML registry information model to determine which classes to include in its registry implementation and what attributes and methods these classes may have—and to determine what sort of database schema its registry implementation may need.

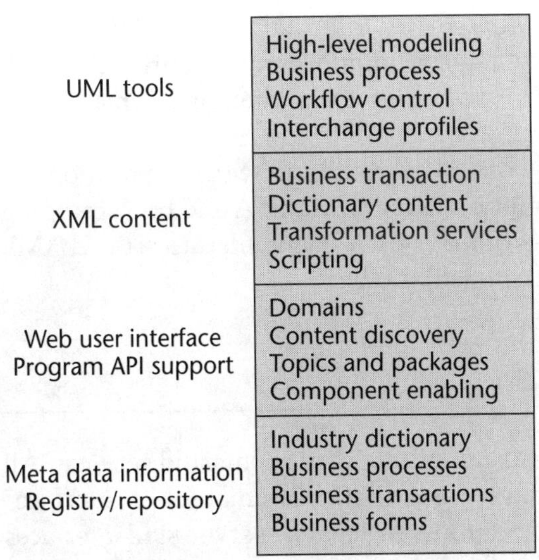

Figure 8.2 The registry as a software stack of services.

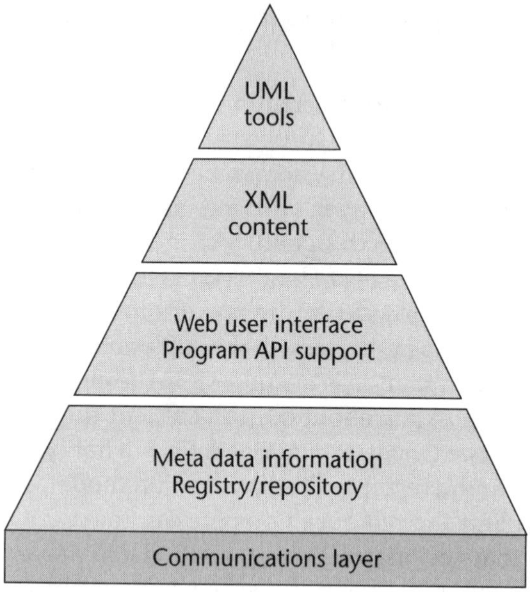

Figure 8.3 The registry as a software service pyramid.

Compliance

According to the *ebXML Registry Services Specification,* a registry implementation complies with the ebXML specification if it meets the following conditions: (1) It supports the ebXML Registry Information Model, (2) it supports the syntax and semantics of the registry interfaces and security, and (3) it supports the ebXML registry DTD. Support of the syntax and semantics of SQL query in the registry is optional.

A registry client implementation complies with the ebXML specification if it meets the following conditions: It supports the ebXML CPA and bootstrapping process, the syntax and the semantics of the registry client interfaces, the ebXML error message DTD, and the ebXML registry DTD.

How the Registry Works

The complete registry system consists of both registry clients and services. All ebXML registry implementations have to support a minimal set of interfaces and corresponding methods as a standard interface. The server-side interfaces are registry service, object manager, and object query manager interfaces. The client-side interface is the registry client interface. The registry applications can be written in a variety of programming language, such as Java, Visual Basic, or C++, to name a few, and may be structured differently depending on the vendor.

There are a few generic objects in the registry design: registry entries, packages, classification nodes, external links, organizations, users, postal addresses, slots (for annotation purposes), and events (for auditing purposes). The registry entry is a basic registry unit for submitting and querying registry objects, containing a crucial reference to the actual document or data. Every repository item is described by a registry entry. For example, a CPP stored in the repository would have a registry entry that tells us how to find the actual CPP stored in the repository.

Registry/Client Communication

The client finds the registry though a transport-specific communication address for the registry, such as a URL or an email address. The choice depends on the communication protocols supported by the registry. If it is HTTP, the client can find the registry by a URL. For example, the client uses the URL of the registry to create a session with the registry. When the client sends a request to the registry, it provides a URL to itself. The registry uses the URL of the client to form a session with the client. For the duration of the session with the registry, messages may be exchanged in both directions. The client can also use the ebXML messaging services to communicate with the registry.

The registry can use a collaboration protocol agreement as a way for the registry client to discover the registry. The collaboration protocol agreement between clients and the registry should describe the interfaces that the registry and the client expose to each other for registry-specific interactions. The collaboration protocol profile describes the party, the role it plays, the services it offers, and the technical details on how those services may be accessed.

An organization can submit objects and query objects using a registry client, as shown in Figure 8.4. The registry and repository supports registration of a business entity, discovery of business partners, configuration of business partner, and exchange of business information. After you discover a service, the collaborating parties need to agree to the terms and conditions of business exchange, which is addressed by ebXML specifications such as business process specification schema, collaboration protocol profile, and collaboration protocol agreement. For example, terms and conditions for the business exchange can include specifying features for the run-time environment, such as nonrepudiation, security, reliability, and message sequence. The ebXML messaging service provides these messaging features as part of the ebXML infrastructure. Messaging communication uses the ebXML messaging services and is not included in the standard registry functionality.

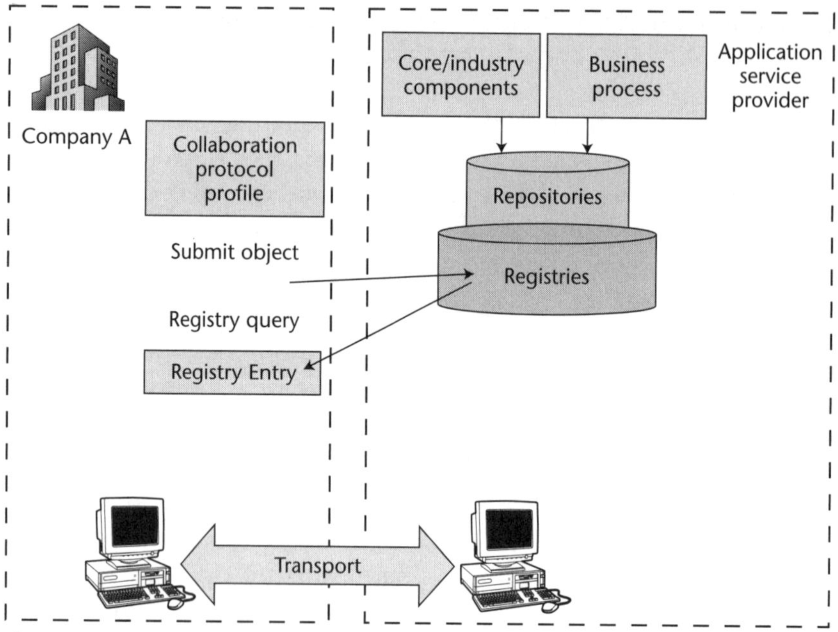

Figure 8.4 A company can submit objects and query objects in a registry.

Registry services may be implemented as a public Web site, as a private Web site hosted by an application service provider, or as a value-added network. For example, suppose two trading partners participate in an exchange hosted by an application service provider. The buyer and seller use the same public registry service provided by a third party. Partners can publish information about their respective business processes via the collaboration protocol profile.

The collaboration protocol agreement is discussed in detail in the next chapter, but basically it works like this: One organization browses the registry classification hierarchy using a registry browser to find its partner. This partner has to meet the organization's criteria based on the collaboration protocol profile in the registry. The two partners can create a collaboration protocol as a basis for ebXML systems interactions. The partners can transact business by posting purchase orders and invoices and arranging shipment and delivery using the ebXML infrastructure.

The registry can be configured in different ways: in a traditional client/server context, peer-to-peer network, or application-to-application. Traditional client/server configurations include using a Web-based application such as a purchasing Web site viewed in Internet Explorer over the Internet, or a specific registry application such as an ebXML browser to access the registry. The registry system can also be used in an application-to-application context, where the registry client resides in a server-side business component such as a purchasing business component. In this configuration there may be no direct user interface or user intervention involved. Instead, the purchasing business component may access the registry in an automated manner to select possible sellers or service providers based on current business needs.

Classification System

A user can browse and traverse the content based on the available registry classification schemes. The registry uses the concept of classification trees, and each branch in the tree is known as a *node*. The starting point in the tree is known as the *root node*. This hierarchical structure is useful for creating a directory of people, places, and things. For example, possible classification systems in a registry include an alphabetical listing by company name, a geographical listing by location, and a numerical listing by telephone number. A collection of terms and definitions relevant to business enterprise forms the enterprise ontology. For example, Figure 8.5 shows a classification tree for different areas in the world, with a root node called geography, and subnodes such as Asia, Europe, or North America.

The ebXML repository stores the connections between an industry language and the core components. A unique identifier (UID) is assigned to each core component. The repository for an industry contains the industry-specific components in addition to the standard core components. Specific industries relate their specific semantic terms to core components. For example, the same core component identifier would apply to an airline passenger, the buyer of a gift, the shipper of a package, and the guest at a hotel. Each repository for the industry or company would store the common identifier and relate it to its specific industry terminology—passenger, buyer, shipper, and guest. Registry items such as core components are assigned UID keys when they are registered in an ebXML registry. These UID keys can be incorporated in XML syntax. These mechanisms can include a reference method, an object-based reference compatible with W3C schema, or a data type based reference. A UID reference is important, since it provides a language-neutral reference mechanism.

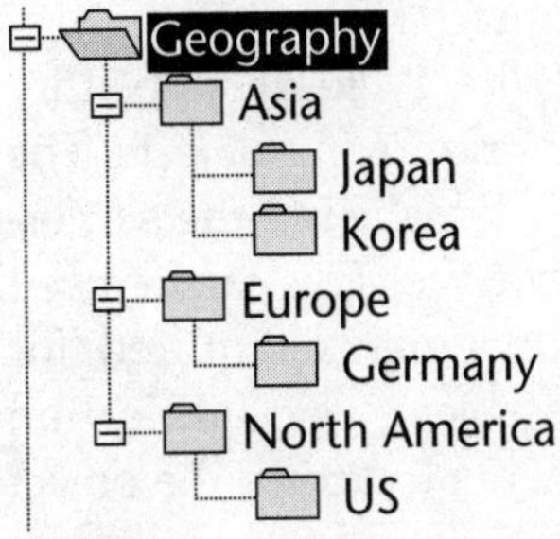

Figure 8.5 A sample classification for places.

Universally Unique ID (UUID)

The *Universally Unique Identifier* (UUID) is assigned to all items within the registry system as a lookup key. This ensures that registry entries are truly globally unique. If a system queries a registry for a UUID, only a single result is retrieved. All objects in the registry have a unique ID based on the UUID, and all conform to the to the format of a uniform resource name (URN) that specifies a DCE 128-bit UUID (see the "References" section for more details). For example, this is a valid UUID:

```
urn:uuid:a2345678-1234-1234-123456789012
```

The registry typically generates the ID for submitted objects. The client may also supply the ID, which must conform to the format of the URN with a DCE 128-bit UUID. If the client supplies the ID, the registry uses it as the ID attribute of the object in the registry. If the ID is not globally unique, the registry issues an invalid ID error. The registry can generate a universally unique id using the DCE 128-bit UUID generation algorithm. Objects can reference other objects using the ID attribute of an object.

Managing Objects in a Registry

Registry services exist to create, modify, and delete registry items and their meta data. As mentioned in Chapter 4, the ebXML registry can contain anything encoded in a binary or text form and has no deep knowledge of ebXML objects. Objects in a registry include a collaboration protocol document, schemas, core component descriptions, and other ebXML documents.

A registry object has four stages in its life cycle: submission, approval, deprecation, and removal. Figure 8.6 shows the typical life cycle of a repository item. The registry attaches XML attributes as meta data to the object for classifying and managing the object. The registry is based on a generic object design, which assumes as little as possible about the objects. Typical objects would be CPPs, CPAs, schemas, specifications, and other documents. Data and documents can be submitted and retrieved as a registry entry. Objects are submitted to the registry as an ebXML message, using the registry DTD.

The *object management service* (OMS) manages the life cycle of repository items, such as submitting objects, approving objects, or removing objects. The registry client can manage the life cycle of repository items using the server-side functionality defined by the object management service. This can be used with all types of repository items, such as XML documents required for ebXML business processes, as well as such meta data objects as classification and association. The *object manager interface* allows clients to access the object management service implementation.

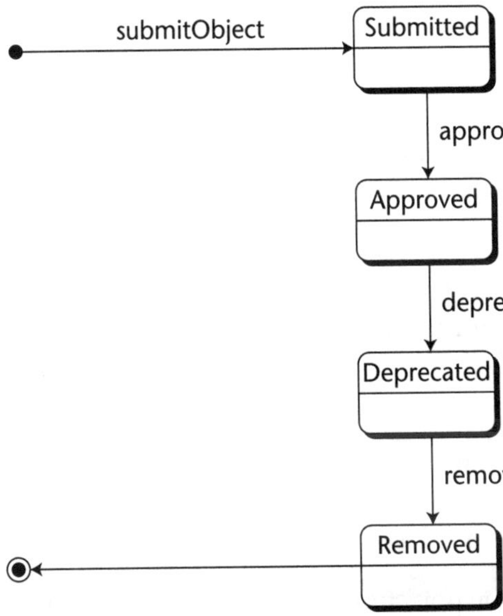

Figure 8.6 Life cycle of a repository item.
Source: "ebXML Registry Specification"

A repository item has a set of standard meta data, defined as attributes of the registry class and its subclasses. These attributes are not part of the actual repository item and catalog descriptive information about the repository item. XML tags called `<ExtrinsicObject>` and `<IntrinsicObject>` encapsulate all object meta data attributes as XML attributes.

The next sections describe the registry service protocols, which perform certain registry actions on repository objects. The registry service protocols include submit objects, approve objects, deprecate objects, remove objects, add slots, and remove slots. If it succeeds, the registry sends the registry response with a status of "success" back to the client. If it fails, the registry sends the response of "failure."

Submit Objects. The registry client can submit one or more repository items to the repository using the object manager on behalf of a submitting organization. The submission process involves the following steps: (1) A submit object request that includes the registry entry list is sent. (2) The registry entry list specifies extrinsic objects or other registry entries such as classifications, associations, external links, or packages. (3) An extrinsic object provides required meta data about the content being submitted to the registry. The extrinsic object is a meta data attribute that is separated from the repository item itself.

Add Slots. Slots can act as temporary storage for adding meta data specified by the user to the registry entries. In this way, they provide a dynamic mechanism for extending registry entries.

Remove Slots. A client can use the object manager to remove slots to a previously submitted registry entry.

Approve Object. A client can approve one or more previously submitted repository items using the object manager. After the repository item is approved, it will become available for use by business parties, such as for the assembly of new CPA/CPP.

Deprecate Objects. A client can deprecate one or more previously submitted repository items using the object manager. A *deprecated object* cannot have new references, such as associations, classifications, and external links. However, existing references to a deprecated object are not affected.

Remove Objects. A client can use the object manager to remove one or more Registry Entry instances and/or repository items. The Remove Objects request is sent by a client to remove registry entry instances and/or repository items. The Remove Objects request includes an XML attribute called *deletion scope*.

Delete Repository Item Only. This deletion scope means the request should delete the repository items for the specified registry entries, but not delete the specified registry entries. This ensures references to the registry entries are valid.

Delete All. This deletion scope means that the request should delete both the registry entry and the repository item for the specified registry entries. The registry entry can be removed using a remove objects request with this deletion scope only if all references, such as associations, classifications, and external links to a registry entry have been removed. Otherwise, removing a registry entry with references raises an invalid request error.

As shown in Table 8.1, the registry uses abstract interfaces instead of concrete classes with attributes to provide an abstract definition without implying any specific implementation. Specifically, they do not imply that objects in the registry will be accessed directly via these interfaces. Objects in the registry are accessed via interfaces. Each `get` method in every interface has an explicit indication of the attribute name that the `get` method maps to. For example, the `getName` method maps to an attribute named `name`.

Table 8.1 Registry Interface and Methods

INTERFACE	METHODS	METHOD DESCRIPTIONS
RegistryService—Can be used by registry clients to discover service-specific interfaces implemented by the registry.		
	`GetObjectManager ( )`	Returns the Object Manager interface implemented by the registry service. This interface provides the publishing interface to the registry.
	`GetObjectQueryManager ( )`	Returns the ObjectQueryManager interface implemented by the registry service. This interface provides the inquiry interface to the registry.
ObjectManager—Can be used by registry clients to submit objects, to classify and associate objects, and to deprecate and remove objects. (Implements the object life cycle management functionality of the registry.)		
	`ApproveObjects (ApproveObjectRequest req)`	Approves one or more previously submitted objects.
	`DeprecateObject (DeprecateObjectRequest req)` [V1.1 will fix a bug and provide a missing UndeprecateObjects-Request]	Deprecates one or more previously submitted objects.

(continues)

Table 8.1 Registry Interface and Methods *(Continued)*

INTERFACE	METHODS	METHOD DESCRIPTIONS
	`RemoveObjects (RemoveObjectRequest req)`	Removes one or more previously submitted objects from the registry.
	`submitObjects (SubmitObjectsRequest req)`	Submits one or more objects and possibly related meta data such as Associations and Classifications.
	`addSlots (AddSlotsRequest req)`	Adds slots to one or more registry entries.
	`removeSlots (RemoveSlotsRequest req)`	Removes specified slots from one or more registry entries.
ObjectQueryManager– Can be used by registry clients to invoke the methods on this interface to perform browse and drill-down queries or ad hoc queries on registry content. (Implements the Object Query management service.)		
	`GetClassificationTree (GetClassificationTree-Request req)`	Returns the ClassificationNode-Tree under the ClassificationNode specified in GetClassificationTree Request.
	`GetClassificationObjects (GetClassifiedObjects-Request req)`	Returns a collection of references to RegistryEntries classified under specified ClassificationItem.

INTERFACE	METHODS	METHOD DESCRIPTIONS
	`getContent ( )`	Returns the content (repository item) catalogued by the RegistryEntry instances specified. The response includes all the content specified in the request as additional payloads within the response message.
	`GetClassificationNodes (GetRootClassification-NodesRequest req)`	Returns all root *ClassificationNodes* that match the namePattern attribute in *GetRoot-ClassificationNodes Request* request.
	`submitAdhocQuery (AdhocQueryRequest req)`	Submits an ad hoc query request.
RegistryClient—The client provides this interface when creating a connection to the registry. It provides the methods that are used by the registry to deliver asynchronous responses to the client. Note that a client need not provide a Registry-Client interface if the CPA between the client and the registry does not support asynchronous responses. The registry sends all asynchronous responses to operations to the onResponse method.		

(continues)

Table 8.1 Registry Interface and Methods *(Continued)*

INTERFACE	METHODS	METHOD DESCRIPTIONS
	onResponse (RegistryResponse resp)	Notifies client of the response sent by registry to previously submitted request.

The ebXML registry has server-side interfaces, which are the registry service interface, the object manager interface, and the object query manager interface. An ebXML registry client has the registry client interface as the principal client-side interface. The registry client can only invoke one method on a specified interface for a given request to a registry.

Searching for Objects in a Registry

For people interacting with a registry such as using a Web browser, certain types of queries can be used to facilitate the discovery process. The registry has a searching capability, using XML to send requests from the client to the registry. This process involves sending an XML document using ebXML messages or using a SQL client to query the registry server. The query syntax used for the registry access is independent of the physical implementation of the back-end system. An ebXML registry has to support both "browse and drill-down query" and "filtered query" capabilities. Another optional search capability is to use Structured Query Language (SQL).

A typical search using XML uses the registry entry query to search and retrieve registry entries. The filter narrows the search criteria, such as organization filter, and returns matches for a specific organization. For example, suppose Big Distributor wants to find Acme Hardware in the registry. This query returns a set of registry entry IDs for items submitted by organizations with the string "Acme Hardware" in their name:

```
<RegistryEntryQuery>
<OrganizationFilter>
name CONTAINS "Acme Hardware"
</OrganizationFilter>
</RegistryEntryquery>
```

For example, by restricting the registry entry filter for only approved items, the search results do not return any registry entry IDs for superceded, replaced, deprecated, or withdrawn items:

```
<RegistryEntryFilter>
status EQUAL "Approved"
</RegistryEntryFilter>
```

Within a query to the registry, we can construct expressions using operators such as OR, AND, and EQUALS. For example, a purchasing manager, using a registry client application, wants to identify all classification nodes that have some given keyword as part of their name or description. The following query identifies all registry classification nodes that contain the keyword "transistor" as part of their name or as part of their description:

```
<RegistryEntryQuery>
<RegistryEntryFilter>
ObjectType="ClassificationNode" AND (name CONTAINS "transistor" OR
description CONTAINS "transistor")
</RegistryEntryFilter>
</RegistryEntryQuery>
```

Using SQL Queries

Using SQL queries to retrieve information requires specific rules for the SQL query syntax, which is a subset of the SQL-92 standard. (See "Structured Query Language—FIPS PUB 127-2" at www.itl.nist.gov/fipspubs/fip127-2.htm for definitions of the terms.) Given the central role played by the RegistryEntry interface, the schema for the SQL query defines a special view called *registry entry* that allows a query against all registry entries regardless of their actual type or table name.

For example, the result will be the set of IDs for all registry entries whose name contains the word "Acme" and that have a version greater than 1.3:

```
SELECT id FROM RegistryEntry WHERE name LIKE '%Acme%' AND
     objectType = 'ExtrinsicObject' AND
     majorVersion >= 1 AND
     (majorVersion >= 2 OR minorVersion > 3);
```

Classification nodes are identified by their ID. However, the nodes may also be identified as a path attribute that specifies an XPATH expression. To get the collection of root Classification Nodes, we can use a SQL query syntax. For example, this query returns all classification nodes that have their parent attribute set to null.

```
SELECT cn.id FROM ClassificationNode cn WHERE parent IS NULL
```

Registry Security

An ebXML registry has to meet requirements to protect the integrity of its contents, authenticate the identity of authorized users, and control access based on defined roles. In ebXML version 1.0, a minimal approach for registry security is based on the philosophy that "any known entity can publish content and anyone can view published content." It is assumed that most registrars may not have resources to validate the content submitted to them. The ebXML registry will generally accept content from any client if a recognized certificate authority digitally signs the content. Submitting organizations do not have to register prior to submitting content. The minimal integrity that the registry must provide is to ensure that content submitted by a submitting organization is maintained in the registry. The registry makes it possible to identify the submitting organization for any registry content.

To ensure integrity, the registry content requires that all submitted content must be signed by the registry client. The signature on the submitted content ensures that the content has not been tampered with. The registry must be able to authenticate the identity of the principal associated with client requests. Authentication is required to identify the ownership of content, as well as to identify what privileges a principal can be assigned with respect to the specific objects in the registry. The registry assigns the default content owner role to the submitting organization at the time of content submission. Clients that browse the registry need not use certificates. The registry assigns the default registry role as "guest" for clients without authentication

The registry must perform authentication on a per request basis. From a security point of view, all messages are independent, and there is no concept of a session encompassing multiple messages or conversations. Session support may be added as an optimization feature in future versions of this specification. The registry must implement a credential-based authentication mechanism based on digital certificates and signatures. The registry uses the certificate from the signature to authenticate the user. Message headers may be signed by the sending messaging service. The payload signature can also be used to authenticate the identity of the requesting client. Message payloads exchanged between clients and the registry can be encrypted during transmission. All content submitted to the registry may be read by a client. Therefore, the registry must be able to decrypt any submitted content after it has been received and prior to storing it in its repository.

The registry creates policy for access control that grants the default permissions to registry users based on their assigned role. The specification defines the following roles in the registry:

Content owner. This is the user that submits content to the registry and has access to all methods on the registry dealing with that content.

Registry administrator. This is a superuser responsible for the management and operation of the registry and who has access to all methods on all registry objects.

Registry guest. This is a user of the registry that has not been authenticated and has read-only access to browse the content.

The registry has to implement the default access control policy, which is as follows: Anyone can publish content, but needs to be authenticated. Anyone can access the content without requiring authentication. The content owner has access to all methods for registry objects dealing with the content. The registry administrator has access to all methods on all registry objects.

Summary

The registry facilitates business partnerships and transactions by introducing standard means of sharing documents and relevant information for transactions. The registry simplifies the consistent exchange of information for business transactions, such as semantic and technical documents. A repository simplifies the process of wading through multiple data formats or proprietary database systems. As a shared semantic registry, the ebXML registry is a cornerstone for shared context in Web services for enterprise application integration. This enables a community of interest around industry semantics, which, in turn, coalesces in whatever forum is the most appropriate to foster new vocabularies, standards, and technologies that will enhance and enable the Web services model.

Web services work well where the parties involved already agree about mutual interests and have the framework for cooperating or collaborating. Web services by itself can automate private, previously negotiated conversations. To move from the private conversations to public and universally interoperable services, Web services needs contractual data (as represented by a collaboration protocol agreement) and a shared semantic registry (as represented by an ebXML registry). In this chapter, we found that the ebXML registry makes possible the idea of unknown but perfectly described capabilities available on the Internet. The registry extends the semantic capabilities of EDI to the Internet, which involves such capabilities as providing remote database lookups, lowering costs in supply chain management, and providing the developer with easier ways to link applications together. The ebXML registries reach beyond Internet business listings and search directories that provide specific, but limited value to an organization. Registries solve the shared discovery problems facing small and large businesses, marketplaces, and technology providers. Registry standards are a major advance, involving cross-industry efforts driven by platform providers, software developers, marketplace operators, and business leaders. The data stored in the registry is for automated application-to-application communication based on Web services. The registry provides a central way to get information about standards and is a single point of access to all markets of opportunity. In the next chapter, we will explore the collaboration protocol agreement and profiles for sharing basic system-level information between ebXML systems.

CHAPTER

9

Trading Partner Profiles and Agreements

"ebXML has opened a whole new era of enterprise alignment by providing a standard way to describe and exchange profiles, agreements, and processes, as well as enabling the mechanics of process alignment between partners. EDIFECS sees this as critical in enabling trading partners to go beyond information alignment into collaborative supply chain optimization."

–Sunny Singh, CEO and founder of EDIFECS

AREAS COVERED IN THIS CHAPTER

- **Interbusiness electronic interactions**
- **The electronic trading partner agreement**
  - **tpaML overview**
- **Collaboration protocol profiles and agreement (CPP/CPA)**
- **Inside the CPA**
  - **Using the CPA**
- **Inside the CPP**

The foundation of the data interchange technologies involves a common language and an electronic contract. The common language, such as XML, can be employed by existing or potential trading partners to specify how they will interact. The electronic contract uses this common language to define and enforce the interaction protocols. In addition, B2B standards such as ebXML set a standard architecture and semantics for business interactions.

What agreement should trading partners have for data interchange? IBM proposed and prototyped the *electronic trading partner agreements,* which define the system level agreement between trading partners. It is a key element for interoperability among B2B system implementations. There is no business information in the TPA, but it contains crucial technical configurations for systems involved in a data interchange. The *trading partner agreement Markup Language* (tpaML) is an XML grammar for expressing electronic trading partner agreements. IBM Research has also designed the *business-to-business protocol framework* (BPF) as a run-time framework to deploy business protocols expressed in tpaML.

The collaboration protocol integrated the ebXML business collaborations (see Chapter 5) with other parts of the ebXML infrastructure. The *collaboration*

THE NEED FOR A STANDARD

According to the U.S. Department of Labor, over half of all activities within a company are related to trading partner interactions. Improving these interactions will change how a company operates, such as reengineering internal processes based on trading dynamics. Within the e-business environment, companies face challenges when integrating their businesses. This integration may be within the enterprise or in the supply chain relationships between many different trading partners. The Web commerce applications are often not integrated to the back-end systems. These internal sets of applications involve complex enterprise resource planning (ERP) and business application systems and multiple operating systems. A solution to this increasing complexity is the development of a shared standard infrastructure with system-level agreements. This provides a technical platform based on open standards, which streamlines key areas of setting up business between trading partners.

Taking the best integration practices, the goal is to create a standards-based infrastructure for trading partners to negotiate an agreement, configure the IT systems with the agreement, and interchange business information. Following are the general principles in designing an agreement between systems in a data interchange:

- ***Open solution.* Partners should not be forced to adopt a common set of hardware, operating systems, middleware, or application software.**
- ***Loose coupling.* Partners should have business processes that are independent of the others.**
- ***Secure.* Partners should have a security framework of control and monitoring, with defined sequences of actions, access, and authentication schemes.**

protocol profile and agreement (CPP/CPA) documents define the system-level parameters for trading partners to transact business in ebXML. This includes partner identification, communications protocol, definition of requests and responses, and security for message exchanges including encryption, authentication, and nonrepudiation.

This chapter is based on information in the *Collaboration-Protocol Profile and Agreement Specification version 1.0* at http://www.ebxml.org/specs/ebCCP.pdf. The information about the TPA is based on the IBM Research technical paper in the *IBM Systems Journal* called "Business-to-Business Integration with tpaML and a Business-to-Business Protocol Framework."

Interbusiness Electronic Interactions

For electronic interactions between businesses, EDI has been the electronic document interchange standard between companies. Increased automation of business processes within a business organization leads to automation of B2B interactions. The automation of business internal processes and integrating application components involve issues such as privacy, autonomy, differences in software platforms, and managing complex interactions.

Companies will implement B2B trading capabilities by modifying their business processes, integrating with external networks, and incorporating infrastructure and process standards using middleware and XML. Component architectures such as Common Object Request Broker Architecture (CORBA) and Enterprise JavaBeans (EJB) provide middleware for integrating application components written in different languages. The CORBA application component interfaces to other components written in a suitable middleware integration language, such as the interface definition language (IDL).

One way for a system to interface with another is to use a common software component called a *software bus*. This requires a shared underlying middleware for distributed applications spanning organizational boundaries. Setting up such a common software bus requires tight coupling of the business partners' software platforms. A software bus may involve complex extended transaction models, which are not appropriate for such business-to-business interactions. The protocols involve tight coupling of operational states across business applications. The application components in an organization may lock up resources in another organization for an extended period of time. This results in loss of autonomy. Hence, the software bus approach is not appropriate as a general solution to the automation of B2B interactions.

Another approach is to use a specific request protocol or standard contract for systems interactions in electronic commerce, supply chain management, and other applications. Contracts describe legally enforceable terms and conditions in all kinds of interactions between people and organizations, such as employment, real estate purchases, and industrial supply arrangements. In e-commerce, the business terms and conditions are covered by a legal contract for the exchange of value between parties.

The Electronic Trading Partner Agreement

A *trading partner agreement* (TPA) is a contract defining both the legal terms and conditions and the technical specifications for both partners in the trading relationship. The American Bar Association published a model TPA for EDI purchase orders, which was adapted to other transactions. The model TPA document had (1) EDI communication terms and (2) underlying trade terms and conditions. Programmers incorporated the TPAs as the part of the technical specifications for the trading system.

However, the TPA may be misinterpreted in usage, resulting in implementation errors in the trading system. By contrast, an electronic TPA automates this process and can be used without human intervention or interpretation. Informal TPAs in EDI often include terms and conditions related to the application issues. A typical paper-based TPA in EDI for purchasing might include business terms such as price lists and delivery time. By contrast, an electronic TPA deals specifically with the technical issues.

The electronic TPA expresses the terms and conditions describing the electronic interactions between businesses. The TPA is the data interchange contract, covering IT procedures ranging from communication protocols to business protocols. Written in human languages that are then converted into code by programmers, the TPA embodies the terms and conditions at the system level as configuration information and code at each trading site. This agreement contains the rules of interaction between the parties and is independent of the internal processes at each party. Each trading system uses the configuration information in the electronic TPA to ensure that the systems are compatible and properly set up. An electronic TPA can be automatically generated at each server. The electronic TPA quickly converts the terms and conditions to code and ensures that the code at each site precisely reflects the actual terms and conditions. It also facilitates negotiation of terms and conditions for certain situations, such as the quick and easy setup of B2B deals.

The essence of the electronic TPA can be characterized in this dialogue between two trading systems:

System 1: "I want to send and receive business transactions with your system. Here is my system profile."

System 2: "OK, but we both have to agree to these terms and conditions for exchanging information. Both our systems have to be configured based on this agreement. We can begin after confirming your agreement."

System 1: "My system is set up according to the agreement. Here is a proposed business transaction..."

The rules specified by the electronic TPA are independent of the business processes at either party. A technical description of the terms and conditions from the TPA is expressed in an XML document, which configures each IT systems to operate under the agreement rules.

The information in the TPA is not a *complete* description of the application, only a *simplified* description of the interactions between the parties. The application business logic still has to handle the complete interaction and support back-end functionality. For example, the TPA may have a request, such as "reserve airline ticket." This ticket reservation functionality needs to be designed, coded, and installed on the server. That functionality may use various middleware functions and back-end processes. The actual implementation details are not visible to the other party through the TPA. The TPA design ensures that each party has complete independence from the other party. This applies for the implementation details, the business processes, and the back-end functions, such as database, transaction monitors, and ERP.

TPA properties include its name, partner names, starting and ending dates, roles, and other parameters. Communication and security properties include communication addresses and protocol such as HTTP and SMTP, authentication and nonrepudiation protocols, and certificate parameters. Error handling rules are various conditions related to error conditions, such as the maximum waiting time for the response to a request. The application program or higher-level application framework handles higher-level issues, such as processing the content of the message payloads.

Now that we've discussed the basics of the electronic TPA, let's look at the actual TPA language, the Trading Partner Agreement Markup Language (tpaML).

tpaML Overview

As mentioned, the electronic TPA is a generated XML document. The TPA document is described by an XML document type definition (DTD) or XML schema document, which defines the tree structure of the TPA tags and XML syntactic rules. Some TPA semantics defined in the tpaML specification are outside the DTD or XML schema, but an authoring tool uses these additional semantics to create a valid TPA. tpaML can support any document format using plug-in parsers and document generators, including EDI messages or XML.

Overall Structure

Each of these tags is the top level of a subelement (subtree of tags). This code snippet of XML shows the overall structure of the TPA:

```
<TPA>
 <TPAInfo> <!-- TPA preamble -->
  ... <!--TPAname, role definitions, participants, etc.-->
 </TPAInfo>
 <Transport>
  ... <!--communication and transport security information-->
 </Transport>
 <DocExchange>
  ... <!--document-exchange and message security information-->
 </DocExchange>
 <BusinessProtocol>
  <ServiceInterface> <!-- for each provider-->
    ... <!--Action definitions etc.-->
  </ServiceInterface>
 </Business Protocol>
</TPA>
```

The `<BusinessProtocol>`, `<DocExchange>`, and `<Transport>` sections describe the processing of a unit of business conversation. As a communication model, the business protocol, document exchange, and transport sections are structured as stacked layers.

Business Protocol Layer

The business protocol layer defines the heart of the business agreement between the trading partners: the services that parties to the TPA can request and sequencing rules for the order of requests. This layer is the interface between the TPA actions and the business application functionality. The `<BusinessProtocol>` tag contains all the business protocol definitions for the business application. The `<ServiceInterface>` tag defines the set of supported service requests for each party. Each service interface contains some overall parameters and the action menu. An example of the business protocol syntax is in this code snippet:

```
<BusinessProtocol>
 <ServiceInterface> <!--one or two-->
  ... <!-- action menu and other definitions-->
 </ServiceInterface>
</BusinessProtocol>
 Action definition ...
<Action>
 <Request>
  <RequestName> PurchaseOrderRequest</RequestName>
  <RequestMessage>PurchaseOrderRequestMessage</RequestMessage>
 </Request>
 <Response>
  <ResponseName>PurchaseOrderResponse</ResponseName>
 </Response>
```

```
<ResponseServiceTime>
 <ServiceTime>3600</ServiceTime>
  <!-- 1-hour maximum time -->
</ResponseServiceTime>
</Action>
```

The <RequestMessage> tag defines the format of the business document in the message. The value may be the URL of the DTD or XML schema for XML documents. The value may be a keyword for an entry in a local dictionary. Sequencing rules specify the order of action requests. For example, the initial action is specified in this code snippet:

```
<StartEnabled>
 <RequestName>action_name</RequestName>
  <!--one for each action allowed as the initial action-->
</StartEnabled>
```

There is one <StartEnabled> tag for each party. One of the actions may be invoked as the first action in a conversation on that server. Within each action definition, a sequencing rule specifies which actions are allowed and not allowed. The sequencing rules are defined in this code snippet:

```
<Sequencing>
 <Enable> <!--actions permitted after this one-->
  <RequestName>name_of_action</RequestName>
   ...
 </Enable>
 <Disable> <!--actions not permitted after this one-->
  <RequestName>name_of_action</RequestName> ...
 </Disable>
</Sequencing>
```

The <Enable> tag specifies which actions are permissible following the action whose definition contains the <Sequencing> tag. The <Disable> tag specifies which actions are no longer allowed after this action. The application framework handles many error conditions, and this is not specified in general in the TPA.

Document Exchange Layer

The document exchange layer defines properties of the documents exchanged by the parties. Any document formats agreed to by the two parties may be used. The document exchange layer accepts a document from the business protocol layer. It can encrypt, add a digital signature, and pass the document to the transport layer for transmission to the other party. The document exchange layer includes the message encoding, such as BASE64, whether or not duplicate messages should be detected, and the message-security definition. Message security may be either or both of digital envelope (symmetric encryption using certificate-based encryption to exchange the shared secret key) and nonrepudiation using certificates.

Transport Layer

The transport layer is responsible for message delivery using the selected communication and security protocols. The communication properties define the system-to-system communication used in the application. These details include the protocol to be used by both parties, such as HTTP and SMTP, each party's address parameters, maximum network delay, and other parameters. An example of the definition is the <Communication> tag for HTTP:

```
<Communication>
 <HTTP>
  <Version>version</Version>
  <HTTPNode> <!--One for each party-->
   <OrgName Partyname=name/>
   <HTTPAddress>
    <LogOnURL>url</LogOnURL>
    <RequestURL>url</RequestURL>
    <ResponseURL>url</ResponseURL>
   </HTTPAddress>
  </HTTPNode>
  <NetworkDelay>time</NetworkDelay> <!--Optional-->
 </HTTP>
</Communication>
```

The transport security tags define the security protocols to be used in transporting messages. Protocols are defined for encryption and authentication. Encryption information includes the name of the encryption protocol and various parameters defining the certificates. Authentication information includes the type of authentication; such as password or certificate; the protocol, such as Secure Sockets Layer (SSL); and the certificate parameters.

Delivery Channels

A delivery channel consists of one transport definition and one document exchange definition. The TPA may include multiple transport and document exchange definitions, which can be grouped into delivery channels with different characteristics. Each request may specify a particular delivery channel, allowing the partners to specify a different path for each message. This design allows dynamic selection of a delivery channel for each message based on conditions such as path congestion and failures.

Role

Roles are defined generic terms, such as buyer and seller. A specific TPA substitutes specific parties for the role parameters. The identification defines the organization names of the parties and contact information, such as email and postal service addresses. It can define an outside arbitrator to be used for settling disputes. The role definitions are included under the <TPAInfo> tag. Each <RoleDefn> tag supplies a pair of role parameters and the actual name. The <RoleName> tag defines the name of each role. The <RolePlayer> tag has a blank value in a TPA template and the name of an actual party in a specific TPA. For example, in the following, the roles are defined for a TPA between a retailer (Acme Hardware) and distributor (Big Distributor) in the tags under <Role>:

```
<Role>
 <RoleDefn> <!--one or more-->
  <RoleName>hardware retailer</RoleName>
  <RolePlayer>Acme Hardware</RolePlayer>
 </RoleDefn>
 <RoleDefn>
  <RoleName>distributor</RoleName>
  <RolePlayer>Big Distributor</RolePlayer>
 </RoleDefn>
</Role>
```

Collaboration Protocol Profiles and Agreement

In ebXML terms, *collaboration* refers to the business process for exchanging messages or establishing other services. The *collaborative protocol* refers to the initial system request or protocol between ebXML systems, based on the more generic TPA and tpaML concepts. As mentioned earlier in the chapter, the original tpaML technology IBM submitted to ebXML for consideration was developed for a general business model called the business-to-business protocol framework (BPF). The implementation was based on proprietary IBM technology, such as WebSphere and Net.Commerce. The ebXML work initially focused on the TPA document. ebXML uses some but not all of the details in the trading partner profiles and agreements. ebXML renamed the concept as *collaboration protocol profile and agreement* because it describes the trading partner capabilities at the system interface level. The collaboration protocol profile and agreement are derived from specific EDI application functionality based on the X12 838 Trading-Partner Profile used in a more automated way of setting up trading relationships in ebXML.

The so-called "protocol" in ebXML is more of a system interface than a communication protocol. In a strict technical sense, the collaboration protocol is not really a protocol, such as HTTP or FTP, but a data structure used at run time to configure systems for data interchange. In the collaboration protocol, the system uses XML documents for company system profiles and system-level agreements between trading partners. This collaboration protocol can be deployed in many scenarios, such as using a peer-peer or client/server architecture.

Mentioned earlier in the book the *collaboration protocol profile* (CPP) describes the company capabilities, such as the supported business processes, transport, security, and messaging protocols. The profile defines the functional and technical support for business processes and roles for the trading partner. A trading partner can express the business processes and business service interface requirements in a way that can be universally understood by other trading partners. Potential trading partners can publish information about their supported business processes and specific technical details about their data interchange capabilities. The XML document is governed by a DTD or schema that specifies the ebXML semantic rules for the CPP.

A *collaboration protocol agreement* (CPA) defines the system-level agreement for data interchange between the trading partners. This is in the form of an agreement documenting the terms from the intersection of the CPPs of the trading partners. The information content of a CPA is similar to the IT specifications included in paper-based TPA documents in EDI. The CPAs do not include legal terms and conditions of a business agreement, which should be defined in the actual business transaction itself. The XML document is governed by a DTD or schema that specifies the ebXML semantic rules for the CPA.

Inside the Collaboration Protocol Agreement

The CPA is an electronic agreement between trading partners, which defines the terms and conditions for document interchange. As an electronic document in XML, it is processed by a computer system for setting up and executing the information exchange. The CPA defines mutual technical capabilities for the ebXML business collaboration. The ebXML systems in both trading partners are configured to use identical copies of the CPA. The definitions in the CPP/CPA specification define only the basic rules. Although the CPA/CPP specification covers the general issues in creating a CPA from two CPPs, it does not specify an actual algorithm, and it leaves the implementation details to software vendors and application developers. A software developer can build a CPP/CPA authoring tool to understand both the semantics of the CPP/CPA and the XML syntax to automatically generate the code, enforce its rules, and interface with the back-end processes.

The intent of the CPA is to provide a system-level agreement that can be understood by people and enforced by computers. A CPA describes all the valid, visible, and enforceable interactions between the parties, and how to execute the interactions. The agreement is independent of the internal processes executed at each party. Each party executes its own internal processes and interfaces according to the business process specification. The CPA does not expose details of internal processes to the other party. The CPA can be formed from the CPPs of the parties involved. The resulting CPA contains only those elements that are in common between the two parties. The two parties then negotiate the parameters to produce a final CPA.

The CPA can be viewed as a result of narrowing subsets. The outermost scope relates to all of the capabilities that a trading partner *can* support, with a subset of what a trading partner *will* actually support. CPA is derived through a mutual negotiation. This narrows the options of what the trading partners *can do* as defined in the individual CPPs into what the trading partners *will do* as defined in the mutual CPA.

Trading partners may register their CPAs in the registry. The CPA can be used by a software application to configure the technical details of conducting e-business in ebXML. A CPA adjusts the business service interface to a set of parameters agreed to by all trading partners in the process, defining a specific business process and its requirements. Essentially a snapshot of the messaging services and the business processes information from the trading partners, a CPA is negotiated after the discovery and retrieval phase. If any parameters contained within the accepted CPA change after the agreement has been executed, a new CPA has to be negotiated again.

The information in the CPA is used to configure the partners' systems to enable exchange of messages in the course of performing the selected business collaboration. Typically, the software that exchanges messages and otherwise supports the interactions between the parties is middleware that can support any selected business. This software may be the ebXML message service handler.

A CPA defines a *conversation* between the trading partners. A unit of business under the CPA, a conversation is a set of related business transactions in the form of message exchange. Many conversations may be running concurrently. Each transaction is a request message from one party and response message from the other party. The CPA may reference more than one business process specification (Process-Specification) document, with each business process specification defining a distinct type of conversation.

The messages in a conversation may be interchanged synchronously or asynchronously. It is up to each IT infrastructure to ensure that the message exchanges adhere to the rules of the CPA. Each party is responsible for maintaining the relationship between messages within a conversation, which is called the *conversation state*. The ebXML business process specification defines the business process model, schema, and patterns. A party is also responsible for its own business process implementations upon receipt of a request message and for generating an appropriate response.

The CPA execution instance represents a single long-running conversation. In the simplest applications, there are two parties involved: a server and a client. For example, in a travel application, a travel agency uses a client and an airline company hosts a server. The airline can ask the travel agency for information about a traveler or itinerary. The parties may exchange roles. The CPA defines the interactions between the travel agent and a hotel company. This process starts where the traveler makes different reservations, continues throughout the check-in processes during the trip, and ends when the traveler checks out at the last stop. The server includes the middleware that supports communication, execution of the CPA functions, interfacing to back-end processes, and logging the interactions for purposes such as audit and recovery. The middleware may support a conversation. To configure the systems for operations, the information in the CPA and Process-Specification documents at each site is configured in the system.

The CPA describes the messaging service and the requirements for business processes mutually agreed to by the trading partners. The CPA includes the following key information, such as overall properties, identification, communication, document exchange, security, roles, business transactions, and comments.

Overall properties. These contain information relating to the overall CPA, such as the duration of the agreement.

Identification. This identifies the parties to the agreement, including nominated contacts with their addresses, as well as other party identifiers, such as registered DUNS numbers.

Communication. This identifies supported communication protocols, including parameters such as timeouts, to ensure interoperability between the parties.

Document exchange. This establishes the messaging protocol to be used in exchanging business documents and includes a description of the set of messages that can be exchanged, along with its encoding and any parameters associated with reliable delivery.

Security. This includes information to ensure a secure interchange of information between the parties—for instance, nonrepudiation parameters such as certificates, protocols, hash functions, and signature algorithms. For a digital envelope, it includes certificates and encryption algorithms.

Roles. Each party is associated with a role defined in the CPP. Generally, the description is defined in terms of roles such as "buyer" and "seller." The CPP identifies which role or roles the party is capable of playing in each collaboration protocol referenced by the CPP.

Business transactions. These are the business transactions or services that the parties agree to interchange. Described are the interfaces between the parties and the business application functions that actually perform the transactions.

Comments. This is a text format used for additional information, such as reference to any legal documents relating to the partner agreement.

Code Listing 9.1 shows the overall structure of the CPA.

To explain some of these XML tags further, we elaborate on the element definitions and their attributes:

<CollaborationProtocolAgreement>. This root element of a CPA has the unique identifier attribute (`cpaid`) for the document. The `id` attribute

```
<CollaborationProtocolAgreement
 xmlns="http://www.ebxml.org/namespaces/tradePartner"
 xmlns:bpm="http://www.ebxml.org/namespaces/businessProcess"
 xmlns:ds = "http://www.w3.org/2000/09/xmldsig#"
 xmlns:xlink = "http://www.w3.org/1999/xlink"
 cpaid="CPA1234"
 version="1.2">
<Status value = "proposed"/>
<Start>1988-04-07T18:39:09</Start>
<End>1990-04-07T18:40:00</End>
<!--ConversationConstraints MAY appear 0 or 1 times-->
<ConversationConstraints invocationLimit = "100"
 concurrentConversations = "4"/>
<PartyInfo>
...
</PartyInfo>
<PartyInfo>
...
</PartyInfo>
<Packaging id="N20"> <!--one or more-->
...
</Packaging>
<!--ds:signature MAY appear 0 or more times-->
<ds:Signature>
...
</ds:Signature>
<Comment xml:lang="en-us">any text</Comment> <!--zero or more-->
</CollaborationProtocolAgreement>
```

Code Listing 9.1 Overall structure of the ebXML collaboration protocol agreement.

value is assigned by one party and used by both parties. The specification recommends that companies uses a uniform resource identifier, such as a Web or email address. The CPA element has a version attribute to provide versioning for a CPA during negotiation between the two parties. The version value is updated with each change to the CPA document, using a value such as "1.0" or "2.1". The root CPA element has namespace declarations for ebXML trading partner specifications and business process models, as well as W3C specifications for digital signatures and XML Linking Language (XLink).

<Status> (required). This element identifies the stage of development for the CPA, with options of `proposed`, `agreed`, or `signed`. The `signed` option can be in the form of a digital signature. In this example, the CPA is proposed by one party and possibly waiting for agreement from another party:

```
<Status value = "proposed"/>
```

<Start> and <End> (required). The `<Start>` element records the date and time that the CPA goes into effect. The `<End>` element records the last date and time that the CPA is valid.

```
<Start>1988-04-07T18:39:09</Start>
<End>1990-04-07T18:40:00</End>
```

<ConversationConstraints> (optional). This element defines parameters for message processing during a conversation between two parties. The *invocation limit* is an upper limit on the number of units of activity covered by the CPA. A *concurrent conversation limit* is an upper limit on the number of conversations between the parties processed anytime. This reflects possible limitations in the capabilities of back-end systems.

```
<ConversationConstraints invocationLimit = "100"
 concurrentConversations = "4"/>
```

<PartyInfo> (required). This element defines the information for each party; one is required for each party using the CPA.

```
<PartyInfo>
...
</PartyInfo>
```

<Packaging> (required). This element defines configuration for the ebXML message headers and payload. It provides the document level properties for security, MIME content types, XML namespaces, security parameters, and MIME structure of the data.

```
<Packaging id="N20">
...
</Packaging>
```

<ds:Signature> (optional). This element signs the CPA using the XML Digital Signature standard. If the digital signature is invalid, the CPA is also considered invalid.

```
<ds:Signature>
...
</ds:Signature>
```

<Comment> (optional). This element provides added descriptive information in text format.

```
<Comment xml:lang="en-us">This is a comment.</Comment>
```

Using the Collaboration Protocol Agreement

The basics of the collaboration protocol are shown in Figure 9.1. Any company may register its profile with an ebXML registry. The registry serves as the repository for XML documents such as the CPPs, CPAs, schemas, and related business process documents. The CPA/CPP are used by the ebXML-compliant systems in the trading partners to initiate and engage in a business transaction. In this section, the term *framework* is used to represent the generic business process code that supports the TPA and the interactions between business partners.

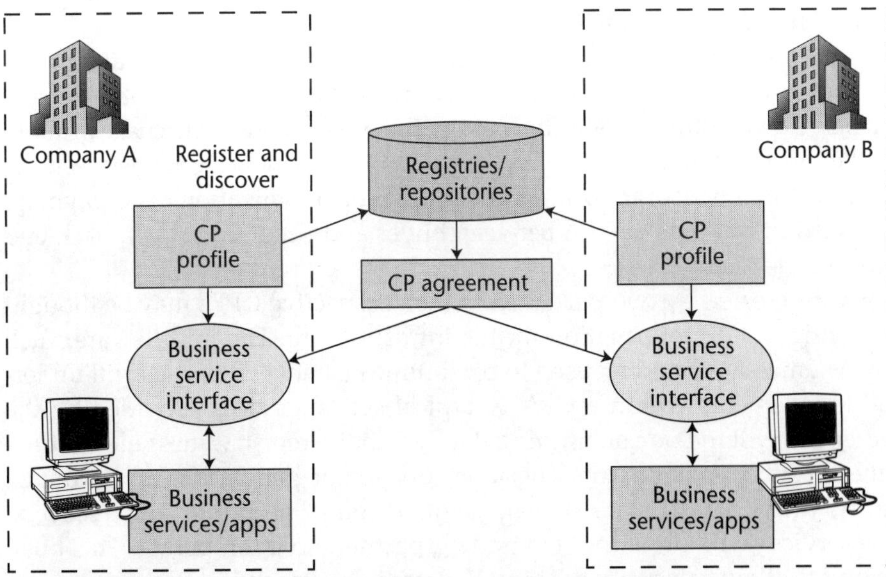

Figure 9.1 Overview of the collaboration protocol and CPP/CPA within the ebXML architecture.

One category of an ebXML trading system is a buy-side business application for merchants supporting business buyers, such as creating purchase order requests. For example, suppose Acme Hardware is looking for a supplier for a widget. By searching in the registry, the purchasing manager discovers and downloads the CPP for a trading partner, Big Distributor. The trading system at Acme Hardware creates a CPA and sends the CPA to the trading system at Big Distributor. Acme Hardware and Big Distributor have identical copies of the CPA as the system configuration for both servers. After this initial system level handshake, Acme Hardware continues with business transactions, such as sending a purchase order for widgets.

This can be extended to other buy-side systems, such as requesting approval of purchase order requests. For example, an ebXML-compliant business system can interact with any ebXML-compliant buying system. The buyer can place orders directly with the merchant server of the seller organization. The buyer can browse a catalogue and place an order with the seller organization using a browser. When the buyer has placed an order, the server of the seller organization sends a partial purchase order to the server of the buyer organization. The buyer validates the purchase order request and transforms it into a complete purchase order, then returns it to the seller. The seller then prepares an invoice, arranges for payment, and ships the merchandise in the order. The payment process handles electronic payments. Using the browser, the buyer can view and update information at the buyer organization server, such as the buyer profile, outstanding requests, and so on. The buyer can also check the status of an order at the seller.

Another example is a business application for merchants for dealing with their suppliers, such as checking for inventory. When a purchasing department buys large volumes for a stock room, the buyer sends a purchase order to the seller and a partial purchase order is initiated. There is a CPA between the servers of the buyer organization and the seller organization. The payment process is not part of the CPA between buyer and seller, but it is a back-end process of the seller.

The CPA created by two parties from their respective CPPs may be thought of as configuration information for the infrastructure. The middleware, such as ebXML message handler, used to communicate between parties will understand the elements within a CPA. A typical set of services provided by the middleware will include submitting the CPA to the registry, message routing, business state transition rule checking, document generation and parsing, security, conversation state management, logging, auditing, and recovery. These services will allow the two trading partners to interoperate. This business process flow can apply to many B2B processes, such as request for quote (RFQ), request for information (RFI), and other processes supported by different CPAs.

The interface to back-end systems can be provided by an extended framework in the business logic that handles incoming requests, such as partial or completed purchase orders. The partners could have different frameworks supporting the CPA standard or could deploy any system implementation consistent with the CPA/CPP specification. This independence provides flexibility for doing business over an open medium such as the Internet. CPA/CPP functions can be provided by plug-ins, using document parsers and generators and security functions. This loosely coupled system provides flexibility for setting up trading agreements where a company can replace suppliers without having to make new IT investments to support the new supplier.

Inside the Collaboration Protocol Profile

The CPP summarizes relevant company data for a company within the ebXML system. The CPP is stored into a registry or similar repository, along with additional documents. When the CPP for the trading partner is in the repository, other companies can find it by using the repository discovery services. This discovery mechanism allows trading partners to find one another and discover which business processes are supported. The CPP definition provides for clear selection of choices in cases where there may be multiple selections, such as between HTTP or SMTP transport. A CPP defines business processes supported by the trading partner and defines the roles within a business process for a trading partner. For example, two roles may be a seller and buyer within a purchasing business process.

The main functions of a CPP include (1) the process specification, which defines supported e-business services; (2) document exchange, which defines the connection between process specifications and transport, such as encryption and digital signatures; and (3) transport, which defines the messaging protocols and services. Code Listing 9.2 shows the overall structure of a CPP.

```
<CollaborationProtocolProfile
 xmlns="http://www.ebxml.org/namespaces/tradePartner"
 xmlns:ds="http://www.w3.org/2000/09/xmldsig#"
 xmlns:xlink="http://www.w3.org/1999/xlink"
 version="1.1">
<PartyInfo>  <!--one or more-->
...
</PartyInfo>
<Packaging id="ID"> <!--one or more-->
...
```

Code Listing 9.2 Overall structure of the collaboration protocol profile. *(continues)*

```
<Packaging>
<ds:Signature>  <!--zero or one-->
...
</ds:Signature>
<Comment>text</Comment> <!--zero or more-->
</CollaborationProtocolProfile>
```

Code Listing 9.2 Overall structure of the collaboration protocol profile. *(continued)*

To explain some of these XML tags further, we elaborate on the element definitions and their attributes:

<CollaborationProtocolProfile> (required). This is the root element of the CPP document. It references three XML namespaces, which are the default ebXML trade partner, the W3C XML Digital Signature, and Xlink namespaces. The subelements of the CPA include a required `<PartyInfo>` tag, a required `<Packaging>` tag, optional `<ds:Signature>` tags with the digital signatures for the CPP document, and optional `<Comment>` tags. A CPP document may be digitally signed, according to W3C/IETF XML Digital Signature specification, to ensure that the document has not been altered and to authenticate the author of the document.

<PartyInfo> (required). This element defines the organization (or parts of the organization) whose capabilities are described by the CPP. The following code snippet shows the overall structure of `<PartyInfo>`:

```
<PartyInfo>
<PartyId type="...">  <!—one or more—>
 ...
</PartyId>
<PartyRef xlink:type="...", xlink:href="..."/>
<CollaborationRole>   <!—one or more—>
 ...
</CollaborationRole>
<Certificate>  <!—one or more—>
 ...
</Certificate>
<DeliveryChannel>  <!—one or more—>
 ...
</DeliveryChannel>
<Transport>  <!—one or more—>
 ...
</Transport>
```

```
<DocExchange>  <!—one or more—>
 ...
</DocExchange>
</PartyInfo>
```

<PartyId> (required). This element identifies the trading partner with a unique string. The values can be UCC/EAN assigned company codes, DUNS numbers (as shown in the following code snippet), or specific industry identifiers, such as carrier codes in air travel or company codes in publishing.

```
<tp:PartyId tp:type="DUNS">123456789</tp:PartyId>
```

<PartyRef> (required). This is a reference using the XLink syntax to Internet accessible information about the trading partner. The value can be a registry or other Internet resources, such as the company Web site, as in the following code snippet:

```
<tp:PartyRef tp:href="http://foo.com/about.html"/>
```

<CollaborationRole> (required). This element describes the business processes supported by the company, as well as its roles in the processes. The ebXML business process specification defines the trading partner roles in the business process. An example of the collaboration role syntax is:

```
<tp:CollaborationRole tp:id="N00">
<tp:Role tp:name="buyer" xlink:type="simple"
xlink:href="http://ebxml.org/processes/buySell.xml#buyer"/>
 <tp:CertificateRef tp:certId="N03"/>
 <tp:ServiceBinding tp:channelId="N04" tp:packageId="N0402">
 <tp:Service
tp:type="uriReference">uri:example.com/services/buyerService</tp:Service>
<tp:Override tp:action="orderConfirm" tp:channelId="N07"
tp:packageId="N0402"
xlink:href="http://ebxml.org/processes/buySell.xml#orderConfirm"
xlink:type="simple"/>
</tp:ServiceBinding>
</tp:CollaborationRole>
```

<Certificate> (required). This element defines digital certificates used by the trading partner for nonrepudiation or authentication. This includes an ID for each certificate and data that describes the certificate, as defined by the XML Digital Signature specification. An example of the certificate syntax is:

```
<Certificate certId = "N03">
 <ds:KeyInfo>. . .</ds:KeyInfo>
</Certificate>
```

<DeliveryChannel> (required). This element defines transport and message protocols that the trading partner supports. A delivery channel has one transport tag, one document exchange tag, and one characteristics tag with security details. An example of the delivery channel syntax is:

```
<DeliveryChannel channelId="N04" transportId="N05" docExchangeId="N06">
 <Characteristics
  syncReplyMode = "responseOnly"
  nonrepudiationOfOrigin = "true"
  nonrepudiationOfReceipt = "true"
  secureTransport = "true"
  confidentiality = "true"
  authenticated = "true"
  authorized = "true"/>
</DeliveryChannel>
```

<Transport> (required). This element describes the details of the messaging transport protocols, such as HTTP, SMTP, and FTP. This tag has the protocols for sending and receiving, an endpoint for the trading partner address as the message recipient (such as http://foo.com/handler in the following example), and security information for each specific way of transport. The overall structure of the transport tag is shown in this code snippet:

```
<Transport transportId = "N05">
<!—protocols are HTTP, SMTP, and FTP—>
 <SendingProtocol version = "1.1">HTTP</SendingProtocol>
 <!—one or more SendingProtocol elements—>
 <ReceivingProtocol version = "1.1">HTTP</ReceivingProtocol>
 <!—one or more endpoints—>
 <Endpoint uri="http://foo.com/handler" type = "request"/>
 <TransportSecurity>  <!—0 or 1 times—>
  <Protocol version = "3.0">SSL</Protocol>
  <CertificateRef certId = "N03"/>
 </TransportSecurity>
</Transport>
```

<DocExchange> (required). This element defines the characteristics of the messaging services used by the trading partner to exchange documents. This tag includes subelements for message encoding, reliable messaging properties, nonrepudiation to verify the sender identity by a digital signature, digital envelope for message encryption, and namespace extensions. The overall structure of the document exchange tag is as follows:

```
<DocExchange docExchangeId = "N06">
 <ebXMLBinding version = "0.92">
 <ReliableMessaging>  <!—occurs 0 or 1—>
 ...
 </ReliableMessaging>
 <NonRepudiation>  <!—occurs 0 or 1—>
```

```
  ...
  </NonRepudiation>
  <DigitalEnvelope>  <!—occurs 0 or 1—>
  ...
  </DigitalEnvelope>
  <NamespaceSupported> <!— 1 or more —>
  ...
  </NamespaceSupported>
  </ebXMLBinding>
</DocExchange>
```

Summary

XML and application middleware are the key capabilities to enabling dynamic business process integration. One missing piece of the B2B e-commerce puzzle was a standard system-level document for the IT terms and conditions. A collaboration protocol originated from an IBM innovation called the trading partner agreement and its associated markup language. Trading partner agreement (TPA) defines the rules of engagement between entities engaging in e-business. The Trading Partner Agreement Markup Language (tpaML) streamlines the process of establishing electronic trading relationships; a process with earlier technologies could take weeks or months. TPA text documents define B2B interchanges based on EDI. IBM has submitted a draft of tpaML to the ebXML initiative for standardization. A standard language for system agreements is a key element of interoperability between the B2B servers of different vendors. ebXML has adopted the term collaboration protocol agreement (CPA) to serve similar system-level functions as the paper-based TPA.

The collaboration protocol profile (CPP) describes what a partner can do at the system level. These capabilities include the supported business process and communication protocols and the security requirements for the message exchanges. The exchange of information between two parties requires each party to know the supported business collaborations of the other party, the other party role in the business collaboration, and the technology details about how the other party sends and receives messages. The CPP describes the company system capabilities for e-business transactions, such as the supported transport, security, and messaging protocols.

A CPA is a document enforcing a trading relationship between two parties. The rules for the tags or the semantics can be defined in the DTD or XML schema. The CPA represents the intersection of the CPPs of the trading partners involved in the data interchange and any additional information based on mutual agreement. The CPA contains the messaging service interface requirements and details about the mutually agreed upon business processes.

The CPA and CPP can be stored in and retrieved from a registry. Having the CPA and CPP in a registry is not a mandatory part of the CPA and CPP creation process, but it is an expected part of ebXML software design. The CPA/CPP specification covers the general tasks and issues in creating a CPA from two CPPs. However, it does not specify an actual algorithm, which leaves the implementation details to software vendors and application developers. The ebXML system functionality includes submitting and retrieving the CPA in the registry, routing messages to their destinations, sequencing rules, business document generation and parsing, security, conversation management, logging, and recovery. Two partners have agreed on a CPA to define how they will interact, but they can choose how to implement the business system. A business system supports many scenarios through the adoption of these open standards.

CHAPTER

10

Implementing ebXML in the Organization

"ebXML is a complement to EDI, not a competitor. We want to bring the benefits of EDI to companies with fewer than 1,000 people that don't have access to EDI."

—Bill Smith, President of OASIS

AREAS COVERED IN THIS CHAPTER

- **Why ebXML?**
  - **Semantics management for XML**
  - **Standard technical infrastructure**
- **From theory to practice**
  - **Managing workflow**
  - **Service provider model**
- **ebXML project life cycle**
  - **Planning**
  - **Pilot**
  - **Implementation**

The ebXML initiative was founded with the mission statement: "To provide an open XML-based infrastructure enabling the global use of electronic business information in an interoperable, secure and consistent manner by all parties."

You may be a customer who wants to use ebXML to establish a relationship with one or more suppliers. Or you are a supplier who wants to use ebXML for a competitive edge. Perhaps you are a supplier with customers who want you to adopt ebXML. This chapter summarizes the business case for ebXML and provides an overview of the process for an ebXML project. We address how to adopt a business strategy based on ebXML and how to use ebXML as a technology platform for enabling business exchanges.

Why ebXML?

The ebXML value proposition is that it provides the business semantics management and the standard technical infrastructure for communication between businesses. Industry standards, both de facto and de jure, are always a compromise that requires consensus.

EDI, the main data interchange standard, has been in existence for several decades, and will not disappear overnight. Why not? First, the large investment in EDI has to be recovered. EDI also offers important insights for the development of new e-commerce frameworks, as it still proves to be valuable in business and technical contexts. By viewing XML as a substitute for EDI, we are discounting the experience built up in the past decades and may have to relearn the lessons of the past. Rather than the radical position "EDI is dead, long live XML," a more moderate attitude may be to view ebXML as the *new* EDI from the same organization that produced EDIFACT. Although we may build from scratch on the technology side, the underlying business processes may not have changed. The experience built up in EDI should be taken into account. According to Peter Jordan, a member of the Global Commerce Initiative (GCI) Board of Directors, "By implementing ebXML as part of our infrastructure, GCI takes advantage of the excellent development work that's being accomplished to streamline many EDI processes and remove waste and redundancy from supply chains."

But what lessons should be learned from EDI when designing *new* ebXML-based architectures? Here are a few:

- Legacy EDI systems requirements should be used as input for setting design goals for ebXML-based systems. We want to retain the goals achieved in EDI and improve upon them.
- Data exchanges should be predictable. We may want to do business with minimal prior negotiation with another company. We should identify any possible constraints and put them into the schema. The ebXML registry and repositories are the schemas for message formats and are stored for common access.
- Unique identifications for data should be used to track the business transactions. As we discuss later in this chapter, namespaces are very helpful for this purpose.

- Common, interchangeable data elements, such as simple items like a date or an address, should be used to interoperate among different industries. This is addressed in the ebXML core components.
- Both parties should acknowledge everything at any time to ensure the state of a transaction. For example, as in ebXML transport mechanisms, there is a difference between sending a receipt acknowledgment and confirming that the received document is understood.
- Redesign business processes and avoid manual processing. An interesting lesson to be learned from EDI history is that significant productivity gains are not achieved by simply pulling the automation trigger. We should ask if and how we can improve the electronic versions of paper documents. *Electronic* should still apply to the transaction processing inside company boundaries. In many companies, incoming EDI data is printed and keyed into other systems. In this respect, ebXML is designed for both external and internal systems.
- Security is much more important in an open Internet environment than in closed VAN-based systems. This issue should be addressed in the foundations. It is not something to add at the end.

In the ebXML framework, many of its principles are based on EDI, such as the *Open-EDI Reference Model*. ebXML has special attention for small companies, which currently cannot afford to build an EDI solution. The goal in ebXML is a data interchange system that has the similar or improved features, but without the drawbacks of EDI.

In addition to ebXML, new foundational technologies enable interbusiness integration in enterprise business processes. Before the Web and Internet, for software vendors to interoperate in cross-network application services was a major challenge. HTTP, SMTP, and TCP/IP standardized lower-level transport protocols for communication. The Web uses HTTP running on TCP/IP. In 1994, TCP/IP was a mature standard as the Web was introduced into the mainstream. Now HTTP is widely adapted as a universal business standard. HTML is primarily the information access and display layer. HTML tags describe the look and feel of the document, and a Web browser can figure out how to present the document. When using a presentation markup language such as HTML, much of the structure and meaning of the underlying data is lost. Enterprise applications still need a shared messaging, data encapsulation, and meta data standard that provides "80 percent of the benefit of SGML with 20 percent of the effort."

As the standard for application-to-application communication, XML is platform-independent and is used for data description in message-passing protocols. XML officially became a standard in February 1998, when the W3C announced that XML 1.0 had reached draft recommendation status and was suitable for deployment in applications. Using meta data in XML, we recognized that the information in a Web site contains data, not just plain text without context.

Shared Context and Semantics Management for XML

XML has been viewed as a kind of semantic magic for interoperability, as the *lingua franca* to enable Web services. XML-based Web services communicate over standard Web protocols using XML interfaces and XML messages, which any application can interpret. This singular view may be flawed. XML provides the primitives for describing larger concepts, and it works by allowing an unlimited number of semantic concepts to be encoded using those primitives. The ability to parse content in XML does not mean universally usable semantics. Any XML parser can declare an XML document structurally valid. This does not mean the recipient will understand the contents of the XML document. XML allows businesses or developer groups to share data if they agree on the data semantics. It enables data interoperability, but by itself it does not create semantic interoperability.

Web services have defined a layered stack built on top of XML to provide coordination and address shared semantics. One example is WSDL, which provides a way to describe the simple aspects of a Web service such as data types, and operations supported by the service, called bindings. Web services by itself does not create a framework in which any two arbitrary applications can interact, because XML does not provide shared languages, merely shared alphabets. The Web services stack pushes this shared semantics problem into higher and higher layers without solving it. Applications operate in a problem domain with narrow semantics. The Web model can be extended into the application domain by implementing it in areas where broad agreement on what and how to communicate already exists. Web services are likely to work best in areas with predefined methods and vocabularies, where the recipient can be counted on to decode the message.

A standard Web service example is stock price retrieval. It is simple and obvious, but not generally representative of real-world problems. Stock prices exist in an extremely constrained world. There is a canonical list of company-to-ticker-symbol mappings, and the types of data are well defined. The stock quote example illustrates Web service technology without solving the problem of shared context, because the coordination has been established in advance.

How can you create interoperability between two parties who have never interacted with one another before without defining in advance the vocabulary they will use to communicate? The vision of Web services as a framework for automated interactions does not address the shared context and coordination issues. A proprietary solution from a single vendor lacks the cross-industry consensus and support to be really open and interoperable. This issue of shared context must be solved using a public standards-based solution. ebXML is a bridge between these islands of semantics. ebXML built a technical architecture based on providing standard semantics for data interchange. The foundation for e-business includes a shared semantic registry, such as the ebXML registry. ebXML has a shared vocabulary and terminology library that serve as a commercial semantics framework. This semantic framework is a set of shared XML vocabularies and the process for defining actual message structures and definitions. This allows applications using ebXML to interoperate among different business systems in commerce.

There are several pieces to this semantic framework: a model about the business process and information models, common business processes, and a set of reusable business logic. ebXML has a discovery mechanism that allows enterprises to find each other and agree to become trading partners. They can use a shared repository for business process models and related message structures—a new set of standard vocabularies to represent all the components of shared context and to define open, vendor-neutral Web services to support the infrastructure. Without standards or conventions for representing this context, every site maintains information in a proprietary format. With shared context, the vision of transparent, dynamic interaction of widely distributed, heterogeneous Web services can be a reality.

Standard Technical Infrastructure

Multiple standards for the universal means to connect business applications over a network have been proposed, including Common Object Request Broker Architecture (CORBA), Distributed Component Object Model (DCOM), UNIX Remote Procedure Call (RPC), and Java Remote Method Invocation (RMI). All of them exist today with their own user bases, but each has failed to gain a broad constituency. CORBA was limited to mostly UNIX systems vendors. DCOM, a Microsoft technology, was predominately Windows based. UNIX RPC, which refers to several flavors of technologies that are available on UNIX systems, was never widely deployed outside the UNIX space. Java RMI technology from Sun is a recent addition, but it may be limited on Windows platforms because of Microsoft's break with Java. These technologies typically did not gain significant market share and critical mass in market momentum, and they do not address data interchange specifically.

The ebXML architecture provides a way to define business processes based on standard patterns and interoperable Web services for the entire e-business relationship. The architecture includes standardized data infrastructure, semantic framework, and shared discovery. This infrastructure uses a standard message transport mechanism with defined interface, packaging rules, and reliable delivery and security. The infrastructure acts as a business service interface that handles incoming and outgoing messages. The architecture develops business messages based on core components to register and discover business process sequences with related message exchanges, to define company profiles, to define trading partner agreements, and to exchange messages using a uniform message transport layer. The architecture supports discovery of a new trading partner and facilitates a working relationship with the technical capabilities of that trading partner, including the business process description, business messages, communications services, and trading-partner-specific extensions to standard process and message standards. The architecture supports identification and downloading of available software components that comply with the business process and messages. It also supports a legal agreement that describes the collaboration between the two parties. The ebXML architecture is overlaid on top of the foundation of commonly used Internet protocols and languages, such as HTTP, HTML, XML, SMTP, TCP/IP, and so on. The architecture can protect investments and avoid proprietary lock-in via a standards-based architecture and hardware, operating system, and programming language neutrality.

Moving from Theory to Practice

It is no secret that "business" people and "systems" people have been in conflict for decades. Reasons for this include differences in knowledge, culture, professional interests and goals, and the alienation that simple physical separation between groups can produce. As an open XML-based framework, ebXML can fundamentally change the nature of the relationship between business and systems people.

The ebXML solution enables businesses to improve collaboration with customers, partners, and suppliers by reducing integration time and expense, compared to existing EAI and B2B solutions. It can result in reduced inventory and transaction costs and improved supply chain efficiency. It can increase revenue via expanded distribution channels and short time-to-market for new value-added services, by enabling public discovery of existing assets. It can enhance customer service levels by allowing customers and trading partner access to core systems. In addition, the ebXML solution can generate new revenue opportunities through creation of private trading networks.

Managing Workflow

ebXML can be used *within* the enterprise as well as between companies, as illustrated in the example in this section. Companies can use the critical-information-path approach to model business processes. A workflow-centric approach in ebXML can use different vocabularies identified by XML namespaces. Middleware tools are used to convert or filter information from one format to another.

The key is to express syntax in ways that are easy and intuitive for people in that work context. This means breaking down business processes into workflow models using XML and ebXML semantics. Each business process can use its own business vocabulary to describe its transactions. Role-based vocabulary allows people to create descriptions of the information they work with that fit their perception of the information. Shipping clerks have a different perspective on information than accountants, while executives have their own perspective. According to his role, a person views detailed information based on a consistent description of his part of the transaction. For example, a shipping clerk does not need to see credit card information to ship orders, and an executive does not need to read through thousands of orders for different parts to understand the sales figures for a given day.

Namespaces identify these vocabularies, or users can keep track of the origins of messages to interpret for their vocabularies. For example, a customer placing an order for goods can send an initial request using an ebXML message with this payload:

```
<order xmlns="http://foo.com/order" id="010000000">
<vendor>foo.com<vendor>
<customer>
<name>John Doe</customer>
<address>123 Easy Street</address>
<city>Gotham City</city>
<state>New York</state>
<zip>00000-0000</zip>
<email>john.doe@hotmail.com</email>
</customer>
<item>
<widget size="large" style="XYZ" quantity="2" unitPrice="$9.95" />
</item>
<shipping delivery="overnight"/>
<payment type="VISA" number="1234 4567 8910 1234" exp="12/03" />
</order>
```

If an automated processor receiving this order has missing or invalid information for the order, such as billing information, it can send an email to the customer to request the information. By storing information about previous transactions, a processor can build maps for converting various external formats to its internal formats. The warehouse receives from the processor an ebXML message with this payload:

```
<order xmlns="http://foo.com/order/inventory" id="010000000">
<ship-to>
<name>Joe Doe</name>
<address>123 Easy Street</address>
<city>Gotham City</city>
<state>New York</state>
```

```
<zip>00000-0000</zip>
<ship-to>
<item aisle="1" shelf="ABC" quantity="2" />
<shipping delivery="UPS_ground" />
</order>
```

The warehouse would retrieve, package, and ship the item. The purchasing department for the company would be informed of the change in inventory with an ebXML message with this payload to update the inventory database:

```
<inventory xm xmlns="http://foo.com/order/inventory" id="010000000">
<item aisle="1" shelf="ABC" quantity="-2" />
</inventory>
```

The warehouse would send a message to accounting to update the accounting system, using an ebXML message with this payload:

```
<order xmlns="http://foo.com/order/accounting" id="010000000">
<shipping status="complete" date="20011221" />
</order>
```

The accounting system would use the order information to bill the customer's account, using an ebXML message with this payload:

```
<order xmlns="http://foo.com/order/receivable" id="010000000">
<bill-to>
<name>Joe Doe</name>
<address>123 Easy Street</address>
<city>Gotham City</city>
<state>New York</state>
<zip>00000-0000</zip>
<bill-to>
<payment type="VISA" number="1234 4567 8910 1234" exp="12/03" />
<amount>$19.98</amount>
</order>
```

After accounts receivable billed the customer, it can send an ebXML message to the accounting and sales systems to update the financial and sales reports. This can grow into a significant web of information flow, using different ways to describe information. Each business process can use its own business vocabulary to describe its transactions.

Middleware can be used to connect different systems, while hiding the complexity of interactions behind a simplified interface. For example, a sales database application asks a sales force automation application to retrieve that table from a marketing database. Using XML, the sales force automation application contacts the customer relationship management application to request the table. The customer relationship management application that receives the request changes into a form appropriate to the marketing database, retrieves the table, and sends the data as XML to the sales force automation application making the request. The application interprets the XML and passes it to the requesting database. Using this approach, the database developers on both sides need only communicate with the middleware. The middleware will convert the request and responses from XML, without having to communicate in proprietary database protocols. The same approach can be used with a variety of different applications, between client and server, as well as peer-to-peer.

Service Provider Model

ebXML can be used *between* enterprises as a service provider model on top of Web services, as illustrated in the example in this section. A service provider model involves a Web service that can understand context and can share that context with other services. It produces dynamic results based on who, what, when, where, and why it was called. It can quickly respond to changing market conditions and customer preferences by using loosely coupled modular services. This is a part of the next generation of networks, a "semantic Web" (the name comes from Tim Berners-Lee, inventor of the Web) where machines talk intelligently with other machines to solve problems. Several technologies have come along, including Web services and the Resource Description Framework (RDF), an XML-based way to integrate information from different sources.

Common understanding is an important building block. For machines to work with each other, they need a common set of words (vocabularies) and rules. Machines will need to grasp relationships the way humans do. The Web has already given us the potential for universal access to information. Web information is simply displayed on screens, using HTML that tells a computer how to show what a server computer is sending out to another machine. What we need to do is devise ways to help machines understand what they're displaying. They can work with each other to process that information for the benefit of the people using the computers. We are not inventing relational models for data, or query systems, or rule-based systems. We are just allowing them to work together in a decentralized system, without a human having to custom-craft every connection.

Who will own the vocabularies? Who will build and maintain them? There is potential for lock-in and monopolization if certain sets of words become popular but proprietary. Industry consortia can create the vocabularies embodied as core components or other semantic constructs. The vocabularies will have to be linked to each other, or put together in ways that machines can subsequently understand so that the machines can answer questions across disciplines and industries.

When we try to connect the various data-handling applications in a company, there is a certain overlap between two systems that creates manual work involving a lot of rekeying and associated errors. This can mean custom programming by a lot of consultants. If all the applications use XML, we only have to handle XML data, not the full range of internal formats in which data used to be stored and transferred. This means that some of the application glue can be constructed using XML tools such as XSLT, the transformation language. To take a query on an XML document, add in some constraints from another document—we can't just merge two queries. Instead, we need to move up a thin layer of interoperability. The relational language for data on the Net is called RDF. XML is made up of elements and attributes that tell you only about how things are written into the file. RDF data is made up of statements where each statement expresses the value of one property. The information from each application is output in RDF. Any query can run over any selection of this data. Filters can be written very simply, as well as converters to extract and calculate the data you need. This is input to the applications that need it.

For example, suppose in an order fulfillment process a customer has ordered different items. At the time of the order, we promised the customer that the goods would be shipped within 2 days. The Web service places the order with your contract suppliers. Procurement determines that there is a supply constraint on one of the items that will prevent you from shipping the entire order. A Web service can determine a course of action by considering the customer profile and past history. It would consider the impact to the bottom line of expediting the missing components or changing factory work orders. The service may consider other parameters, such as cost of inventory, cost of space, estimated shipping charges, and expected delivery times. The service might send an inquiry to the customer using an ebXML message, voice response message, fax, or some other delivery as defined in the customer profile.

ebXML Project Life Cycle

The ebXML project life cycle covers three major stages: planning, pilot, and implementation. Each can been separated into several major activities, as described in the following sections:

Planning. In this stage, we plan the ebXML program and prepare the organization to adopt it.

Pilot. This is an initial step to get the ebXML program into operation with a pilot program for a small group of key trading partners.

Implementation. In this stage, we establish a complete continuing ebXML program.

Planning

The main purpose of the planning stage is to understand the investment in people, hardware, software, and processes to maximize cost savings and other benefits. Business and technical issues in the planning stage include training of both management and employees, adapting to the cultural change from a traditional paper-based operation to an electronic process, upgrading and revising business systems to integrate ebXML, and working in partnership with other trading partners. The network potentially may involve hundreds of other businesses, all at differing stages of ebXML development and knowledge. The functional business manager should take the lead role in defining the business specifications for the new systems. The IT manager evaluates the work required and assigns the design and development tasks to a team of IT analysts and developers.

A project champion, such as a project manager (a so-called ebXML "guru"), should be responsible for working with stakeholders to identify the project goals and respond to users' needs. The right person will have the skills and attitude to address the full range of business and technical issues. This requires a unique combination of knowledge, experience, and leadership ability.

The project manager should be empowered to operate across functional areas, to participate in industry action groups, and to set strategies and deadlines for the project. The project should have executive sponsorship at the highest levels. This ensures that functional managers fully participate in the ebXML project.

In addition to the overall project manager, a steering committee should be formed to represent operational groups that will be affected by the project. These representatives must have direct input into the planning process. At an early stage, it is vital to set goals for the ebXML project, such as reducing internal costs, reducing lead time between order and receipt of goods and parts, and reducing errors in orders and shipments. These benefits are achieved over the long run as business processes are modified. There are indirect benefits to be gained in the process of integrating more closely with trading partners.

The definition of objectives should also include definition of project scope. This is a useful approach given that most businesses will constantly be changing and upgrading the businesses with ebXML and related technologies. Another important set of early planning decisions is deciding on the selection of information systems and technologies. The ebXML system should be compatible with the existing and planned business systems. Find out what EDI, Internet, and ebXML standards are used in the industry, particularly by potential trading partners. Joining an industry group involved in ebXML can help you learn about common standards in your industry. By taking an active role in the standards-setting process, you can also ensure that your needs are met.

Another early step is to train the trainers—that is, train project leaders on the system fundamentals including self-instruction, literature, and practice on the actual system screens. In addition, a group of IT analysts should be tasked with assessment and recommendation of solutions to the implementation team. This begins with the assessment of the company's capabilities in communications, operations, and processes. Internally, data from trading partners has to be sent to various locations through an internal network. Externally, communications need support linkage with a synchronous or asynchronous protocol and sufficient bandwidth for the anticipated data traffic. The IT analysts should prepare a time and cost estimate for the additional capacity and plan to incorporate them prior to initial pilot testing. The assessment should include the impact that ebXML will have on the operational processes. Using the projected volumes and number of trading partner transactions, the operational capacity required should be estimated in sample scenarios based on such factors as computer storage and processing capacity, bandwidth connection with external trading partners, staffing levels, and operational time.

Many companies find that the additional workload and responsibilities of handling and controlling multiple data transmissions from and to multiple trading partners in an ebXML environment decrease operational efficiency. A third-party service can serve as a communications intermediary.

The IT analysts prepare a list of pros and cons of working with trading partners directly or through a third party. If the recommendation is for the use of a third party, the recommendation list should include business and technical requirements and issues. This can be included in the request for a proposal to be sent to potential third-party service providers. Responses to the requirements and issues will help the implementation team evaluate candidates.

The costs of an ebXML project include labor as well as hardware and software. Also included are travel expenses to attend industry meetings, as well as costs associated with site visits to trading partners and training tools such as seminars and subscriptions.

One of the first steps in the planning phase is collecting information from users. This information is used to develop standard formats to meet the needs of all users within the affected organizations. Collecting input from large numbers of users in multiple organizations can be difficult, often more politically than technically so. Not all users may care about the project, and they may not freely cooperate. It may take a team of people to make the necessary contacts, and team members themselves may have different perspectives on the project.

Surveys may not be enough to collect the materials needed for interchange requirements. Interchange in one area may depend on another area. Surveying isolated user groups may not capture the dependencies. People may also be inadvertently excluded from the survey, but in fact have requirements for using the structures. A good place to begin is with existing interchange standards, such as the ebXML specifications. Standards can provide the stable bedrock for the technical constraints of the project. The interchange standards are designed for information between legacy systems and applications and modeling the input and output of these systems.

The focus here should be on the flow of information rather than the demands of particular users. Using platform-specific vocabularies on a project that involves multiple platforms may not work. Focus instead on the collective, rather than specifics. Describe the data—not the way it is represented in a particular document presentation, database table, or application structure. An important first step is to have project participants agree on names for things. Then the participants can plan out the structure using those names, along with more precise descriptions of the contents.

Finding a common vocabulary keeps a project from getting stuck in the particular visions of its varying participants and encourages participants to compromise with each other. By creating different views of the same information

STANDARDS VERSUS FLEXIBILITY

XML provides a foundation grammar for the structure as well as labels for information. The basic structure in XML is a system for helping applications comprehend the meaning of a document as a standard across organizations and processes.

Standardization has been a critical aspect of getting information into and out of computers. It is used to convert the blizzard of information in the real world to an understandable stream of information stored on computer systems. Information modeling involves converting information from the intuitive format that people use to a logical format that computers can manage and process. Critical tools for reducing information into computer formats include creating unique identifiers, assigning structures, and reducing ambiguity. Computers with limited memory and processing power are limited in their capacity to understand natural languages. XML can provide a key set of tools so that users can move closer to role-based vocabularies without the requirements of natural language processing.

XML provides a solid set of structures that computers can recognize. Labels and structures provide recognized information that computers can use to convert input into internal structures for additional processing. The easiest applications to write are those built to handle a single set of labels and structures. However, this is not useful when working with a different set of structures. DTDs provide a limited range of flexibility, with features like optional and repeatable content models.

Building more flexible systems means planning workflow from input to internal structures to output that adapts to different requirements and business scenarios. In some cases, the application itself may be able to create new and different workflow, sometimes with human help.

for each audience, we can use XML to resolve any remaining conflicts. For instance, this meta data could be made available as explanations of data fields to end users, which would de facto turn the schema into a data dictionary. Though end users are not supposed to understand the schema language itself, the language syntax should be application-readable.

In a B2B context, schemas communicate the structure of our documents to business partners. This puts even bigger pressure on their readability, both to humans and computers. The ideal of a truly self-explanatory information model should be attained as closely as possible.

Pilot

Ideally, the pilot program should be set up with a half dozen trading partners and should be scheduled with a specified duration of three to six months. Solicit the support of the trading partners identified as key participants in the program.

A key person should be the pilot lead, who is responsible for administration of the pilot plan and for tracking progress. As tasks are completed successfully, the pilot lead updates the project status and records any issues as comments attached to the task.

The pilot plan structure contains all of the steps or tasks needed to set up, test, and evaluate the hardware, communications, software, and process with each trading partner involved. Milestones are defined as a group of associated pilot tasks with a specified partner. For example, a milestone can be to "interpret and process invoice transaction from trading partner into the receiving invoice processing application" or to "test in parallel processing transaction with trading partner in both manual process and automated processes."

At the end of the scheduled duration period, the pilot can be evaluated to determine its success or failure. If successful, the milestones achieved so far should be converted into a phased production implementation. Additional steps and phases should be added as necessary. Predefined success criteria and schedules for the pilot program help maintain project momentum.

Conformance testing uses a large set of documents for extensive processing to determine whether the system is going to work. The size of the set of test documents depends on the size and complexity of the document structures. The set should always include both documents that should work and those that should not. Testing failures and their impact on receiving applications is critical. Not everyone will send documents that conform precisely to the standard. Testing the tools that generate XML in the specified format is also important. To test the XML generation application, we have to build validating applications that check generated documents against the constraints in the specification, including the DTD. The testing process generates different types of results. This may require changes in the XML generators or receivers. This may also suggest that the specification needs to be changed, perhaps clarified to remove ambiguities or loosened to support more possibilities. With real-world implementations, it will be easier to refine the document structures.

Implementation

A major part of the implementation program will be to encourage trading partners to do business electronically via ebXML. Working with trading partners to develop new business practices helps ensure support for ebXML.

Some techniques for implementing ebXML programs are as follows:

- A marketing program to promote ebXML adoption for trading partners. For example, a company prepared a presentation that explained how ebXML would work, what the hardware and software requirements would be, and what benefits the partners would expect to realize from using trading with ebXML infrastructure.
- Using the current systems in place, work with trading partners to leverage current investment and build cost-effective systems for messaging and translation.
- To schedule its implementation rollout, one company encouraged trading partners to commit to implementation deadlines.
- Another company selected trading partners to attend a marketing seminar on ebXML. The executive responsibility for purchasing worked with purchasing account representatives to educate and inform the sales staff in trading partners' organization.
- The CEO was a visible advocate of ebXML, both within the company and outside to trading partners.
- A company offered incentives to trading partners for signing up, such as a favorable partner status.
- Another company made follow-ups by phone, mail, and meetings. Potential trading partners often face inertia and require extensive follow-up to help them understand benefits clearly.

Once the system is in place and working, the goal is to extend it to more trading partners. Many suppliers are looking for opportunities to improve business relationships with their customers and may already have e-commerce systems in place. The key is working with your trading partners. Industry conferences are an excellent forum for communicating with potential trading partners

If you adopt ebXML simply as a technology to be handled by technical specialists, you've lost of sight of the most important principle behind ebXML: that it is not just a technology, but a new way of doing business. Even if you adopt ebXML, you will lose ground to competitors who see the technology as a way to improve their entire operations and build strong new relationships with their business partners.

A way to frame the business strategy is to show how ebXML provides a competitive edge. ebXML is not just a technology to improve efficiency and productivity; it can be used to form a central part of your business strategy for B2B transactions, including time-to-market, relationship building, and fostering standard practices.

- ebXML is a way to do business in an environment that places a premium on speed.
- ebXML is a way to develop relationships with customers and suppliers that turns all of you into parts of an organic whole, pursuing common goals, rather than individual businesses each pursuing its own objectives.
- ebXML can become the way to renew standard business practices to take full advantage of current technology.

When a product vendor implements its ebXML system, it usually is not just a response to the technology, but to market needs for better service to its customers and lower cost of transactions. For example, a record company implements an ebXML system to ensure every outlet has the right number of Britney Spears' new album when it is released, in order to better track the sales and inventory of CDs in retailers such as Wal-Mart. The product mix at each store can be varied to match customer preferences and to minimize costs of holding inventory or returned goods. When a participating store sells a pair of Britney Spears CDs, a barcode is scanned at the register. The customer, the price, quantity, the title selection, and sales volume are recorded in the store's system, and the information is sent by an ebXML messaging system to the record label, which can ship additional supplies to match customer preferences. The advantage to the retailer is that there is always a good selection on the shelves. The tracking of customer preference and adjusting selection of popular titles in the store can increase sales dramatically, and the retailer can operate with smaller inventories and lower overhead. The record label has placed itself in a position of active partnership with its retail outlets. The system provides a means to improve sales and customer service.

A major challenge to a trading program in ebXML is ensuring the cooperation of trading partners. The partners may have issues with the technology, the costs, or the business reorganization needed. Some examples of incentives for joining the trading community are improving operations, reducing inventory costs, and improving efficiency by automating labor-intensive tasks. A large corporation with numerous small trading partners can subsidize the investment required, or partner with an application service provider that can convert the initial cost into an incrementally small subscription fee. This is a proactive approach that can help expand the trading community. Using incentives and subsidies to encourage trading helps a large company to improve its efficiency, and in the long term, justify the investment via cost savings and revenue increases.

Summary

The EDI development process and standardization took many years, and it is unlikely that standards for a more complicated and complete set of transactions would emerge overnight. Revolutions tend to evolve, with long-term commitment winning out over short-term fervor. For something as big as the Internet, it would take many years for all the implications to work themselves through the economy. The time-consuming route to integrating e-commerce with the core business is a valuable business proposition. Slower integration allows businesses to see what customers are doing across all channels. ebXML can bring many benefits, but the payoff may be long term. Expectations have to be in line with reality. And ebXML is not just a technical matter involving only the IT organization

The value proposition of ebXML is that it provides the consistent business semantics and the standard technical infrastructure for exchanges between businesses. Bringing the right people together in the implementation process can be the difference between success and failure. The functional areas, application software, communications, legal, and trading partner representatives must all be involved in the implementation process to develop a complete business and technical specifications. A pilot plan takes the project from the implementation phase to production. Online trading with a half dozen partners is a milestone, but building a trading community with most of the potential trading partners is the final goal in realizing the full potential of ebXML.

APPENDIX

Additional Resources

ebXML Resources

The official ebXML Web site

www.ebxml.org

OASIS

www.oasis-open.org/

Web Services Architect—Articles—An Introduction to ebXML

www.webservicesarchitect.com/content/articles/irani02.asp

developerWorks—XML—Understanding ebXML

www-106.ibm.com/developerworks/library/x-ebxml/index.html

ebXML—A Critical Analysis

www.metronet.com/~rawlins/ebXML0.html

XML-based EDI Resources

ANSI ASC X12

www.x12.org/

DISA

www.disa.org/

European Committee for Standardization's Information Society Standardization System (CEN/ISSS) European XML/EDI Pilot Project

www.cenorm.be/isss/workshop/ec/xmledi/isss-xml.html

EEMA EDI/EC Work Group EDIFACT-based XML/EDI effort

www.edi-tie.com/edifact/xml-edi.htm

Common Business Library (CBL)—developed by Veo Systems (acquired by Commerce One)

www.veosystems.com/

www.cbl.org/

Commerce XML (cXML)—jointly developed by Sterling Commerce and Ariba Systems

www.cxml.org/

BizTalk—Microsoft's B2B framework

www.biztalk.org

Open Applications Group—A consortium developing XML standards for integrating MRP and intra-enterprise applications

www.openapplications.org/index.htm

RosettaNet

www.rosettanet.org/

W3C XML Group

www.w3.org/XML

XML/EDI Group
www.geocities.com/WallStreet/Floor/5815

CommerceNet's XML/EDI Task Force
www.commerce.net/services/portfolios/edi/xml-edi/index.html

OO-EDI and XML (TMWG discussion paper)
ftp://www.eccnet.com/pub/xmledi/Uml-xml.htm

TMWG report to UN/ECE/CEFACT on XML and EDI
www.unece.org/trade/untdid/download/99cp16.pdf

Microsoft Web Workshop on XML
http://msdn.microsoft.com/workshop/xml/default.asp

e-Commerce Resources

Open Business on the Internet
www.openbuy.org

Open Trading Protocol (OTP)
www.otp.org

Web Services Resources

Brief History of SOAP
http://xml.com/pub/a/2001/04/04/soap.html

Sun's white paper on Web services
http://java.sun.com/xml/webservices.pdf

Glossary

Abstract class A class that cannot be directly instantiated. Contrast Concrete class. (UML Glossary V1.3)

Abstraction The essential characteristics of an entity that distinguish it from all other kinds of entities. An abstraction defines a boundary relative to the perspective of the viewer. (UML Glossary V1.3)

Active class A class whose instances are active objects. (UML Glossary V1.3)

Actor Someone or something outside the system or business that interacts with the system or business. (Rational Unified Process Terminology)

Agency assigned ID Identifier used to recognize the information entity within the specified controlling agency. (CC/Core Component Terminology)

Aggregate [class] A class that represents the "whole" in an aggregation (whole-part) relationship. (UML Glossary V1.3)

Aggregate core component Defines a functional unit representation form that contains embedded information entities. (CC/Core Component Terminology)

Aggregation A special form of association that specifies a whole-part relationship between the aggregate (whole) and a component part. (UML Glossary V1.3)

Application An application is software that may implement a service by processing one or more of the messages in the document exchanges associated with the service. (ebXML Glossary)

Architecture The architecture of a software system (at a given point in time) is its organization or structure of significant components interacting through interfaces. (Rational Unified Process Terminology)

Authorization A right or a permission that is granted to a system entity to access a system resource. (IETF RFC 2828)

Authorization process A procedure for granting authorization. (IETF RFC 2828)

Basic core component A meaningful piece of business information of a simple type—that is, not containing other components. (CC/Core Component Terminology) See also Basic Information Entity.

Basic information entity Defines a component that contains data but does not have embedded information entities. (CC/Core Component Terminology)

Behavior The observable effects of an operation or event, including its results. (UML Glossary V1.3)

Business A series of processes, each having a clearly understood purpose, involving more than one organization, realized through the exchange of information and directed toward some mutually agreed upon goal, extending over a period of time. (Open-EDI Reference Model Standard—ISO/IEC 14662)

Business library A repository of business process specifications and business information objects within an industry, and of common business process specifications and common business information objects that are shared by multiple industries. (TA Specification Terminology)

Business activity A business activity is used to represent the state of the business process of one of the partners. For instance, the requester is either in the state of sending the request, in the state of waiting for the response, or in the state of receiving. (BPM Specification Terminology)

Business collaboration A coordinated execution of a process or exchange of information between one or more business entities under a defined set of rules. (TA Specification Terminology)

Business collaboration knowledge The knowledge involved in a collaboration. (TA Specification Terminology)

Business context Defines a context in which a business has chosen to employ an information entity. (CC/Core Component Terminology)

Business document The set of information components that are interchanged as part of a business activity. (CC/Core Component Terminology)

Business entity Something that is accessed, inspected, manipulated, produced, and worked on in the business. (UMM)

Business operational view (BOV) A perspective of business transactions limited to those aspects regarding the making of business decisions and commitments among organizations, which are needed for the description of a business transaction. (TA Specification Terminology)

Business partner An entity that engages in business transactions with another business partner(s).

Business process The means by which one or more activities are accomplished in operating business practices. (UMM)

Business Process and Information Metal Model An extension to the UML meta model that includes business process domain specific syntax and semantics for specifying a business process and information model.

Business process interface The definition of how to interact with one partner role in order to make a partner perform a desired service.

Business process qualifier Identifies the generic type of the subprocess that applies to the context. An example is whether it is part of a request/ response sequence, a simple notification, and so on. (CC/Core Component Terminology)

Business process specification A declaration of the partners, roles, collaborations, choreography, and business document exchanges that make up a business process.

Business process type Type of ebXML business flow design pattern that is used to represent the business process. (CC/Component Use Terminology)

Business profile Describes a company's ebXML capabilities and constraints, as well as its supported business scenarios.

Business rules Rules, regulations, and practices for business. (UMM)

Business service interface A software component that exposes an interface for one or more roles in an ebXML collaboration. (TA Specification)

Business transaction A logical unit of business conducted by two or more parties. The community, the partners, and the process are all in a definable and self-reliant state prior to the business transaction, and in a new definable and self-reliant state after the business transaction. In other words, if you are still waiting for your business partner's response or reaction, the business transaction has not been completed.

Choreography A declaration of the activities within a collaboration and the sequencing rules and dependencies between these activities.

Class A description of a set of objects that share the same attributes, operations, methods, relationships, and semantics. (Rational Unified Process Terminology)

Class diagram A graphical representation that shows static structure of concepts, types, and classes. Concepts show how users think about the world; types show interfaces of software components; classes show implementation of software components. (UML Glossary V1.3)

Code A character string (letters, figures or symbols) that for brevity and/or language independency may be used to represent or replace a definitive value or text of an attribute. Codes usually are maintained in code lists per attribute type, such as color. (ebXML CC Dictionary Naming Conventions)

Collaboration Describes a pattern of interaction among objects; it shows the objects participating in the interaction by their links to each other and the messages they send to each other. (Rational Unified Process Terminology)

Collaboration diagram A graphical representation of a collaboration. (Rational Unified Process Terminology)

Collaboration protocol The protocol that defines for a collaborative process. 1. The sequence, dependencies, and semantics of the documents that are exchanged between parties in order to carry out that collaborative process, and 2. The messaging capabilities used when sending documents between those parties. Note that a collaborative process may have more than one collaboration protocol by which it may be implemented. (CPA Specification Terminology)

Collaboration protocol agreement (CPA) Information agreed between two (or more) parties that identifies or describes the specific collaboration protocol that they have agreed to use. A CPA indicates what the involved parties will do when carrying out a collaborative process. A CPA must be representable by a Document. (CPA Specification Terminology)

Collaboration protocol profile (CPP) Information about a party that can be used to describe one or more collaborative processes and associated collaborative protocols that the party supports. A CPP indicates what a party "can" do in order to carry out a collaborative process. A CPP must be representable by a document. While logically, a CPP is a single document, in practice, the CPP may be a set of linked documents that express various aspects of the capabilities. A CPP is not an agreement. It represents the capabilities of a party. (CPA Specification Terminology)

Collaboration process A shared process by which two parties work together in order to carry out a process. The collaborative process may be defined by an ebXML collaboration model. (CPA Specification Terminology)

Common business process A business process that is used with reasonable frequency in a business community.

Communication protocol envelope The outermost envelope of an ebXML message. For example, HTTP or SMTP. (Messaging Service Specification Terminology)

Concrete class A class that can be directly instantiated. (UML Glossary V1.3)

Conformance Fulfilment of a product, process, or service of all requirements specified; adherence of an implementation to the requirements of one or more specific standards or technical specifications. (ISO Guide 2)

Constraint A condition or a restriction. (UMM)

Controlling agency Agency responsible for controlling the content of a basic information entity. (CC/Core Component Terminology).

Core component Lowest-level, industry-neutral building blocks that are used within the construction of ebXML business processes. (CC/Core Component Terminology)

Core library Contains data and process definitions, including relationships and cross-references, as expressed in business terminology that may be tied to an accepted industry classification schema or taxonomy.

Data type A type of data to be used to represent the content of an information entity. This can be specified in XML Schema or ISO 8601. (CC/Core Component Terminology)

Digital signature A digital code that can be attached to an electronically transmitted message that uniquely identifies the sender. (Digital Signature Scheme ISO 9796)

Distributed registry Federation of multiple registries that behave logically as one registry. (TA Specification Terminology)

Document type definition (DTD) Allows different instances of documents of the same type to be automatically processed in a uniform way. (XMI Glossary: OMG)

Domain aggregate core component Complex component required within a business domain. The term "complex" will be removed once it is replaced by "aggregate" in all related documents. (CC/Core Component Terminology)

Domain basic core component. Basic component required within a business domain. (CC/Core Component Terminology)

ebXML infrastructure The full complement of technical specifications encompassed within the ebXML framework. (Technical Architecture Terminology)

EDIFACT WorkingGroup (UN/EWG) To develop and maintain UN/EDIFACT, the support of harmonized implementations and the use of multi-lingual terminology. (UN/EWG)

Electronic business (e-business) A generic term covering information definition and exchange requirements within and between enterprises by electronic means.

Electronic commerce (e-commerce) Doing business electronically. This includes the sharing of standardized unstructured or structured business information by any electronic means. (UN/CEFACT SIMAC)

Electronic data interchange (EDI) The automated exchange of any predefined and structured data for business among information systems of two or more organizations. (Open-EDI Reference Model Standard—ISO/IEC 14662)

Element An atomic constituent of a model. (UML Glossary V1.3)

Encryption Cryptographic transformation of data (called "plaintext") into a form (called "ciphertext") that conceals the data's original meaning to prevent it from being known or used. If the transformation is reversible, the corresponding reversal process is called "decryption," which is a transformation that restores encrypted data to its original state. (IETF RFC 2828)

Entity context Defines a context which a managed core component has been associated with. (CC/Core Component Terminology)

Extensible Markup Language (XML) XML is designed to enable the exchange of information (data) between different applications and data sources on the World Wide Web and has been standardized by the W3C. (UN/CEFACT SIMAC)

Extension Expansion of the information entity definition when applying a component in a business message. (CC/Core Component Terminology)

Functional services view (FSV) A perspective of business transactions limited to those information technology interoperability aspects of IT systems needed to support the execution of open-EDI transactions. (Open-EDI Reference Model, ISO/IEC 14662)

Functional set A set of managed core components that can be used within a business document to serve a specific type of business activity. (CC/Core Component Terminology)

Functional unit A set of information entities that can be used within a business document to control a business activity. (CC/Core Component Terminology)

Implementation An implementation is the realization of a specification. It can be a software product, system, or program. (NIST)

Industry classification Identifies the industry sector in which the context is being employed within a predefined set of sector identifiers. (CC/Core Component Terminology)

Industry classification qualifier New levels of sub-classification that need to be used to further qualify the context in which the data is being used. If Other has been selected for the Industry Classification, a new industry is proposed for addition to the Industry Classification. (CC/Core Component Terminology)

Information entity rules Identifies rules to be applied to a managed core component used as part of the aggregate information entity. (CC/Core Component Terminology)

Information identifier. Identifier used to uniquely identify an embedded information entity. (CC/ Core Component Terminology)

Inheritance The mechanism by which more specific elements incorporate structure and behavior of more general elements related by behavior. (Rational Unified Process Terminology.)

Instance An entity to which a set of operations can be applied and which has a state that stores the effects of the operations. (Rational Unified Process Terminology)

Interaction diagram Shows how several objects collaborate in single use case. (UML Glossary V1.3)

Managed core component Generic term that covers both an aggregate information entity and a basic information entity. (CC/Core Component Terminology)

Message envelope A communication independent envelope, specifically MIME multipart/related, that contains the two main parts of an ebXML compliant message (the header and payload containers). (Messaging Service Specification Terminology)

Message header A specification of the structure and composition of the information necessary for an ebXML messaging service to successfully generate or process an ebXML-compliant message. (Messaging Service Specification Terminology)

Messaging capabilities The set of capabilities that supports exchange of documents between parties. Examples are the communication protocol and its parameters, security definitions, and general properties of ending and receiving messages. (Messaging Service Specification Terminology)

Messaging service A framework that enables interoperable, secure, and reliable exchange of messages between trading partners. (Messaging Service Specification Terminology)

Messaging service layer Enforces the "rules of engagement" as defined by two trading partners in a collaboration protocol agreement (including, but not limited to, security and business process functions related to message delivery). (TA Specification Terminology)

Method A regular and systematic way of accomplishing something; the detailed, logically ordered plans or procedures followed to accomplish a task or attain a goal. (Rational Unified Process Terminology)

Minmax constraints Indicates the maximum and minimum number of occurrences of the information entity that are permitted within this aggregate information entity. (CC/Core Component Terminology)

Official constraints Identifies formal constraints that apply to the business context. (CC/ Core Component Terminology)

Open-EDI Electronic data interchange among multiple autonomous organizations to accomplish an explicit shared business goal. (MoU)

Package A general-purpose mechanism for organizing elements into groups. Packages may be nested within other packages. (Rational Unified Process Terminology)

Package diagram Shows groups of classes and dependencies among them. (UML Glossary V1.3)

Party An entity such as a company, department, organization, or individual that can generate, send, receive, or relay documents. (CPP & CPA Specification Terminology)

Party discovery process A collaborative process by which one party can discover CPP information about other parties. (CPA Specification Terminology)

Payload A section of data/information that is not part of the ebXML wrapping. (Messaging Service Specification Terminology)

Payload container An optional container used to envelope the real payload of an ebXML message. If a payload is present, the payload container must consist of a MIME header portion (the ebXML Payload Envelope) and a content portion (the payload itself). (Messaging Service Specification Terminology)

Payload envelope The specific MIME headers that are associated with a MIME part. (Messaging Service Specification)

Permitted value The set of possible data values with the data type. If the data is the coded data, the permitted values are assigned to a code list. (CC/Core Component Terminology)

Process core component Use of a core component in a particular business context with modification(s). (CC/Core Component Terminology)

Region Identifies the geopolitical region in which the information entity can validly be used. (CC/Core Component Terminology)

Registry A mechanism whereby relevant repository items and meta data about them can be registered such that a pointer to their location, and all their metadata, can be retrieved as a result of a query. (TA Specification Terminology)

Registry authority A superuser who maintains registry. (Defined in ISO11179)

Registry clients An application that makes use of services offered by a registry using the messaging services. For example, the ebXML registry and the ebXML messaging services. (TA Specification Terminology)

Registry entry Meta data that catalogs registry items.

Registry infrastructure provider An entity that provides a registry/repository to store profiles, CPPs, and so on.

Registry interface A set of registry services that provide access to registry content to clients of the registry is defined in the ebXML Registry Services Specification. (TA Specification Terminology)

Registry item The content registered in a repository. (TA Specification Terminology)

Registry service A way of providing access to registry content to clients of the registry. (ebXML Registry Services Specification 222)

Repository A location or set of distributed locations where repository items, pointed at by the registry, reside and from which they can be retrieved. (TA Specification Terminology)

Representation type Type of data to be used to represent the content of an information entity. (CC/Core Component Terminology)

Role The named specific behavior of an entity participating in a particular context. A role may be static (e.g., an association end) or dynamic (e.g., a collaboration role). (UML Glossary V1.3)

Scenario A formal specification of a class of business activities having the same business goal. (ISO 19735 Part I)

Security model A schematic description of a set of entities and relationships by which a specified set of security services are provided by or within a system. (IETF RFC 2828)

Security policy A set of rules and practices that specifies or regulates how a system or organization provides security services to protect sensitive and critical system resources. (IETF RFC 2828)

Sequence diagram A diagram that shows object interactions arranged in time sequence. In particular, it shows the objects participating in the interaction and the sequence of messages exchanged. (Rational Unified Process Terminology)

SIMPL-EDI Subsets of UN/EDIFACT messages especially designed for SMEs.

Simple electronic business (SEB) The application of simplified business processes, using core application data and new and existing standardised techniques that support paperless and efficient operations. (UN/CEFACT SIMAC)

Simple Electronic Business Defines simplest processes and their required core data, allowing the exchange of the minimum data to effect a business transaction electronically. (UN/CEFACT SIMAC)

Specification schema An additional view of a meta model.

Stereotype core component. Information entities (components) that are independent of business context. (CC/Core Component Terminology)

Submitting organization Any organization that submits a repository item to be registered in a repository. The submitting organization will be the intellectual property owner of the repository item. (OASIS)

Substitute core component Use of a core component in a particular business context without modification. (CC/Core Component Terminology)

Supply chain A sequence of events that may include conversion, movement, or placement and that adds value to goods, products, or services. (UN/CEFACT SIMAC)

Unified Modeling Language (UML) A set of diagrams that communicate requirements regarding a business process.

Unique identifier (UID) The abstract concept of utilizing a standard mechanism and process for assigning a sequence of alphanumeric codes to ebXML registry items, including core components, aggregate information entities, and business processes. (CC/Core Component –Terminology)

Universally unique identifier (UUID) An identifier that is unique across both space and time, with respect to the space of all UUIDs. A UUID can be used for multiple purposes, from tagging objects with an extremely short lifetime, to reliably identifying very persistent objects across a network. (DCE 1.1: Remote Procedure Call. Open Group Technical Standard. Document Number C706. The Open Group [Reading, UK: August 1997]).

Use case Defines a sequence of actions a system performs that yields an observable result of value to a particular actor. It is used to structure the behavioral things in a model.

Use case model A model that describes a system's functional requirements in terms of use cases. (UML Glossary V1.3)

Vulnerability A flaw or weakness in a system's design, implementation, or operation and management that could be exploited to violate the system's security policy. (IETF RFC 2828)

Workflow The sequence of activities performed in a business that produces a result of observable value to an individual actor of the business. (Rational Unified Process Terminology)

References

Books, Articles, and White Papers

Barton, J., S. Thatte, and H. Nielsen. "SOAP Messages with Attachments." October 9, 2000. www.w3.org/TR/SOAP-attachments

Box, D., D. Ehnebuske, G. Kakivaya, A. Layman, H. Nielsen, S. Thatte, N. Mendelsohn, and D. Winer. "Simple Object Access Protocol (SOAP) v1.1." W3C Note. May 8, 2000. www.w3.org/TR/SOAP

"Business Process Analysis Worksheet and Guidelines." Version 1.0. ebXML Technical Report. May 2001. www.ebxml.org/specs/bpWS.pdf

"Business Process and Business Information Analysis Overview." Version 1.0. ebXML Technical Report. May 2001. www.ebxml.org/specs/bpOVER.pdf

"Catalogue of Context Drivers." Version 1.04. ebXML Technical Report. May 2001. www.ebxml.org/specs/ccDRIV.pdf

"Collaboration-Protocol Profile and Agreement Specification." Version 1.0. ebXML Technical Specification. May 2001. www.ebxml.org/specs/ebCCP.pdf

"Context and Reusability of Core Components." Version 1.04. ebXML Technical Report. May 2001.www.ebxml.org/specs/ebCNTXT.pdf

"Core Component and Business Process Document Overview." Version 1.05. ebXML Technical Report. May 2001. www.ebxml.org/specs/ccOVER.pdf

"Core Components Specification Documentation." Version 1.8. February 2002. www.ebtwg.org/projects/documentation/core/CoreComponentsTS1.80.pdf

"Core Component Structure." Version 1.04. ebXML Technical Report. May 2001. www.ebxml.org/specs/ccSTRUCT.pdf

"Core Components Dictionary." Version 1.04. ebXML Technical Report. May 2001. www.ebxml.org/specs/ccDICT.pdf

"Core Components Discovery and Analysis." Version 1.04., ebXML Technical Report. May 2001. www.ebxml.org/specs/ebCCDA.pdf

"Database Language SQL—Part 4: Persistent Stored Modules (SQL/PSM)." ISO/IEC 9075-4:1996.

"DCE 128-Bit Universal Unique Identifier." www.opengroup.org/onlinepubs/009629399/apdxa.htm#tagcjh_20;www.opengroup.org/publications/catalog/c706.htm; www.w3.org/TR/REC-xml

"Document Assembly & Context Rules." Version 1.04. ebXML Technical Report. May 2001. www.ebxml.org/specs/ebCCDOC.pdf

"ebXML Business Process Specification Schema." Version 1.01. ebXML Technical Specification. May 2001. www.ebxml.org/specs/ebBPSS.pdf

"ebXML Catalog of Common Business Processes." Version 1.0. ebXML Technical Report. May 2001. www.ebxml.org/specs/bpPROC.pdf

"ebXML Glossary." Version 0.99. ebXML Technical Reference. May 2001. www.ebxml.org/specs/ebGLOSS.pdf

"ebXML Messaging Service Specification." Version 1.0. ebXML Technical Specification. May 2001. www.ebxml.org/specs/ebMS.pdf

"ebXML Registry Information Model." Version 1.0. ebXML Technical Specification. May 2001. www.ebxml.org/specs/ebRIM.pdf

"ebXML Registry Services Specification." Version 1.0. ebXML Technical Specification. May 2001. www.ebxml.org/specs/ebRS.pdf

"ebXML Requirements." Version 1.06. ebXML Technical Report. May 2001. www.ebxml.org/specs/ebREQ.pdf

"ebXML Technical Architecture Risk Assessment." Version 1.0. ebXML Technical Report. May 2001. www.ebxml.org/specs/secRISK.pdf

"ebXML Technical Architecture Specification." Version 1.04. ebXML Technical Specification. February 2001. www.ebxml.org/specs/ebTA.pdf

"E-Commerce and Simple Negotiation Patterns." Version 1.0. ebXML Technical Report. May 2001. www.ebxml.org/specs/bpPATT.pdf

Frier, A., P. Karlton, and P. Kocher. "The SSL 3.0 Protocol." Netscape Communications Corp. November 18, 1996.

"Guide to the Core Components Dictionary." Version 1.04. ebXML Technical Report. May 2001. www.ebxml.org/specs/ccCTLG.pdf

Hoffman, P. "SMTP Service Extension for Secure SMTP over TLS." January 1999.

"ISO 11179 Information Model." http://208.226.167.205/SC32/jtc1sc32.nsf/576871ad2f11bba785256621005419d7/b83fc7816a6064c68525690e0065f913?OpenDocument

"Joint W3C/IETF XML-Signature Syntax and Processing Specification." www.w3.org/TR/2000/CR-xmldsig-core-20001031/1871

Leyland, Valerie. *Electronic Data Interchange: A Management View.* 1994. Prentice Hall.

McDougall, Paul. "Decoding Web Services." *Information Week.* October 1, 2001.

"Naming Convention for Core Components." Version 1.04. ebXML Technical Report. May 2001. www.ebxml.org/specs/ebCCNAM.pdf

Naujok, Klaus-Dieter and Ralph Berwanger. "Global E-Commerce Standard Ready to Roll." *Interactive Week.* May 2001. http://www.zdnet.com.au/newstech/ebusiness/story/0,2000024981,20225538,00.htm

"OASIS Information Model." www.nist.gov/itl/div897/ctg/regrep/oasis-work.html

"Official Names for Character Sets." IANA (edited by Keld Simonsen, et al.). www.iana.org/assignments/character-sets

"Overview of ebXML Architectures." Ed. Mike Rawlins. July 19, 2001. www.rawlinseconsulting.com/ebXML2.html

"Simple Object Access Protocol (SOAP) v1.1." W3C Note. May 8, 2000. www.w3.org/TR/SOAP

"Structured Query Language." FIPS PUB 127-2. www.itl.nist.gov/fipspubs/fip127-2.htm.

Tapscott, D., D. Ticoll, and A. Lowy. *Digital Capital.* Cambridge, Mass: Harvard Business School. 2000.

"Using UDDI to Find ebXML Reg/Reps." ebXML white paper. May 2001. www.ebxml.org/specs/rrUDDI.pdf

"W3C Recommendation: Extensible Markup Language (XML) 1.0." Second Edition. www3.org/TR/REC-xml

"W3C Recommendation: Extensible Markup Language (XML) 1.0." Second Edition. October 2000. www.w3.org/TR/2000/REC-xml-20001006

"W3C Recommendation for Namespaces in XML: World Wide Web Consortium." January 14, 1999. www.w3.org/TR/REC-xml-names.

"W3C XML Linking Candidate Recommendation." www.w3.org/TR/xlink/

"W3C XML Schema Candidate Recommendation." www.w3.org/TR/ xmlschema-0/; www.w3.org/TR/xmlschema-1/; www.w3.org/TR/ xmlschema-2/

"XML Path Language (XPath)." Version 1.0. www.w3.org/TR/xpath

"XMTP: Extensible Mail Transport Protocol." www.openhealth.org/documents/xmtp.htm

Request for Comments (RFC)

821. "Simple Mail Transfer Protocol." J. Postel. August 1982.

822. "Standard for ARPA Internet Text Messages." D. Crocker. August 13, 1982. www.w3.org/Protocols/rfc822/

1766. "Tags for the Identification of Languages." Edited by H. Alvestrand. March 1995. www.cis.ohio-state.edu/htbin/rfc/rfc1766.html

1827. "IP Encapsulating Security Payload (ESP)." R. Atkinson. August 1995.

2015. "MIME Security with Pretty Good Privacy (PGP)." M. Elkins. October 1996.

2045. "Multipurpose Internet Mail Extensions (MIME). Part One: Format of Internet Message Bodies." N. Freed and N. Borenstein. November 1996.

2046. "Multipurpose Internet Mail Extensions (MIME) Part Two: Media Types." N. Freed and N. Borenstein. November 1996.

2068. "Hypertext Transfer Protocol—HTTP/1.1." R. Fielding, J. Gettys, J. Mogul, H. Frystyk, and T. Berners-Lee. January 1997. www.w3.org/Protocols/rfc2068/rfc2068

2246. "The TLS Protocol." Version 1.0. Dierks, T. and C. Allen. January 1999.

2277. "IETF Policy on Character Sets and Languages." Edited by H. Alvestrand. 1998. www.cis.ohio-state.edu/htbin/rfc/rfc2277.html

2278. "IANA Charset Registration Procedures." Edited by N. Freed and J. Postel. 1998. www.cis.ohio-state.edu/htbin/rfc/rfc2278.html

2279. "UTF-8, a transformation format of ISO 10646." F. Yergeau. January 1998. www.ietf.org/rfc/rfc2279.txt

2311. "S/MIME Version 2 Message Specification." S. Dusse, P. Hoffman, B. Ramsdell, L. Lundblade, L. Repka. March 1998.

2312. "S/MIME Version 2 Certificate Handling." S. Dusse, P. Hoffman, B. Ramsdell, and J. Weinstein. March 1998.

2616. "Hypertext Transfer Protocol, HTTP/1.1." R. Fielding, J. Gettys, J. Mogul, H. Frystyk, L. Masinter, P. Leach, and T. Berners-Lee. June 1999.

2387. "The MIME Multipart/Related Content-Type." E. Levinson. August 1998.

2392. "Content-ID and Message-ID Uniform Resource Locators." E. Levinson. August 1998.

2396. "Uniform Resource Identifiers (URI): Generic Syntax." T. Berners-Lee. August 1998.

2402. "IP Authentication Header." S. Kent and R. Atkinson. November 1998.

2554. "SMTP Service Extension for Authentication." J. Myers. March 1999.

2617. "HTTP Authentication: Basic and Digest Access Authentication." J. Franks, P. Hallam-Baker, J. Hostetler, S. Lawrence, A. Leach, E. Luotonen, and L. Stewart. June 1999. www.faqs.org/rfcs/rfc2617.html

2633. "S/MIME Version 3 Message Specification." Edited by B. Ramsdell. June 1999.

2817. "Upgrading to TLS within HTTP/1.1." R. Khare and S. Lawrence. May 2000. www.faqs.org/rfcs/rfc2817.html

2818. "HTTP Over TLS." E. Rescorla. May 2000.

3023. "XML Media Types." Edited by M. Murata, S. St. Laurent, and D. Kohn. January 2001. ftp://ftp.isi.edu/in-notes/rfc3023.txt

Index

A

abstract service interface, 85
Acme Hardware, ebXML, 91–92
aggregate core component (ACC), 123
aggregated business information entity (ABIE), 123
aggregated components, 122–23
Amazon, B2C e-commerce, 6
American Iron and Steel Institute (AISI), 28
American National Standards Institute (ANSI), 28–29
American Paper Institute (API), 28
analysis worksheets, 78
ANSI X12 standard, EDI, 28–29
application programming interface (API), 11–12
applications, data-handling, 229
application service, 12
application service provider (ASP), 9
architecture, 70–73, 75–87, 89–92, 155–57
association attribute, registry services, 182
asynchronous messaging, 144
attachments, SOAP message, 152–53
attributes, 35–37, 182–83, 190
auction model, B2B e-commerce, 7
auditable event attribute, registry, 182
authentication of receiver/sender, 89
automated payment system, B2C, 6
Automobile Industry Action Group (AIAG), 28

B

B2B system implementation, 200
back-end system, 9
binary collaborations, 105–6
binding, WSDL document element, 60
BizTalk standard, 17, 20, 94–95
body extensions, SOAP, 162
business document flow, 109–13
business information entity (BIE), 122
Business Operational View (BOV), 75–76
business process, context category, 131
business process analysis worksheet, 78
Business Process and Information Meta Model (BPIMM), 81–82
business process model
  architecture element, 80, 81–83
  binary collaborations, 105–6
  business process specification schema (BPSS), 102–4
  business service interface (BSI), 101
  collaboration, 100–2, 104–8
  collaboration protocol agreement (CPA), 103
  document type definition (DTD), 102–4
  interchange activities sequence, 113–16
  multiparty collaborations, 107–8
  schema, 102–4
  transactions, 100–2, 108–13
  value chain integration, 99
Business Process Modeling Language (BPML), 14

business process specification schema (BPSS), 76, 82, 102–4
business service interface (BSI), 101
business-to-business (B2B), 5–12
business-to-business protocol framework (BPF), 200
business-to-consumer (B2C), 5–6
business webs, B2B e-commerce, 8

C

catalogs, 78
Chemical Industry Data Exchange (CIDX), 28
claims processing, component service, 49
classes, 121
classification attribute, registry, 182
classification node attribute, registry, 182
Classification of the Purposes of Nonprofit Institutions Serving Households (COPI), 132
classification system, registry, 187–88
clients, registry service, 185–87
collaboration protocol agreement (CPA), 80, 88–89, 103, 185, 208–15
collaboration protocol profile (CPP), 80, 87–89, 215–19
collaboration protocol profile and agreement (CPP/CPA), 201, 207–19
Collaboration Protocol Profile and Agreement Specification version 1.0, 201
collaborations, 100–2, 104–8
collaborative protocol, 207
Commerce Daily, B2B e-commerce, 6
CommerceNet standard, 18
Common Gateway Interface (CGI), 11
common languages, uses, 199–200
Common Object Request Broker Architecture (CORBA), 10, 201, 225
compliance, registry services, 184
component objects, 121
components, *vs.* objects, 121
composite objects, 121
consumer-to-consumer (C2C), 5
content owner, registry services, 196–197
context, 122, 129–138
context-free core components, 122
context rules, 134–38
contract, electronic, 200
core components, 80, 83–84, 120–28, 130–40
Core Component Technical Specification, 126–27
currency conversion, 49

D

data elements, EDI, 28
data interchange technologies, 199
Dell Computer, 6–7
digital signatures, 89–90, 168–69
Distributed Component Object Model (DCOM), 10, 145, 225
DirectX, Microsoft API, 11
document envelope, 112, 149–50
documents, 60, 109–13, 138–40
document type definition (DTD), 37–38, 102–4,
Dollar Rent-A-Car Systems, Inc., 62
domain component, 122
dynamic services, B2B e-commerce, 12

E

eBay, e-commerce business type, 4
ebXML
  business/customer collaboration, 226
  defining business processes, 225
  following an order, 226–29
  reasons for selection, 17–20, 222–23
  service provider model, 229–30
  workflow management, 226–29
  worksheets, 78
ebXML project, 231–37
ebXML registry, shared semantics, 225
e-commerce, 4–6, 78, 241
EDIFACT standard, 18, 29
e-hubs, business-to-business (B2B), 8
Electronic Data Interchange (EDI), 14–15, 19–20, 26–31, 222–23
electronic exchange, 13
electronic interaction, 201–2
electronic interchange, 13
electronic marketplaces, B2B, 8
Electronics Industry Data Exchange (EIDX), 28
electronic trading, 13
electronic trading partner agreements, 200
electronic trading standards, 15–17
email, message service type, 144

enterprise application integration (EAI), 9
Enterprise JavaBeans (EJB), 202
enterprise resource planning (ERP), 9–10, 200
enterprises, using ebXML between, 229
enterprise standard, platforms, 72
error handling, message services, 157, 167
exchange model, 7
Exchange Server, Web services tool, 13
Extensible Markup Language (XML)
  allowable content types, 40
  attribute rules, 41–42
  attributes, 35–37
  attribution declaration, 41
  body element, 36
  checking with parser software, 38
  comments, 34
  common language, 199–200
  containers, 34
  content model, 39
  content providers, 40–41
  data interchange solution, 73
  document structure, 33–42
  document type declaration, 38
  document type definition (DTD), 37–38
  ebXML component, 4
  vs. EDI, 14–15
  element declaration, 39–41
  element naming rules, 36
  elements, 35–37
  element structure, 39–41
  epilog element, 36
  grammar, 38
  HTML integration, 14, 32–33
  information integration, 229
  markup tags, 33
  message services integration, 146–47
  meta data, 32
  namespaces, 42–43
  occurrence indicator, 39
  prolog element, 36
  schemas, 42–43
  SGML integration, 31–33
  shared content, 33, 224–25
  smart data, 14
  special characters, 40
  standardization *vs.* flexibility, 233
  standards, 43
  validation, 38
  vocabulary, 31
  W3C's 1.0 specification, 33
  XLink, 14
  Xpointer, 14
external identifier attribute, 182
external link attribute, 182

F

frameworks, 71, 93–96, 214
freight transactions, EDI automation of, 27
Functional Service View (FOV), 75–77

G

GE, B2B e-commerce, 5
geopolitical, context category, 131–32
Global Commerce Initiative (GCI), 21, 222
Global Commerce Internet Protocol, 21
goals, message services, 154–55
grammar, XML, 38
Green Pages, UDDI registry system, 58

H

Harmonized Commodity Description and Coding System (HS), 132
header container, message service, 160
header extensions, SOAP, 161–62
header parsing, 156
header processing, 156, 160–61
headers, 144, 148–49
horizontal Web sites, 7
Hewlett-Packard (HP), use of Web services, 61
HTML, XML, 14, 32–33
HTTP protocol, Web services, 48–49
hub model, 7–8

I

IBM, use of Web services, 61–62
IBM MQSeries, 144
identifiers, core components, 124–26
implementation, ebXML project, 235–37
industry, context category, 133
informed decisions, e-commerce benefit, 5
infrastructure, ebXML, 225–26
instances of a class, 121
integration, B2B e-commerce, 8–9
integrity, ebXML security, 89
interaction protocols, 200
interbusiness electronic interaction, 201–2

intermediary, B2B e-commerce, 7
International Standard Industrial Classification (ISIC), 133
Internet Engineering Task Force (IETF), 89–90
Internet Inter-ORB Protocol (IIOP), 145
Internet search engines, 177
interoperability, 11, 224–25
invocation (call) process, SOAP, 56
ISO 3166, Country Codes, 132
ISO 11179, naming conventions, 84
ISO Open-EDI Reference Model, 75–76

J

Java 2 Enterprise Edition (J2EE), 10
Java API for XML Messaging (JAXM), 57
Java API for XML Registries (JAXR), 179
Java Message Service (JMS), 144
Java Naming Directory Interface (JNDI), 57

L

language translation, 49
life cycle, 188–89
Lightweight Directory Access Protocol (LDAP), 178
loosely coupled, 145

M

mail user agent (MUA), 164
manifest, message services, 154
mapping, messaging service protocols, 85
markup tags, XML, 33
message-oriented middleware (MOM), 144
message package, 56–57, 154, 157–59
message service interface (MSI), 157
message services
  architecture element, 80, 84–85, 155–57
  asynchronous, 144
  design criteria goals, 154–55
  digital signatures, 168–69
  duplicate message handling, 166–67
  ebXML, 153–63
  email, 144
  error handling, 157, 167
  error reporting, 167
  failed delivery, 167
  formatting messages, 157–61
  header container, 160
  header parsing, 156
  header processing, 156, 160–61
  headers, 144
  lost messages, 166
  mail user agent (MUA), 164
  manifest, 154
  message handling, 163–69
  message package, 154, 157–59
  message service interface (MSI), 157
  message status request, 165
  message transfer agent (MTA), 164
  payload, 144
  ping/pong service, 165–66
  reliability, 156–57
  reliable messaging, 164–67
  vs. remote procedure call (RPC), 144–46
  security, 156, 167–69
  SOAP extensions, 161–63
  transport interface, 157
  XML language integration, 146–47
message transfer agent (MTA), 164
messages, 54–55, 60
messaging service layer, 85
messaging system, 144
meta data, 32, 87, 174–75
Metals Aluminum Association (MAA), 28
methodology, core component, 84
Microsoft, use of Web services, 61–62
middleware, 10
mission statement, ebXML, 221
mixed content, XML, 40
multiparty collaborations, 107–8
Multipurpose Internet Mail Extensions (MIME) object, 154

N

namespaces, 42–43, 149–50, 227
National Institute of Standards and Technology (NIST), 20
National Office Products Association (NOPA), 28
National Retail Merchants Association (NRMA), 28
.NET framework, middleware, 10, 61
nonrepudiation of origin, security, 89
nonrepudiation of receipt, security, 89

O

Object Management Group (OMG), 10, 145
object management service (OMS), 188
object manager interface, 188
Object Request Broker (ORB), 145
objects, 120–21, 188–95
occurrence indicator, XML, 39
official constraints, context category, 133
one-to-one selling, 6
OnSale, B2B auction model, 7
Open Buying on the Internet (OBI), 18
Open-EDI, 19
Open-EDI Reference Model, 223
open standards, 17
operation, WSDL document element, 60
Oracle9*i* Application Server, 62
Oracle, use of Web services, 61–62
Oracle Dynamic Services, 62
organization attribute, 182
Organization for the Advancement of Structured Information Standards (OASIS), 20, 21
origin nonrepudiation, security, 89

P

package attribute, registry services, 183
parser software, 38
Partner Interface Processes (PIPs), RosettaNet, 95
partners, context category, 132–33
Passport, Microsoft Web service type, 49
payload, 144
payload container, SOAP, 162–63
Petroleum Industry Data Exchange (PIDX), 28
pilot program, ebXML project, 234–35
ping/pong service, messages, 165–66
planning, ebXML project, 231–34
platforms, 72
policy compliance, e-commerce benefit, 5
Polymerland, B2B e-commerce, 6
ports, WSDL document element, 60
port type, WSDL document element, 60
positional format, 29
process architecture, 79
process context, 131
product architecture, 79
product catalogs, 6
product classifications, 132
productivity, e-commerce benefit, 4–5
prolog, XML document element, 36
property context, 131
proprietary standards, 17

Q

queries, 186, 195

R

real estate, e-commerce business type, 4
receipt nonrepudiation, security, 89
receipts, acknowledgment, 111–12
receiver authentication, security, 89
registry, architecture element, 80, 85–87
registry administrator, 197
registry browser, identification, 128
registry entry, 87, 195
registry guest, security, 197
Registry Information Model (RIM), 183
registry model, registry services, 179–81
registry services
  add slots protocol, 190
  approve object protocol, 190
  attributes, 182–183
  business semantics, 173–74
  classification system, 187–88
  client communications, 185–87
  collaboration protocol agreement, 185
  compliance, 184
  configuration methods, 186
  content owner, 196
  deletion scope, 190
  deprecate objects protocol, 190
  directory model, 178
  distributed Internet registries, 179
  interface/methods, 191–94
  Internet search engines, 177
  meta data, 174–75
  object life cycle, 188–89
  object management, 188–94
  object management service (OMS), 188
  object manager interface, 188
  object searches, 194–95
  queries, 186
  registry administrator, 197

registry services *(continued)*
registry guest, 197
registry model, 179–81
remove objects protocol, 190
root node, 187
security, 196–97
shared context, 174–75
shared semantic discovery, 176–78
software service pyramid, 184
software stack of services, 183
submit objects protocol, 189
supported processes, 181–82
who should use, 172–73
reliability, message services, 156–57
Remote Method Invocation (RMI), 225
Remote Procedure Call (RPC), 54–55, 144–46, 225
repository, architecture, 80, 85–87
repository meta data, 123
Resource Description Framework (RDF), 229
root node, registry services, 187
RosettaNet standard, 18, 20, 95–96

S

sales channels, e-commerce benefit, 5
schema, 42–43, 102–4
searches, registry services objects, 194–95
Secure Sockets Layer (SSL), 90
security, 89–92, 156, 167–69, 196–97
Security Assertion Markup Language (SAML), 51
semantics management, XML, 224–25
semantic Web, 229
sender authentication, security, 89
service provider model, ebXML, 229–30
services, 5, 60
shared context, 33, 174–75, 224–25
shared semantic discovery, 176–178
shipping, component service type, 49
shopping basket, B2C e-commerce, 6
Simple Object Access Protocol (SOAP), 19, 50, 54–56, 144, 147–53, 161–163
smart data, XML concept, 14
SOAP Messages with Attachments (SwA), 148, 152–53
software bus, system interfaces, 201
software enablers, B2B e-commerce, 9
Southwest Airlines, use of Web services, 62
special characters, XML content, 40
SQL queries, 195
SQL Server, Web services tool, 13
Standard Generalized Markup Language (SGML), 31–33
Standard International Trade Classification, 132
standards
ANSI X12, 28–29
BizTalk, 20
CommerceNet, 18
EDI, 19–20, 26–31
EDIFACT, 18, 29
Open-EDI, 19
open *vs.* proprietary, 17
RosettaNet, 18, 19–20
Universal Product Code (UPC), 21
X12, 18
XML, 43
XML/EDI, 19
states, business process model, 114–15
Sun Microsystems, 10, 61
supply chain management, 8
syntax, expressing, 227–29
system capabilities, 134

T

Techniques and Methodologies Working Group (TMWG), 20
Tibco Rendezvous, 144
time limits, transactions, 111
trading partner, 13, 235
information, 80
trading partner agreement (TPA), 202–3, 224–25
Trading Partner Agreement Markup Language (tpaML), 87, 200, 203–7
Transaction Authority Markup Language (XAML), 51
transaction processing, 27, 51–53
transactions, 100–2, 108–13
Transportation Data Coordinating Committee (TDCC), 27
transportation industry, EDI use, 27
transport interface, message services, 157
types, WSDL document element, 60

U

UN/CEFACT Modeling Methodology (UMM), 76–79
Unified Modeling Language (UML), 61–62, 76–79
Uniform Resource Identifier (URI), 127
Uniform Resource Name (URN), 127
unique ID (UID), core components, 127
United Nations Centre for Trade Facilitation and Electronic Business, 20, 21
United Nations Standard Product and Service Code (UN/S1PSC), 132, 133
Universal Description Discovery and Integration (UDDI), 50, 57
  registry services, 58, 179–81
Universal Product Code (UPC), 21
Universal Unique Identifier (UUID), 127, 188
UPS, horizontal logistics example, 8

V

validation, 38
value-added network (VAN), 14, 27–28
value-added supply chain, 4
value chain integration, 99
variables, 121
vendors, Web services user, 62
Verticalnet, B2B e-commerce, 5
vertical Web sites, B2B e-commerce, 7
VisualStudio.NET, 12–13, 61
vocabularies, 31, 227–30
Voluntary Interindustry Communication Standard (VICS), 28

W

W3C, 20–21, 33, 89–90
Web services
  application-to-application communications, 49
  business-to-business (B2B), 12–13
  component services, 49
  HTTP protocol, 48–49
  Java Naming Directory Interface, 57
  reasons for using, 63–64
  semantic Web, 229
  server-to-server communications, 49
  transaction processing, 51–53
  users, 61–62
Web Services Description Language (WSDL), 50, 60–61, 179, 224
Web sites
  BizTalk framework, 94
  business process specification and DTD, 100
  core component tools/references, 124
  CPP/CPA Specification version 1.0, 201
  Messaging Service Specification version 1.0, 144
  MIME information, 153
  Overview of ebXML Architecture, 79
  SOAP Note on W3C, 54, 153
  Using UDDI to Find ebXML Registry/Repository white paper, 85, 179
  XML-based EDI resources, 240–241
WebSphere Private UDDI Registry, 62
WebSphere Studio, 62
White Pages, UDDI registry system, 58
Wholesalers Stationers Association (WSA), 28
workflow, managing, 226–229
worksheets, ebXML analysis, 78
World Wide Web Consortium (W3C), 20–21, 33, 89–90

X

X12 EDI standard, 18, 28–29
XLANG, WSDL extension, 61
XLink, complex linking, 14
XML. *See* Extensible Markup Language (XML)
XML/EDI, B2B e-commerce standard, 19
XML Encryption, 89–90
XML Key Management Specification (XKMS), 51
XML Signature, 89–90
Xpointer, complex linking, 14

Y

Yahoo, B2C e-commerce, 6
Yellow Pages, UDDI registry system, 58